ARMAGEDDON AVENGED

THE ARMAGEDDON TRILOGY

BOOK THREE

C L CABRERA

To my #BooktokBesties, #Bookstagramers, #Poetsoftwitter, and everyone that I found decades ago on writing sites that don't exist anymore, thank you for traveling this road with me. I am so proud to be part of these creative communities.

To my alpha, beta, and ARC readers, critique partners, and street team. May you be as loved as Lex and get away with as much as Raphael.

To myself. Girl, you did the damn thing!

CONTENT WARNING KEY

Your mental health is important to me. Please review the content warning key. You will find corresponding symbols at the beginning of each chapter.

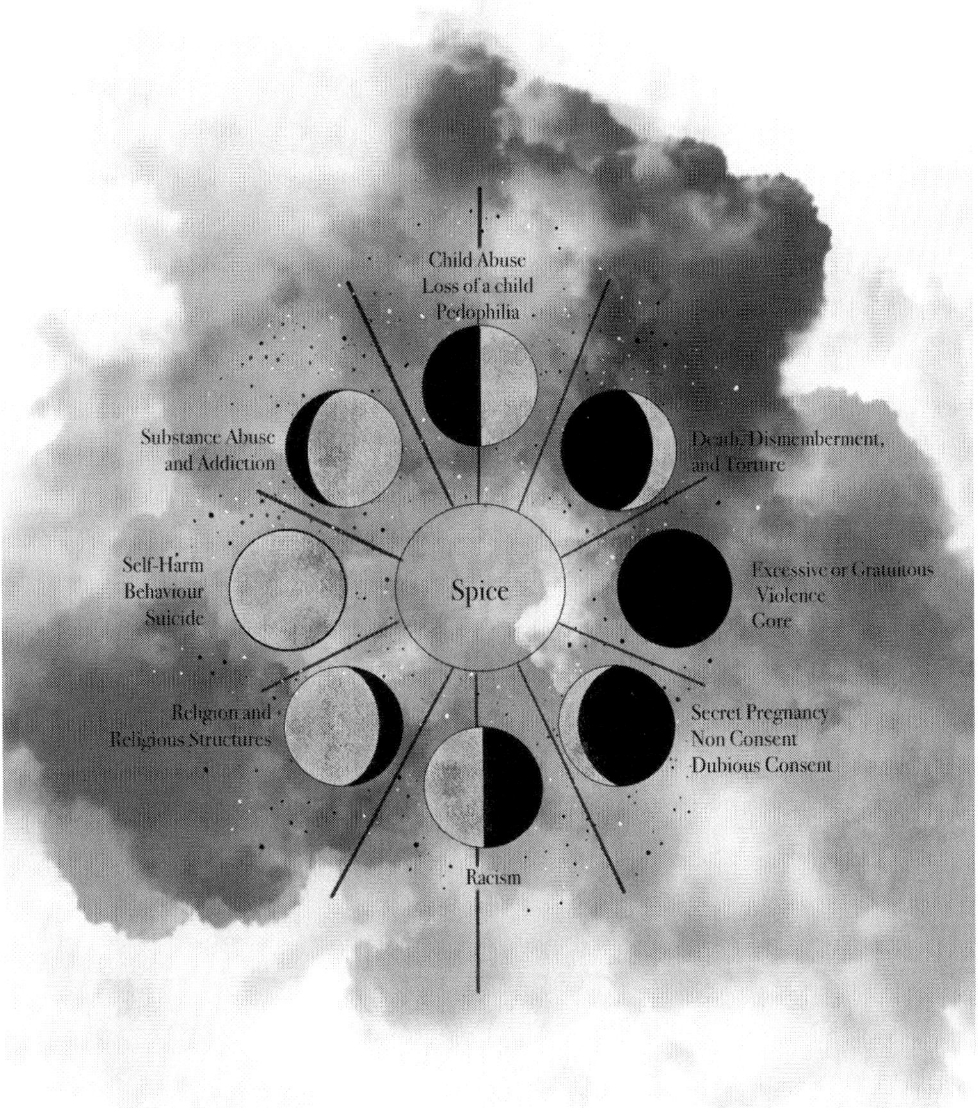
Child Abuse
Loss of a child
Pedophilia
Substance Abuse
and Addiction
Death, Dismemberment,
and Torture
Self-Harm
Behaviour
Suicide
Spice
Excessive or Gratuitous
Violence
Gore
Religion and
Religious Structures
Secret Pregnancy
Non Consent
Dubious Consent
Racism

THE PROPHECY

From the water, she will rise
Born of Death
Raised in Love
Above her, her white horse
He will find her
She will break him
Beside her, the red one
He will wake her
She will hate him
Before her, the black horse
He will protect her
She will save him
Behind her, her pale one
He will betray her
She will forgive him
Angel, Fallen, human, muse
They will gather
For she is Armageddon
The entrance to Heaven

BONUS CONTENT

To find an Armageddon Awakened's playlist, angel lore, audiobook samples and more, scan the QR code below:

LUC 23:34

Forgive them; for they know not what they do.

Prologue

RAPHAEL

Gabriel's frame darkened the corridor. His dead eyes and expressionless face warmed his father's heart. This is how the Dominion preferred his son. Cowed.

"Heel." Raphael pointed, his lips curling into a smile as Gabriel limped to his place beside him and fell to his knees.

Blood splatter spotted the boy's button-up. He'd thrown his tie over his shoulder; the wrinkled silk matched his disheveled hair.

"You look like death, son." Raphael laughed and the angel pushed his fingers through those black curls, leaving a trail of gore behind. "Now it's worse. Hold this." Raphael handed Gabriel his scalpel, removed his gloves, and bent over his chosen one. He fixed the tie first.

The surgical table rattled and a moan filled the air.

"Silence!" Raphael barked. He waited for silence before combing his son's hair. He'd neglected Gabriel since their recent fight. He hadn't planned on using his son's hex again. He'd been so well behaved, but that changed when the Dung family heir wormed her way into Gabriel's life. The boy always had an affinity for the lowly creatures in the world. Raphael would need to take care of her soon. The woman had challenged him. No one challenged him. Not his siblings, not his son, and certainly not some broken muse. Anyway, he dusted Gabriel's shoulder off. His son deserved better.

Raphael stiffened when his victim let out a long, low whine. He straightened, his eyes cutting the female. "Can't you see, we're having a moment?"

The cuffs around her wrists clinked against the metal table, sounds escaped around the gag in her mouth.

Raphael gritted his teeth, his lips turning up. "First you want me to stop and when I do, you start begging for attention." The Dominion opened his hand, turning back to his son. "I'll need that scalpel back."

Gabriel's hand tightened around the handle, his eyes narrowing and then instantly emptied. He placed the blade in his father's hand.

"Thank you, son." Raphael returned to the table and his victims' screams rose to a new crescendo. "Oh stop. You won't remember this." Raphael shoved the female's cheek making her face the opposite direction, and studied the pink healing skin. "Now remind me, where were we?" His hand slid against her tears as she struggled. "God damn, you're disgusting. Angels really shouldn't have this much bodily fluid." He wiped his hand off on his lab coat before pulling on a pair of gloves. He'd left the key to all of his problems inside her centuries before and now it was time to retrieve it.

In fact, he'd left several keys inside her. Angels healed so quickly that he couldn't be sure if her body would retain any of them. So far, he'd palpated the muscle compartments where he'd left behind fragments. He'd opened up her neck and checked along the knuckles of her spine. He'd cracked joints and explored their cavities, but nothing. Raphael was nothing if he wasn't patient. He'd find it eventually, he felt its Scientia, he knew her angel body had retained at least one piece.

He rested his hand on her chest. "We've been friends for a long time, haven't we?"

She nodded, more tears falling.

"You trust me, don't you? You've always trusted me. We've been through a lot together."

She averted her eyes but dipped her head in an affirmative.

"See? Which means you can stop struggling, right?"

She nodded, her chest still heaving.

"Perfect." He slipped his hand between her legs, pressing a thigh until they fell apart. "I've heard this doesn't have to hurt. But last time." He shook his head. "You weren't on your best behavior."

It started with a tremble and soon she jerked and shook, her body arching off the table.

Raphael folded his arms and waited as the angel writhed on the table. A flash beside him caught his eye and he turned. Gabriel's watch had caught the light. "Son? I almost forgot you were there." Raphael pulled off his lab coat and rolled up his sleeves. "Why don't you give me a hand here."

Gabriel moved to his feet and came to the other side of the table.

"Don't just stand there. Hold her legs."

The female shook her head chanting something close to the word "Please." She implored Gabriel with her dark eyes. Her body curled toward him. It amused Raphael the pair might be friends outside of this room. If anything, he knew the female respected Gabriel. There was something so satisfying about the betrayal on her face as his son pinned one leg to his hip and shoved her opposite knee into the table with such force it popped.

The Dominion's hand slipped between her legs again. "One finger, two finger, three finger, four. Like it or not, it's time to explore." The female form interested him, especially their anatomy. It was like God built a pocket just for Raphael to hide his secrets in. "Five finger, six finger, seven finger, eight. Shut. The. Fuck. Up, for Heaven's sake." He bit out the last words, his forearms tensing as he leaned in.

Raphael's smile faltered when Gabriel turned away from the struggle with his nose wrinkled. Was the boy experiencing emotions? Did Raphael need to strengthen his hex? The Dominion had used the magic sparingly over the years, but he knew of nothing stronger than its magic. Gabriel's face smoothed and Raphael's worry melted away. His son was strong. If changes in expression were the only hint of resistance, then Raphael's had nothing to worry about.

His finger snagged on something sharp. There. Wedged in her cervix like a splinter was the bone he'd planted in the days of Saxons and Kings that rose and fell as fast as flies. Raphael trapped the sliver between his fingers and pulled. The bone loosened, but his fingers slipped. "Damn it, Gabriel, open her legs wider."

Gabriel grunted, fighting with the angel's legs as he forced them further apart.

Raphael tried again, bracing her hip with his free hand. "There!" The bone came loose and he pulled his hand free, holding his prize in the air. "Now we're talking." He squinted at the bone. It looked so different, encapsulated with tissue, blood, and mucous. He'd been different then too. He never would've expected it to take this long for technology to catch up with his plans. "C'mon on, son, let's add this to the virus." Raphael left his victim tied to the table, chest heaving, and betrayed eyes trained on Gabriel.

Raphael entered the lab, the precious bone fragment squeezed in his fist. Sometimes he felt like time repeated itself. He remembered collecting the bone and all the tears and grief that had accompanied the moment he smothered the life out of the infant it belonged to. The babe had barely lived and the humans surrounding it acted as though Raphael had pulled the sun from the sky. What a waste. *Emotions, that is.* The energy it took to sob. To beg. Even human anger disgusted him.

He'd always been a simple angel. He never questioned if what he did was right or good or whatever the humans would label his deed the day before he finally snuffed them from existence. Why would he question things? God had made him this way. He was an immortal made of cunning and wrath and God didn't make mistakes.

He settled into the rolling chair before his standing desk, where he kept the centrifuge and the chemicals he needed to break the bone down into its simplest form. Glue. That's what humans were—sticky, stinking sacks of flatulence and opinions. Of course, he'd seen this from the beginning. As he watched the bipedal being of earth transform the grunts into words and their hunts for food into murder. Speaking of God's mistakes. He'd never stoop so low to describe humans as mistakes. They had a purpose. Entertainment. Raphael pulled a glass dish from the drawer and found a file. The metal grating against femur filled the room and Raphael wished he'd grabbed a mask. The dust he created mostly fell into a pile of white shavings, but a fine powder floated in the air and he couldn't help but imagine the little bits of infant he was breathing in. And that's what all the tears had been for. The creature had barely lived before he put it to better use. Did it really deserve all the wailing and whining that accompanied its death?

He set the file down and reached for a spoon with a long handle and a beaker, before scooping the shavings into the glass container.

He splashed a solution on top of the bone and pulled the Bunsen burner forward. There was something satisfying about breaking down a tiny human just to inject it into another larger yet just as stupid human. "What do you think Gabriel? Who should be the first one to receive this new and improved virus?" His son remained standing against the wall where Raphael had left him. He appreciated his silence most of the time, but in truth he missed their verbal sparring. His chosen one was articulate, and he took full credit for it. "How about your girlfriend?"

Gabriel continued to stare into space.

Raphael cleared his throat. "Who do you belong to?"

"Alexis O'Conner, the woman I love."

The Dominion groaned. Every time Gabriel gave him that answer he puked a little in his mouth. He needed that Muse gone, and he needed her gone yesterday. That's that. He was decided. He'd give the whore the first dose. He didn't know which he preferred.

Chapter 1

Three weeks later . . .

Wylie

Wylie wiped at her cheeks as she walked out of the dining room. She didn't know where she was going, but she couldn't sit still. She couldn't be alone. *Samael's wings?* The few bites of meatloaf she had swallowed crawled up her throat. *"Commit to memory the Dominion Samael for soon he will be no more."*

She walked into the family room, her arms wrapped around her middle as she held herself together. A basket of game controllers and a large television took up the opposite wall. She jumped when she turned. Somebody was there. Red light spilled through the shutters pointing to David. She'd forgotten about him. He sat on the couch with his head in his hands.

"David?"

Her muse stood, forced a crooked smile on his tear-stained face, and opened his arms. Wylie rushed into them. The last few weeks came crashing down on her. Ariel's empty eye sockets. That extra heartbeat as Lex came at her. Gabriel, Zeke, Luc. She squeezed her eyes shut against her tears. "I'm sorry." *Samael's wings!* She pushed her forehead into David's chest. Samael losing his wings was worse than losing limbs. No, it was more like cutting her Mexican pride away or slicing out her nursing skills. And he did it for her. A being that existed before God made the world was cutting off his wings for her. "Fuck, I'm so sorry."

David pulled her closer, remaining silent. His emotions mingled with hers. Regret and fear and sorrow swirled around them. His tears fell into her hair while his muse magic held her as tightly as he did. What were they going to do? How were they going to survive this? Would anyone survive this?

They rocked each other for a long time, keeping their thoughts to themselves, holding tight to their injured bond. They broke apart at the sound of heavy boots.

"Where is everyone?" Shafer marched into the room. "Oh, shit." His eyes narrowed on Wylie. "I didn't realize you two—"

"We're not," Wylie pushed her curls from her face.

"You're not?" He gestured at her hand still resting on her muse's shoulder.

She snatched it back, her eyes passing over David's raised brows. "I just lost my niece or nephew and David lost a friend. We—"

"Don't explain yourself to me, just tell me where everyone went. Luc called me, but I can't sense him." He closed his eyes. "That's not it. It feels like he's everywhere. There's some big magic happening in Hell right now."

Wylie covered her face with her hand ignoring the accusations in his eyes. "They're doing a transfer of power."

Shafer's jaw dropped. "From who to who?" The black of his tattooed arm shifted.

"From Samael to me."

Shafer blew out a sigh of relief before turning to David. "You better sit then."

"Why, what's going to happen?" Wylie folded her arms. She wasn't up for any more surprises that night.

"Where do you get all your Scientia?"

Wylie's eyes closed slowly, her brow creasing. "You can't be serious."

"Oh, I'm pretty sure that's why Luc had me come here." Shafer took off his cowboy hat and set it on the end table. "Dude, this is going to suck for you."

David, sat shaking his head until his eyes widened and his body stiffened. "What about Jane? How is this going to affect her?"

"She'll be fine. When an angel dies, their muse barely notices. You on the other hand . . ." Shafer squatted next to the couch, looking up at David. "Samael's about to dump a shit-ton of Scientia into you." The demon shook his head. "Why did we think this was a good idea?"

This was it. Time for Wylie to decide. Was she going to support Samael in his decision, even when she thought it was rash and wrong? *"It's been my honor to serve you as a Dominion."* Damnit, she had to trust him. Had to believe in his sacrifice. She needed to embrace his blind faith, because it was born of something innate and powerful and beyond her comprehension. "I trust Samael with my life."

"I do too, but do you trust him with his life?" Shafer shrugged, tilting his head toward her muse. "No offense David, but I heard you're kinda a douche."

"Samael loves David. He'd never do anything to hurt him."

Shafer patted the empty couch cushion. "Either way, you should probably lay down. I'll try to help as much as I can." His eyes lifted to Wylie. "You too. We need to drain the Scientia as quickly as it enters your muse."

Wylie's lips flattened. She sat next to David, resting her hand on his thigh. The familiarity between them returned. She didn't think it would ever go away. But there was something new between them now, and that *thing* was about to cut off his wings.

David shook his head, leaning back into his seat. He gripped Wylie's hand. "Just make sure I can get back to Jane." He let go and it went to the top of his head, rubbing the hair that had grown back in. "The world's falling apart. I can't leave her alone." He closed his eyes.

The crimson light filtering through the window shifted and Shafer lifted his head. "It's time."

David's brows kissed, his jaw ticking. A minute ticked by and then another. "I don't feel—" Thunder clapped in the distance, and David's body jerked to the side, every muscle tensing. His back and legs locked straight and a gush of wind shoved Wylie away. A guttural cry of pain escaped the muse and then . . .

"What should I do?" Wylie shouted over the storm that burst from David's chest. Pictures flew from the walls. Lamps and vases shattered. David screamed and screamed.

"Help him!" Shafer pushed through the twisting wind and took hold of David's arm. His long hair tore from its tie and whipped through the air. His eyes widened, the sclera turning black. "Satan's staff, hurry!" His nostrils flared.

Wylie crawled to David who'd fallen sideways onto the couch, his body remained rigid, his shouts becoming grunts. Her head bowed against the foreign objects leaving slashes on her face. Her fingers wrapped around David's ankle and power unlike any she'd ever experienced entered her.

Wylie's body did the work her mind couldn't comprehend. She sucked in the Scientia. Into her lungs, through her skin. It zinged through her veins, warming her flesh. It was everything, her air, her peace, the healing she'd searched for. The magic pulled at her as if she were a magnet. She climbed up David's leg, ignoring the black sand flying off of Shaffer and joining the tornado that had formed on David's chest.

Wylie's cheek rested on David's abdomen. Her unblinking eyes stared at the power. She reached for it, her hand shaping the air, guiding the storm to her face. She didn't understand what she was doing, but her lips parted, reminding her of the times she'd sucked fire into herself to prevent it from spreading.

The power tasted like Samael's lips and David's . . . David's . . . This wasn't right. This wasn't her, but she couldn't get enough.

Blind to her surroundings, she swallowed and swallowed, her body pressing into David's. A hand tangled in her hair pulling her closer and she clung to her muse, both afraid of herself and hungry for more.

The door.

The door.

Fire. Death. Four horses.

White.

Black.

Red.

Pale.

Fire and ash and ice.

Lifeless green eyes.

Wylie woke with a start. Her skin buzzed, and her mouth tasted like shit. Her chest hurt. It felt like someone had stabbed her in the back or shoved her in the chest or both at once. She groaned, her eyes fluttering open. "David?" A hand grazed her cheek.

"Are you okay?"

Wylie scrambled off David's lap and fell off the couch. She landed on her hip, pain and shame hitting her at once. "What just happened?" She pushed out of David's reach, her hand covering her mouth as the dream fog transformed into memories. Her hands clinging the familiar planes of David's body.

"It's okay, Wylie. I'm okay." A blush crept up his scalp. "You helped me."

"I knew Samael was powerful, but Devil's Spawn, David's lucky you hulked out Wylie." Wylie'd forgotten Shafer was there.

"Hulked out?" Wylie rubbed her chest with a shaking hand. Her skin and teeth vibrated.

"I think we met your demon."

"Demon?"

"My what?"

David and Wylie asked at once, their eyes meeting and then rushing back to Shafer.

"You were welcomed into the family just a few hours ago. Did you forget?" Shafer shook his head, putting his cowboy hat back on. "We should meet them; they'll all be a mess."

David helped Wylie from the ground and though a mountain of words grew between them, she remained silent as they followed Shafer out of the house. They found the demon standing under the eaves, his eyes wide.

Wylie followed Shafer's gaze, noting the demons standing on their porches. The neighborhood bustled with activity. Children jumped and twirled, skipped and splashed. "What is everyone doing?"

"It's raining."

Wylie almost laughed, if people reacted like this to rain where she was from, they'd get nothing done. "Why?"

"It's never rained in Hell before." Shafer's eyes cut from Wylie back to the view. "Look, there they are." Shafer broke into a run, pausing to open the gate and then continued down the sidewalk.

At the end of the block Kami leaned against the weight of a duffle bag. A giant lion walked at her side. Shafer rushed to the Queen of Hell, taking the duffle bag from her.

Wylie stepped into the rain, her feet breaking into a sprint as she recognized the sandy haired male draped on the lion's back. Blood ran down his naked back and saturated the lion's mane. She met them at the gate, her breath catching as she held it open. She took in his back, the exposed bone left behind.

"Wait." The lion paused and Wylie fell to her knees, resting her hands on his shoulders. She closed her eyes and forced her healing power into him, but no matter how she tried her Scientia refused to penetrate his skin. "It's not working." She lifted her head. "Why isn't it working?"

"Scientia won't work on him. He's given it up and all its benefits," Kami said, pushing past Wylie to the door. She pat David's shoulder. "He knew what he was doing when he brought you here, didn't he?"

David's jaw ticked once before a mask of professionalism fell over his face. He allowed the lion to pass before turning to Shafer. "What kind of first aid supplies do you have?"

"We have everything."

"Everything, huh?" David turned to Wylie. "Go with him, you know what I'll need." He followed close behind the Queen of Hell, pushing up his sleeves as he walked.

Wylie listened for Shafer's thoughts, but his mind was a steel trap. "Why would you have all these supplies in hell?"

"Believe it or not, we bleed too." Shafer swung open a door to reveal the concrete floors of a garage. On a workbench in the corner sat Beelzebub Belby and Zeke, both leaning over a crystal in the latter's hands.

"Wy-yee!" Zeke popped up from his seat.

Wylie bit her lip, her hands coming up before the boy could rush her. "Sorry, buddy, I have to hurry and help Shafer now."

"C'mon, Zeke," Belby called. "I haven't shown you the rubies yet."

Wylie forced a smile as he hopped back onto the bench and Luc's father pulled the kid closer.

"Here." Shafer gestured at the cabinets along the back wall.

Wylie immediately threw doors open and began shoving supplies in her pockets. Three types of sutures, bottles of lidocaine, a needle, and syringe.

Shafer held up a duffle.

"Good, thanks," Wylie stuttered, her hand trembling as she grabbed a pack of gauze. "We still need—"

"Got it, just go."

Wylie didn't answer, she just turned on her heels and ran, back into the hall toward Samael's cries of pain. She blinked tears from her eyes as she forced her way into the room. Samael flailed on the bed until David pulled his hands away. The doctor knelt next to him, his hands covered in blood. Wylie's muse turned to Luc. "We're going to need restraints. I can't sew a moving target."

"Let me talk to him." Wylie placed all her supplies next to David and sat by Samael's head. She leaned close to his ear as he brushed the long blonde strands from his pale face. His body stiffened, his eyes wild and unfocused. Again, she tried to force her Scientia into him. Nothing. She brushed his cheek and started singing, just as she had, or Roberto would. "My sunshine, my only sunshine."

He reached for her, and she took his hand. His eyes closed and Wylie sang as David reached back into the wound. "It's shredded. What did you guys use, a hack saw?"

Luc shrugged. "What, should we have consulted with you before we cut his wings off?"

"Probably." David dabbed at the broken flesh as Shafer stalked into the room and dropped the duffle at the foot of the bed. "Sedate him or restrain him. Lidocaine ain't gonna cut it. Wylie, he's bleeding and human. I need your help. He needs a blood transfusion."

"I've been a medic in a few wars. I'll start an IV, give him Ativan."

Shafer's head dipped, his eyes connecting with Wylie's. "You helped Ariel. I'll help him."

Wylie nodded, turning Samael's arm over for Shafer before rounding the bed to kneel across from David. A lump grew in her throat as her eyes landed on Samael's back. "Shit."

David nodded. "We'll have to do layers. If you start irrigating, I'll look at what we have there. I hope he's up to date on his tetanus."

Luc snorted from his spot at the foot of the bed and Kami settled into the armchair next to the bed. "Do you really think, now's a good time to joke, doctor?" The queen asked.

"Not joking. It would be a shame for him to die of lock jaw after surviving this." He handed Wylie some fluid before picking through the instruments in the duffle. Her heart slowed as she fell into her role. She'd worked across from David for so long she didn't have to read his mind or his mood. When he opened his hand, she knew what he wanted. His eyes narrowed, and she held up a light. Blood splashed his face and Wylie wiped it away. And when David hit skin Wylie let herself look at Samael again. He may no longer be a Dominion, but he'd always be the angel who'd found God when he pressed his lips against hers.

Chapter 2

Lex

Lex sat in line, tugging on her septum ring. Anger made it impossible to sit still.

"How long have you been waiting?" asked a man with a clipboard and a fabric-covered cart.

"For–fucking–ever," she said through gritted teeth.

"Are you hungry?"

"No." Lex's voice had returned to its former glory, but she had no space in her heart for celebration, nor did she care to answer a fucking survey.

He checked a box on his paper. "Tired?"

"No." Someone coughed in the row behind her. Her eyes narrowed as the plastic chair next to her creaked. Its inhabitant shifted again as she peeked over the clipboard.

"Cold?"

Lex snorted. "No."

"Bored? Homesick? Sad?"

"Fucking pissed. Can you check a box for that?" Lex had spent her entire time in this waiting room creating new combinations of swear words. How the fuck did she end up in this place? She'd paid her fucking dues. She'd had a shitty life and just when things started looking up, she ended up here.

The man threw back the cover and reached into his cart. "I have something for that." He passed her a tablet and a pair of headphones. "This will let you view earthside. There's a channel for every loved one you left behind. Hopefully, it will give you some peace."

Lex clutched them to her chest, her mind reminding her where the hurt had been. Gabriel. His hand on her belly. The stars. Yes, she hadn't even said goodbye. Fuck, she needed to stay angry. She couldn't fall to pieces in this new place. No one had threatened her, but she wasn't about to look weak in front of, what was it? A hundred people?

". . . those are the only rules. Do you understand?"

Lex scowled. She hadn't heard a word, but she'd thank the bastard before she'd ask him to repeat himself. She put the headphones around her neck, ready for the man to leave her alone so she could explore the tablet.

"The other matter we must discuss is your . . ." The man lowered his voice. "Your pregnancy." He clicked his tongue. "It will progress faster while you are here."

"My pregnancy?" Lex stood, her eyes landing on the roundness of her belly, the tablet slipped from her fingers. The wire, connecting the headphones, prevented it from crashing to the ground. Her hands flew to the now obvious bump, her throat closing to breath. *Our baby.* She was going to have this baby without Gabriel? For the first time she wondered if she was actually in hell. No one had moved from their seat since she got here, nor did they communicate with each other. She'd done the same, averting her eyes whenever they connected with others.

"So, I'm going to have this baby." She'd found her breath only for it to be stolen again. "Are you guys going to let me keep it?" Her eyes flew around the room in search of a weapon. Nothing. Just her chair. She'd go MMA on these motherfuckers if they tried to take her baby. Gabriel's baby. She'd already killed herself to keep it from becoming a zombie. There wasn't much she wouldn't do.

"Of course." The man smiled, but Lex refused to find comfort in those laugh lines. "Once you have your baby you can move on. That's why time runs faster here, so you won't have to wait as long."

"Why am I waiting?" Lex turned her body slightly, just in case she'd need to reach for the chair. She waved her hand at her silent neighbors. "Why are we waiting?"

"There's no pain in heaven." The man lowered his voice, his hand coming up non threateningly. "So, in your case, you need to give birth before you enter."

"Give birth? While I'm waiting? What the fuck is this place?"

"This is The Grand Queue. We have a medical facility and anything else you may need while you're here."

Lex blinked. "It doesn't matter what you have here. I'm alone. I can't have a fucking baby by myself." The shifty woman next to her stiffened, her snooping coming to an abrupt end. She must know something.

"You're allowed, visitors. We already have two names for you." The man flipped through a few pages on his clipboard. "Dung and John?"

Lex sat down, her eyes rolling at her mother's name. "Fuck! My mom and my brother?"

"They are both very excited according to my notes. John plans to bring his husband."

"Husband?" Lex's voice broke on the second syllable.

"Yes." The man flipped another page, nodding. "The two of them live in a very nice area. They plan for you to stay with them." He flattened the clipboard against his chest when Lex didn't respond. "Now, if you don't have any other questions I'll move on."

Lex flipped the man off. "Go then." She folded her arms and glared at the man as he stopped in front of the woman who couldn't keep her eyes to herself.

"Carol, right?"

Lex picked the tablet off the ground and slid the headphones over her ears as the black screen showed her an unscarred face. Who was she anymore? She turned the device on with the press of a button. The first image showed her father sitting at his desk, checking his emails. She'd failed that man too. She swiped left. David was in his hospital, his hands in the pockets of his white coat. He'd let the hair on the top of his hair grow in and dark circles around his eyes made her wonder if he was mourning her or still torn up about his break up with Wylie. *Fucking bitch.*

Lex's hand shook as she swiped again.

Gabriel's handsome face had grown gaunt and ashen since she saw him last. His suit had crease lines throughout. Had he slept in it? His usually well-manicured beard was too long, and he hadn't gelled his curls into place.

"Gabriel is still mourning his loss and has asked me to make this announcement in his stead." Raphael gestured behind him. "Isn't that right, son?"

Gabriel nodded; his ebony eyes empty of their usual passion. Lex adjusted the screen, panning out so she could see the crowd gathered around the basketball court. Tables lined the wall. Men and women in scrubs hustled around the tables, drawing up a clear liquid into vials.

"We've preemptively created a vaccination for a virus that was made by the US government to kill all muses. They believe they would rid themselves of angels by killing off our muses."

A murmuring grew thick as the crowd turned to each other. That fucking bastard! She gritted her teeth against the urge to shout at the screen.

"Gabriel and his team of scientists have worked night and day to create this vaccine for you. To remain in the compound this immunization is required."

The asshole was so low that he'd threaten these people with homelessness in order to coerce them into letting him inject them with poison.

"Our medical personnel will raise their hands. Please create orderly lines—"

"But what if we don't want your vaccine?" A man in the crowd asked.

Raphael smiled, he straightened, lifting his chin. "Well, how would my son handle this?" Raphael turned back to Gabriel. "Oh look, he has nothing to say. Are you interested in being an example of what happens when you question Rapheal the Dominion, Azarias the Harold, God's Help?" His teeth gleamed under the harsh fluorescent lights of the gymnasium as he grinned. "Because I'm more than willing to teach you."

The man looked around him. His neighbors averted their eyes and, taking several steps away from him. Some even made their way to the table, lining up like dumbasses. The man turned back to Raphael, his eyes narrowing. "Are you threatening me?"

"No, child, I'm ending you."

With a squelch, the man exploded. Brain matter and blood splatted onto those who hadn't moved far enough away, screams rendered the air, and muses rushed for the doors, finding them locked. Angel wings appeared as Gabriel's bodyguards corralled the humans toward the vaccinations and their deaths. How were they letting this happen?

"Help!"

Lex zoomed in on Gabriel. "Don't let this happen," she whispered, her anger from the moment before turning into years and years of unshed tears. "Please, Gabriel. Baby. Don't let them do this."

Her angel stood, unblinking and she ran her finger over his body. He stiffened. "That's it, baby. Look at me." She wiped her eyes. His head tilted to the side. "Stop him!"

The person next to her scooted away, the legs of their chairs screeching on the olive-green tiles. Lex ignored the woman and started shouting in earnest. "Gabriel! You promised! You fucking promised! Stop that bastard!"

Someone cleared their throat next to her and one of the men with the carts hurried down the aisle toward her. Lex stood, her eyes glued to the screen, studying the slight wince on Gabriel's face, the way the corners of his eyes crinkled every time she raised her voice.

"Ma'am, if you are going to continue to shout, we're going to have to ask for the screen back."

Lex ignored him, hurrying in the opposite direction. "Gabriel! Wake the fuck up! Gabriel, you promised." She walked into an usher in the same baby blue uniform, she hadn't seen him coming from the opposite direction.

"Please, ma'am, hand over the tablet."

"Fuck off!" Lex shoved the man aside. She didn't know where she was going but, she knew if she kept at it, Gabriel would wake. He'd already responded to her. She saw it on his face. He'd heard her. She just needed to be louder. He—

Lex ran into a wall. She lifted her eyes from the screen as large arms wrapped around her, pinning the tablet between their bodies.

"Now, ma'am, I'm going to ask that you calm down."

Lex kicked and bashed her head against the man's chest, but he was a marshmallow, a very large unmoving marshmallow. "Fuck you! You, asshole! Let me go! Let me go!"

“I’m just going to hold you here until you stop.” The man flinched away as Lex’s arm escaped his grip. “Please, ma’am, I don’t want to hurt you.”

She struggled for days. It was probably minutes, but it felt like fucking days. “Gabriel needs me,” she said, her body going limp. “You don’t understand.” Her throat tightened around a sob. “I left him all alone and he needs me.” She sagged into the man’s firm hold the tablet still pinned to her chest. “I told him I loved him, and then I left him. I left him, and now I’ll never see him again.”

The man’s bear paw of a hand patted her back, letting her spew her nonsense and her tears all over him. The man cleared his throat in between her cries. “My name’s Justin, and I’m going to hold you up until you can do it yourself.”

Chapter 3

Gabriel

"You promised!"

Gabriel woke with Lex's uninjured voice in his head. His shoulders and knees ached. His side burned with the other-worldly pain his father often unleashed upon him, but the agony consuming him had nothing to do with his surroundings. *Lexy*. He choked on a shuttered breath, as he closed his eyes against the gray of the dungeon walls. He wanted to rest his thumbs in the places between the slant of her eyes and the curve of her cheeks. He wanted to taste the scar on her lips. He wanted to see her purple stained fingers against his skin. Run his nose along the nape of her neck and breathe in her lavender shampoo. But he'd never do any of those things again.

He shook his head, sweat splashing onto the stone from his unkempt curls. He blinked against the light and he pushed his body from the ground. Once on his knees he pulled off his wrinkled jacket and threw it on the stone floor, the black outline of his father coming into focus. "Raphael?" His name came out in a rasp, as if he hadn't spoken in days.

"Good. You're awake." The Dominion stepped up to the bars separating them. The angels flanking him held their distance, their fear leaking off of them like piss. "For old time's sake let's just let bygone be bygones and get back to our mission."

Gabriel studied his father, but only saw the blood splattered on the wall where Lex had . . . Raphael needed to die. He reached out his hands, stepping closer, his head hanging low. "Father?"

"Yes, son, I'm here."

Gabriel lunged, caught Raphael's lapels and dragged him into the bars. He pressed his forehead into his fathers, and taking a page from Wylie's book, shoved all of his pain into the Dominion.

The angel gripped Gabriel's wrists. If anguish was a weapon, he'd surely be dead. Raphael pulled himself free and dusted off his suit. "Think carefully about what you do next. I can have you back under my control in a second."

Gabriel screamed, his body shaking with the force of it. He loathed this angel. He loathed the fact that he'd served him all these years. How dare he call him son after killing Gabriel's only happiness. His eyes locked onto Raphael's, and he stepped back. Smiling that sick grin he'd stolen from the Dominion, he fisted both hands. Raphael's angel guards crumpled into a mass of feathers and blood so quickly they made no sound but gurgles and splats.

"That was childish of you." The Dominion stepped to the cell door and unlocked it. "We don't have time for your theatrics. This is the end days; we'll soon be rid of the muses." The door squealed as it opened. "I know this place can't hold you, I was just hoping to minimize the mess." He gestured at the angel piles. "I'd prefer to have the real you at my side, instead of the puppet version I've had to put up with over the last week."

Gabriel folded his arms, setting his teeth, his mind racing through his options. He'd killed Dominion's before, but it hadn't been easy or fast. Decapitation by ice might be the quickest option, but could he do it before Raphael took control of his body again? His body. His brows came together, he'd almost missed his father's message. These bars weren't his prison, his body was. Gabriel looked down at his wrist. His watch was gone. He closed his eyes. "Just kill me."

Raphael laughed. "And waste millennia of planning? I think not." The Dominion shook his head. "Binah, talk some sense into him."

It took all of Gabriel's strength not to fall to his knees when the closest thing he had to a friend stepped out of the shadows. "I'll talk to him," she said.

Raphael nodded. "I need a break from his abrasive attitude. Don't leave his side." Raphael strolled out of the room without a backward glance.

"You?" Gabriel stiffened as Binah entered his cell. He put up a hand and she stopped. "Is this the truth? Were none of my angel's loyal?"

The Virtue shook her head, her beaded braids clicking with the movement. She held a finger to her lips. "You're a figure head, not a leader." Binah pointed at her head and then pulled her ear. *We can't talk here.* She thought in circles.

She'd never been talented in telepathic reading. He narrowed his eyes, studying her. Her midnight skin creased over the concern on her face. He remembered calling for her in those moments of panic before Lex herself. She never came. He'd always known the angels who followed him had followed Raphael first, but he'd never suspected they would turn their backs on him that quickly. *Fuck them.* That's what Lex would say. The only thing that mattered any more was putting down the monster he called father. "Move."

"Look at yourself." Binah took a few cautious steps. "You're barely standing. Let's get you cleaned up."

Gabriel straightened, crystals forming on his skin. It'd been decades since their power dynamic shifted and he became the one giving orders. "Clean me up? Who do you think you're talking to?" A sword formed in Gabriel's hand, and he stepped into ready position.

Binah gave him a bored look. "While I appreciate the gesture, I'm not going to fight you." Binah lunged without pulling out a weapon of her own. She ducked, the first blow slicing the air above her, and slid on the ground under his guard.

Gabriel's second strike froze when Binah fisted his pant leg and projected them.

They landed on soft mud. Gabriel's heavy breaths echoed, and his blade evaporated as dizziness hit him. He braced the wet reaching walls of a cavern. Gabriel growled into the darkness. "Where have you taken me?"

"Hear me out." Binah turned on a flashlight, stepping back until an arm's length separated them. "You need my help."

Gabriel lifted his chin, unable to stand upright yet, he bared his teeth. "Take me back."

"You've missed a lot." The flashlight's beam traveled up the stone. Condensation dripped down, leaving green and yellow trails. "You can't kill Raphael."

"I can, and I will."

Unphased by Gabriel's raised voice, Binah pulled out a map, her eyes scanning the paper. "Not if he's controlling you." Her southern twang bounced around the cavern as she pulled out her compass and compared it to the map. "This way."

"Why?" Gabriel pressed his forehead into the cold stone with a groan. "Where are we? What is this place."

"Tennessee. We're in some caverns under the Appalachian Mountains. Did you know these were here before Noah?"

Gabriel's eyes drifted shut, and he slid sideways. A sharp rock tore his palm. He jerked upright with the new pain. He ran his fingers through the blood. He'd give anything to stain his hands with his father's blood.

"Gabriel, focus. I brought you here because I wanted you to have a choice."

Option one: Run. Just project to wherever you'd planned to take Lex. Wait things out. Raphael has a lot of enemies. Someone will eventually put him down." She snorted. "Or you can be the angel I know you are and stay at Raphael's side until I get this little mind control thing fixed."

"Stay at his side?" Anger etched lines into Gabriel's face, disgusted by the idea. "Stay at his side?" His fists clenched. He'd forgiven the angel over and over, for big insults and invisible aggressions, he'd let his 'father' burn his first love to death. But Raphael had exhausted all filial ties when he sunk that needle into Lex's leg. The urge to punish the Dominion transcended vengeance. The moment Gabriel opened his eyes the compulsion to coax cries of agony out of the angel had ingrained itself into his soul– stronger than a temptation, more insidious than addiction, as involuntary as his heart beats.

"You've asked more of the angels you've led."

Binah's head tilted as she squinted into the darkness. She nodded to herself, returning her map to her pocket. "Now move, we don't have a lot of time." Binah took off toward a tunnel with a low ceiling.

Gabriel followed, too tired not to.

After a few steps, he fisted the back of Binah's shirt pulling her to a stop. "How can I trust you? Especially after advice like this."

"You don't have much of a choice. I'm the only one willing to risk my neck for you." Binah pulled away, but Gabriel held fast.

"And why is that? How does helping me benefit you?"

For a moment silence stretched between them, only interrupted by the dripping stalactites. "Raphael released the virus." More silence. "It's the strain he tested on Lex. We have three months until he turns our little problem into a pandemic. And then, we might as well join Lex."

Gabriel let go, and Binah powered ahead, leaving Gabriel to digest what she told him, pretending she hadn't noticed his rising temper.

"That's why he's thinking this is over. That's why he thinks he's won. We don't have much time. I may have wanted free will, but I still love the human race. I see that part of myself in you." The light bounced off the wall next to Gabriel as Binah looked over her shoulder at him. "These people are under your protection. You need to get back in there and keep them safe."

Gabriel came to a stop and slammed his fist into the wall. "*Putain!*" Dust rained down. "Binah, I'm no one's hero. The world can burn for all I care. I've given enough." His head hung as he covered his face with his hand.

Binah tapped his shoulder with a flashlight. "Here, hold this," Binah said, shoving it into his chest.

He scowled at it and she shook her head shoving the flashlight under her arm as she dug through her bag.

"I know what you need." She pulled out a pack of cigarettes, balanced one on her lip, and lit it. "Here."

He took it and studied his fingers. The last time they held a cigarette, they were covered in blood. "You're wrong," he whispered, his hand trembling. "You don't know what I need." His words echoed around them. He didn't need a smoke. He didn't need food or water or sleep. Lex would never have any of those things again. His baby . . . His heart spasmed in his chest. His baby never had a chance at life. He smashed the cigarette in his hand, letting the cherry burn his palm. All he wanted was Raphael dead. "You're wasting my time." He looked down at his watch less wrist, and found no comfort there. "I'm going back."

"Please, don't. I promise you it will be worth it." Binah turned to him, but continued walking backward.

Their eyes met and before he knew it, one foot in followed the other as he followed his friend. "I can't do it, Binah. I—" His hand shot out and he grabbed Binah's shoulders, yanking her to him. "Watch out!"

She blinked up at Gabriel and then looked over her shoulder. "Well, shit." Her voice cracked over the words as she aimed the light at it. A pit stretched out behind her; the bottom not visible in the darkness. "That would've hurt." She snorted. "No wonder the map wants us to take a left. Funny, it didn't say anything about that." She gestured behind her with her thumb.

Gabriel shoved her aside and stared into the abyss. He shivered. He was cold. For the first time in his life, he was cold. "Raphael has to die." The beam bounced over Gabriel and to the passage to his left.

"And he will."

"I don't trust you!" he shouted.

Binah folded her arms. "I've served Raphael since before you were born, that's how I know what power he uses to control you. You don't have to trust me to use me. I'm helping, that's all that matters."

Gabriel shook his head. Nothing mattered.

"You stood behind Raphael as he forced the muses of your compound to receive a 'vaccination.'" Binah took the light and turned back to the path. "You know what happened after. The bleeding, the fevers, the hunger." Her back tensed, her feet moving away from him. "Ten percent of the humans received a placebo. So, when they started getting sick, he expressed his regret for not immunizing everyone sooner. Most of the medical team fell sick too. He had them shipped out. Taken by the bus load to other hospitals. Where it could spread. This all happened in less than a week."

Gabriel dropped to a crouch, the blood tears which had stained Lex's face replaced his sight.

"Gabriel, come with me." Binah rested a hand on his back. "When I gave up my muse for free will I didn't sign up for this fucked up world Raphael is creating. He's taken someone from me too. I want him dead just as much as you do."

Gabriel rubbed his naked wrist. "Answer me this: why should I care?"

"Because that's what Lex would have wanted."

He winced, shaking his head. "Don't say her name."

"She wanted you to protect the muses. She didn't believe in many things, but you, she believed in you. Don't let her down."

"Oh, fuck you." Gabriel ran his fingers through his hair, his mind showing him Lex's sharp eyes, her tiny hands, the way the scar on her lips pulled when they pursed. He fucking hated it, but Binah was right. His girl had believed in his cause almost more than he had. Gabriel lifted his head. "Okay, you've got my attention."

"Let's move then." She stood, consulted her map and took off without him. "I think I know how to stop Raphael from controlling you."

Gabriel gritted his teeth. If she could do that then he didn't have a choice. He rose to his feet and followed. They came to a fork in the path and Binah took another left. The walls and the ceiling closed in on them as they walked. "Are you going to tell me what the plan is?"

"Sure, but first—" Binah raised the light to the ceiling, searching until it landed on archaic symbols gouged into the stone. The letters could have been a precursor to Arabic. A line at the top of each letter connected them "—Israfil," she whispered. The Virtue rushed to the spot. "One, two, three—"

"Binah," Gabriel growled as she counted her steps.

She held up a finger. Her feet stopped when she hit seventy-seven. Her light beam swept along the floor, the walls, and then the ceiling, where it landed on the same word, with its sweeping lines and thin curves.

"Binah?"

The Virtue huffed as she hopped, her arm raised above her head, her finger mere inches from the symbols. "Can you reach it?"

Gabriel's head tilted back, and his hand ran along the letters. "What does it mean?"

"Raphael."

Gabriel dropped his arm, his jaw tightening.

Binah's head swiveled on her neck. "That should've been good enough?"

Gabriel's eyes closed as he shook his head. "What?"

"Your touch should have activated it." As if she spoke the disturbance into existence the ground rumbled and clumps of dirt rained from the ceiling. Heavy footfalls echoed through the tunnel.

Gabriel crossed his arms over his bare chest. "I am past impatient." The temperature dropped.

"I'll explain everything," Binah said, stepping behind the male. "After you take care of them." She pointed at the giant figure moving in the darkness.

Gabriel shook his head in annoyance when a man-shaped pile of clay stepped into the tapering beam of the flashlight. Its boulder-sized fists dragged on the ground. It lurched forward on legs as thick as a large man's chest. Raphael's symbol glowed on its forehead, and a mouth formed on its otherwise featureless face as its jaw dropped. His muddy form rippled. The sound between a roar and an earthquake came crashing out of him.

"Damn it, Binah." Gabriel fell to a knee, flattened his hand on the ground, and closed his eyes, forcing his Scientia into the earth. The freeze hit the creature's feet first, and soon the thing froze in place, ice crystals painting patterns along its surface. Gabriel returned to his feet. He turned to Binah. "Now, tell me—"

A crash interrupted his demand. The frozen beast shattered, and its twin walked over him, absorbing the broken pieces. Binah cringed. "There'll be six more of those."

Balling his hands into fists, Gabriel marched forward. He ducked when the creature's tree trunk of an arm swung at him. The angel sprung up and tapped the muddy beast's shoulder. The thing instantly stiffened. Gabriel's elbow swung into the side of its head and shards of it smack into the wall and bounced onto the ground. He continued forward.

He dodged the next creature's blow, his hand shooting out. His palm smacked into where the beast's nose should be. The thing exploded. The tinkling sound of falling glass announced its demise.

Gabriel made quick work of the rest. He found himself at the end of the tunnel. A rockslide prevented him from continuing. He turned back to Binah, who scanned their surroundings with her flashlight. "Well?"

"They were supposed to clear the way for us." She chewed on the inside of her cheek.

Gabriel ran both of his hands through his hair. "Do I have to do everything?" He slapped the wall and pushed his ice into the stone, filling all the crevices. "There." He turned to his left and traced the wall with his hands. "Here," he whispered. The mud and stones crumbled under his touch, leaving behind a hole only large enough for a child to crawl through.

Binah laughed. "I knew I was going to need you for all this Indiana-Jones-shit."

"I'm not going in there." Gabriel leaned against the wall, his eyes fluttering shut.

"You wouldn't fit anyway." She waved him away. "Why don't you take a seat while I finish this. Raphael has had you busy over the last week. You probably need a break."

Gabriel grunted, withholding his snide remark and sat. He curled against the cool, wet stone and listened as Binah climbed into the hole and then into whatever lay behind it. Darkness engulfed him and he held himself, the vision of starlight and vows of love playing in his head. Those tiny heartbeats. *Those tiny heartbeats!*

A screech broke him from his thoughts. Gabriel rolled his eyes. Binah might be a Virtue, but she wasn't useless. His head fell back against the stone, his eyes closing again. Multiple crashes in quick succession rang out and his ears popped as the air around him changed. *Shit.* He jumped up as a gust of wind and dust flew out of the hole.

A dozen or so pairs of footfalls echoed in rapid succession, and another scream came seconds before Binah dived out of the hole, something large and square shaped in her arms. "Run!"

A shadow appeared behind her as Gabriel grabbed her nape and projected them up. They landed in snow. Gabriel's knees buckled. He took Binah down when he fell, and the wooden box flew from her hands. It landed with a plop. Both angels snapped in its direction. Binah's eyes widened. "It can't get wet." She scrambled to it.

Gabriel rolled onto his back, the cold like a thousand razor blades on his skin. The night sky, overtaken by clouds and a flurry of flakes, weighed down on him. He didn't think he could move. Maybe he never would.

Binah stepped next to Gabriel's head, blocking his view. "We have to go." She crouched and steadying the wooden box in one hand, she touched his shoulder.

The third projection sent Gabriel's head spinning. He squeezed his eyes closed, his body instantly reaching out for any muse in the area. He recognized the Scientia of the handful of muses he found. He jerked to sitting. "Are we back at the compound?"

"No, we're at a safe house."

The poster-clad walls of a dorm room crowded Gabriel more than the stone tunnels of whatever cavern Binah had brought him to.

Binah handed the box to Gabriel. "Dry this, but not too much. That thing is fragile."

"Talk." Gabriel sucked the moisture from the box as Binah dug through the closet. He smoothed his hand over the wood where a trumpet was carved into the grain. There was something about it that vibrated with power.

"You are holding four scrolls that belong to the book of Enoch." She tossed a shirt at Gabriel. "Raphael hid it in the Apalachees before the Great Flood."

Gabriel set the box on the floor at the sound of his father's name. "And why should I care?"

"Because those scrolls have the answers to break the hex Raphael has over you." She tossed a pair of sandals at him. "Will these fit?"

"How do you know what hex Raphael is using?"

Binah pushed her beaded hair off her shoulders and sat next to Gabriel. She studied the box, her hands reverently tracing the trumpet. "Because the same hex was used on me. I received mine from Laoth, before she came to our side. Her hex was weaker than Raphael's. Mine was only meant to inflict pain. Yours was originally to keep you quiet."

"You'd think I'd remember this."

"You were a baby." Binah's light brown eyes met Gabriels. "To perform the hex, Rapheal had to cut back the flesh of your back and carve his name into the bones of your ribs." Binah pointed at her ribcage. "I remember mine. It was not a pleasant experience."

"How do you know about this?"

"He bragged about it. He'd grown tired of your crying. I wasn't there, but there are stories of your muse nursemaid dying in an attempt to prevent him from cutting you."

Gabriel blew out a breath, he remembered the first time Lex saw it happen. She wouldn't go into detail about what she saw, but he knew he was covered in blood. He hated that she'd seen him like that. He was the stability in their relationship. "What does it look like, when he takes control?"

"As a baby or a toddler, he only used it to quiet you. When you were a teenager, he'd have you kneel for hours whenever you were late or if you spoke out of turn."

Gabriel gritted his teeth. If these angels were so loyal, then why was he hearing of this for the first time now? "And over the last week?"

"I think you know."

Gabriel bit his tongue until he tasted blood. He rubbed his wrist, missing his watch. "When did it start?"

"When you moved Lex into your room."

The male he called father had cut a screaming infant open to get it to stop crying. He'd made him believe that his biggest foe was Gabriel's own flesh and blood, sabotaging any chance Gabriel had at finding love or peace or happiness.

Gabriel thought back to the day he introduced Lex to Raphael. He'd been so proud to have her on his arm. The woman had something he'd never seen before. She was stronger than anyone he knew. Stronger than his father, stronger than him. A true warrior. They were the same in so many ways, but she came out of the storm of life a beacon that he could never take his eyes off—the mother of his child.

His child.

He remembered how disgust tightened Raphael's jaw the moment he saw her. Gabriel knew if he had to choose between the two of them it would be Lex. It would always be Lex. It still was Lex. But did it matter anymore?

Binah blew out a breath. "If you went back to him. You could keep the muses safe. You could slow his progress and give me time to discover a solution to this hex."

"These scrolls are older than you. How did you know where to find them and what they were?" Gabriel recalled very little about the book of Enoch. He knew it to have the story of the fallen angels and the apocalypse.

"Let's just say, I know the angel the scroll was written about."

"A fallen?"

Binah smiled. "The queen of hell herself. I'm not sure if she is pro-you or anti-Raphael, but I can tell you where I stand." She stood, putting her hand out for Gabriel to take. "I'd follow either of you to war, but you're the one I want to follow into peace."

Gabriel took Binah's hand. "So, back to the compound?"

"Yes, let's go home. You must take back your throne."

Chapter 4

Samael

"The door."

Agony and Wylie's voice woke Samael. He groaned, his face in a pillow, and fear like he'd never known tightened his chest. Explosions and battlefields flashed in his mind replacing her voice. His teeth clenched. Where was he? A swirl of questions sharpened his senses, but he still felt like his ears were plugged. He heard no thoughts and any other sounds were muffled by the four walls surrounding him. A lamp at the bedside left a yellow filter over the dark gray wallpaper and wood floors. What happened to his vision? Had he been injured?

Something to do with Raphael. Something to do with his wings. Something to do with—

"You died!" Wylie hiccupped. Was she crying?

Beside him, the bed moved and his racing heart reminded him of how defenseless he was. How numb and confused he felt. How easy it would be for someone to take his life right now. The sheets rustled and his hand shot out tightening around soft flesh. His foggy head swiveling slower than his body's training.

"Wylie?" He'd crawled on top of her before he knew what he was doing. Her hips pinned between her thighs. The whites of her eyes flashing in the darkness as they opened. He swayed, going down to his forearms.

"Samael, I was just having a bad dream. We're okay." A hand cupped her cheek, those ebony eye's cleared, piercing him. *Trust me,* they said.

"You're okay." Her hand dropped to his shoulder.

He froze, his arms shaking. He couldn't move.

"You're bleeding."

Indeed, he felt it. Blood dripped from his back and around her head like a crimson halo. He needed to give her something, he struggled to remember. The blood— his back— his wings. He turned his head and wretched off the side of the bed.

She stroked his hair and never once complained as his body weight fully rested on her.

Merda, now he knew why he couldn't see. He was human.

Wylie helped him settle back on his stomach and sat on the bed beside him, reaching for the nightstand. "We're at Luc's house in hell. You looked pretty bad for a while. We didn't want to expose Zeke." She wiped his forehead with a damp washcloth. "Your fever broke this morning, but you're still bleeding. I've been so worried."

With each word, he felt his anxiety ease. She was answering all his questions as if she were reading his mind. And maybe she was. He couldn't tell. His eyelids grew heavy. She was beautiful. And it wasn't just her raven curls or broad cheeks that made him think so. It was the way her body talked his into stillness. The way her voice replaced the terror he'd woken with.

She stretched beside him, her head resting on a pillow as she studied him with a crease between her brows. He licked his lips, memorizing her face between blinks. He'd never questioned why God chose Wylie, but now he understood his decision. This woman could do anything, including bring him peace when he'd given his away.

"You should call Luc."

She paled. "Are you sure?"

"It's the only way."

She closed her eyes as she pulled her phone from her pocket. "I hate this."

Samael wished he were stronger, but his limbs felt so heavy, and he knew it was from the blood loss. "You don't have to stay."

She took his hand, squeezing his fingers. "Of course, I do. I'd do it myself but . . ." She looked down at her hands.

"I chose this."

She nodded, the screen of her phone lighting up her the tears in her eyes as she sent Luc a text.

The door opened without a knock, and even through the haze Samael saw the dreaded crow bar. Luc's eye bounced over the bed. "Fuck." The prince sat at the edge of the bed. "You should've called me sooner."

"Let's get this over with." Samael pushed his face into the pillow, holding his breath as Wylie heated the metal in Luc's gloved hands.

Samael couldn't open his eyes. Pain. His back. And there . . . in his lower belly. Between his legs? He ached. Something strained that he'd never felt before. He rocked against pillowy warmth that pressed into him. The emptiness of his missing soul would've immobilized him if it weren't for the urgency of his hips. His hands shook as they came to life, his eyes opened to the darkness. He couldn't see. His eyes were too human now. He squeezed them shut, panic constricting his throat.

He folded forward, looking for comfort and finding it. Her hair tickled his nose. Wylie. His fingers tangled in those curls. Wylie's curls. Wylie's soft body. *God, Wylie.* He breathed her in. Was he dreaming? How often had he wondered what it would be like to do this very thing? Her ass pressed against the throb taking over his body as she stretched against him. He wrapped his arms around her waist. He needed her. She moaned as he pulled her closer.

"Wylie, Wylie, Wylie." His unused voice chanted her name in a gruff prayer.

She turned to him. "You're awake?" Her hands rested on his chest and it took all of his dampened senses not to take them and guide them down his body to the part of him that was about to explode.

"It hurts." He gritted his teeth against sounds he'd never made before. "Please."

"Let me turn on the light." Her sleepy voice was the only medicine he needed. Her voice and her body.

He shook his head. "No." He didn't know what he wanted, but something in the back of his mind told him that once the light came so would reality. He reached for Wylie, fumbling, his knuckles brushing against her stomach, and then her breasts, until he held her face. His thumb ran over her lips. "Remember our kiss?"

She smiled against his touch. "I should really check out your back."

There were so many things he should be doing right now. He should be asking how long he'd been in this bed? What did his fellow angels know? But he wasn't a general anymore, and he trusted her. So, he refused to feel anguish of loss in his first moments of freedom. He was a man with an ache, and he'd woken up next to the most beautiful female to ever exist. "Wylie, I want you."

"Samael?" She melted into him, her head tilting up, her cheek resting against his and suddenly she was rocking too. The two of them in the dark, his hardness pressing between her thick thighs. Damn whoever invented clothes.

Maybe he did need light. If only to see the way her brows furrowed with worry for him again. His lips found hers. Their mouths parted and he breathed in her breath, a shiver wracking his body. Her breasts heaved against him. He didn't need to go to heaven as long as he lay in her arms.

Her tongue pressed into his mouth, and Samael mimicked its movement, thankful for the darkness. Anymore sensations, and he'd surely die. He measured her body with his hands, memorizing its curves and softness, finally understanding what he'd been craving for all these months, and at the same time questioning why this symphony of pleasure had been withheld from him.

He froze when her delicate fingers traveled down his abs and wrapped around his cock. "Is this what you want?" She asked, squeezing.

He answered with an involuntary thrust, his pulse jumping to the surface of his skin.

She pressed her face into his chest. "Samael." She spoke his name into his heart, her hand moving faster and the darkness of the room flashed white. Is this how it feels to be an instrument? "Promise me you're done making sacrifices." Her hand stopped, and he opened his mouth to promise the world only to taste her mouth again.

Her other hand joined the first and his head fell back, his answer lost. She kissed his cheek, his neck, his collarbone, as she worked him. A part of him floated, barely tethered by moans, and then he exploded. His hips jerked of their own accord. In fact, he wondered if he'd ever control them again or if she owned them now.

His breaths slowed as he nuzzled her neck. *"Amor Vincit Omnia."*

"Rest." Her fingers brushed over his shoulder in slow circles until his muscles loosened and exhaustion slowed his racing heart.

He jerked awake when the door flung open. Samael's body moved of its own accord as he drowsily jumped to his feet and stood between Wylie and the door.

The lights turned on. "Well, you two look friendly."

White flashes swam in Samael's vision, and Wylie's arm wrapped around his middle, guiding him back onto the bed.

"Whoa, man." Luc held his hand over his eyes. "I can't unsee that."

"Yes, close your eyes, boy, or I'll make you eat them." The paleness of Samael's face and the growl of his belly made his threat so much less believable. Sweat broke out on his forehead, and Wylie pressed his chest until he lay on his side. She smoothed her hand over his shoulder before covering him with the sheet.

"Bro, you can't talk to me like that in my own house." Luc shook his head as he plopped to the high-backed reading chair in the room's corner. "I have some news that can't wait." He leaned back, crossing his legs and threading his fingers together. "Baton Rouge is under quarantine."

Wylie froze. "What do you mean, quarantine?"

"I mean America is building a wall around Louisiana."

"An actual wall?"

The prince shrugged.

"*Merda*." Samael covered his face with his hand. He needed to heal faster. Why was he still so affected?

"We knew this was coming, but we didn't expect things to move this fast. I wish we could've stopped it, but we're doing our best to slow things down. God's army is a lost puppy without the two of you though. They can't decide if we're on the same team or not."

"What does that mean?" Wylie's back straightened.

"It means: Fucking Madoc." Luc leveled his gaze with her. "We need to get back Earthside."

Wylie rubbed the wrinkle in her brow, her eyes closing. "What about the thing you and Gabriel did? You know where you promised to keep me here forever."

"You think I would've entered into a pact if I didn't know a way out of it?"

Wylie's eyes opened. "I don't know much about you."

"Oh, cuz, we have a lot of catching up to do. If you're going to be part of this family, you'll . . ."

Samael's focus faltered as he studied the worry written on Wylie's face. He thought of their moments in the dark. Did it mean anything? Had it even been real? And now that he'd tasted her, he'd give anything to do it again. He lifted his hand, reaching for one of Wylie's black curls, but folded his arms instead. With the weight of their problems, those moments all felt like a dream. He had no right to touch Armageddon. He should be grateful for the time she'd given him and face reality. Losing his Scientia hadn't affected his mind though. He'd been caring for humans since before their ancestors learned to walk on two feet. God's Army still needed him. He lifted his chin. She needed him out of this bed and back in working order. "So, there is nothing keeping us here?"

Luc stopped mid-sentence his eyes sliding to Samael. "We could leave today."

"Samael's still healing." Wylie shook her head.

"He just threatened to eat my eyes. I think he's fine."

"What's the loophole?" Samael asked. This wasn't up for debate; the longer they stayed here, the further the virus would spread.

Luc leaned forward a smile crossing his face. "Raphael made a mistake when he didn't tell Gabriel about his broken pact."

Wylie shifted in her seat. "From when he killed my father."

Asmodeus. Samael remembered the story about the demon who'd traded his seed for a throne in hell. When Raphael refused to come through with his side of the bargain, he'd lost his mind reading abilities and received a visit from Luc. Raphael's sin had been twenty-eight years ago and now it was finally coming back to haunt him.

"So, we have a free pass, my pact with Gabriel is no longer binding."

"It's kinda funny that Raphael's punishment for breaking his promise is to have you break yours."

"A promise and a pact are two different things. To Demon kind pacts are like marriages. For us, death is the only way out."

"That doesn't sound like a marriage."

No retort came as Samael's eyes drifted shut.

"I agree with Wylie, you need more time," Luc said, his voice bringing Samael back from dreams of duty. "My mother's worried about you too."

Samael forced his teeth to unclench. "She shouldn't worry. I'm not the first angel to go through this."

"But you're the oldest angel to do it. The queen regent wants you to talk to my grandfather."

Samael shifted, blinking against fatigue. He was just so tired. "Your grandfather? My brother doesn't want to see me."

Luc scoffed. "My grandfather gets along with everyone."

"Lucifer started the largest war between angels. I'm going to have to disagree with you." Samael shook his head, forcing his eyes to stay open this time.

"In any case, my mother asked my grandfather to swing by and talk to you. You know, since he had a similar situation."

"Similar?" Samael groaned. He needed to sleep, not listen to this child moon over his grandfather.

"You know, the whole wing thing."

"Wing thing?" Samael grumbled. "Is that what we're calling it?"

"He said he'd come."

Samael made the smallest effort to turn to Luc. "Is he still mad at me?"

"That's beside the point. He said he'd come."

Wylie patted Samael's shoulder. "I think we should let him sleep."

His eyes were already closed. "Thank you, sunshine."

"Sunshine?" Luc laughed.

"Don't you start, *Luci*." Wylie's voice accompanied the feel of a blanket sliding up to Samael's shoulders. "So, Satan, the actual devil, Lucifer the first is stopping by to cheer up Samael?"

"It's more likely he'll try and recruit Samael." Luc's voice traveled to the door as he spoke.

"Do you think he's going to be okay?" Wylie's question was the last thing he heard before he fell into oblivion.

Chapter 5

Wylie

Wylie took the opportunity to get off the bed and actually stretch. "How did you and Samael get so close?" She studied Luc's face in search of her own. There was so much she didn't know about the heir of Hell, but she saw hints of shared genetics scattered across his features.

"It's a long story." Luc leaned against the door frame; his auburn eyes as intense as ever. "We need to talk about Earthside."

Wylie crossed the room. They did need to talk about Earthside and God's Army and exactly what would be expected of her now that she carried Samael's power around her like a cloak? "Then let's talk."

"The angels need you." Luc opened the door and gestured for her to exit.

Wylie spared one more glance on her sandy haired benefactor and walked past her cousin into the darkened hall.

"Samael is welcome to stay as long as he needs, but you should go back. This is your show, Wylie, and you're missing it." The door clicked closed behind them

"You're right." Her eyes lingered on the doorknob, her thoughts on Samael. She wouldn't be able to hide behind him anymore.

His hand landed on her shoulder and she turned to him, the dim lighting of the hallways hollowing his cheeks. "The humans are hosting a Summit. They've invited angel leaders. That means you."

A silence stretched between them. She wasn't exactly surprised. Samael had made it clear from the beginning that he expected big things from her, but she didn't think it would happen so quickly. "Do the angels know this?"

"They were the ones who told me."

Her eyes wandered back to the door Samael slept behind. He'd been so weak, so vulnerable. Could she really leave him? When the prophecy was about to come true. She needed him too. He was her white horse.

"My grandfather will be here in a few days. I think you should stay to meet him. He's your grandfather too. I'm taking you home after, with or without Samael."

She swallowed her apprehension. "We won't have to leave him." She'd start a rehabilitation program for Samael tonight. She didn't want to leave him here. She had something she needed to work out for herself too. "I've been having these dreams."

Luc made his way down the hall. "What dreams?"

"About the prophecy. You know the Armageddon one."

"Yeah, and?" He didn't stopped walking as she spoke, and she hurried to catch up.

"I still don't know who all my horses are."

"And that's a problem?" Luc stopped at the top of the stairs, looking over his shoulder. "It doesn't say anywhere in that prophecy that you'll know who your horses are."

The doorbell rang and their heads snapped up at once. Without intention Wylie's Scientia rushed down the stairs, up the walls around her, and beyond, creating a map of Luc's home in her head. She braced the wall as an image of a woman at the front door replaced the image of the map. She squeezed her eyes shut, pushing the familiarity the female brought with her. She wasn't used to how active Samael's Scientia was. Hers didn't do anything unless she made it, but the Dominion's power was permanently on automatic with new skills making themselves known multiple times a day.

"What are you doing?" Luc's head tilted.

Wylie shook her head as her sight returned. "Checking the door, apparently." She shivered. "What's she doing here?"

Luc's mahogany eyes bounced between hers until the doorbell went off again. "Let's find out."

Her cousin understood her more than she'd ever expected. The Demon handed out purpose and distractions like candy and she ate it up. "Sure."

He led her to the curved stairs and to the entryway, his long legs making her wonder if her height came from his side of the family. He held up a hand and she paused several paces back.

Luc opened the door and Samael's Scientia jumped out of Wylie and like an over-eager puppy, rushing past Luc to circle his guest, knocking her onto her knees before Wylie could reel it back.

The female tilted her head, her wings blinking into existence behind her. Her hazel eyes met Wylie's and her lips parted. "She's changed."

"Binah, old friend, no need to kneel for me." Luc put out his hand, pulling the angel up when she took it.

"We've taken turns kneeling in each other's courts over the centuries. But this time I wasn't kneeling for you. Where's Samael, and why is she wearing his Scientia."

Wylie folded her arms. She remembered this angel. It was hard to forget her with her height and midnight skin. She'd accompanied Gabriel when he'd first visited her. She'd held David over the edge and threatened to drop him. "Luc, you know this angel works with Gabriel, right?"

"Excuse my cousin. They don't teach manners Earthside. Come in." He stepped aside and gestured for Binah to enter.

Wylie didn't budge. "Why is she here?"

"I made it very clear, I'm not on your side." Luc shrugged. "I'm not on his side. I'm on my side. And if I want to have your brother's little buddy over *in my house,* I can. Now, step aside."

Narrowing her eyes, Wylie stepped away from the door. Was Luc betraying them?

"Alexis wore my name on her face. Let's save each other some time and assume I know everything she did." Luc's shoulder brushed against Wylie's when he opened the door wider for Binah to enter. *I'm glad you're here for this. The fight between you and your brother has gotten out of hand.* He pushed the thought into Wylie's head, his eyes never falling from Gabriel's second as she strolled into his house.

Binah took off her hat, holding it to her chest. Her head tilted back as she admired the crystal chandelier that dominated the vaulted entryway. "I'm not here for pleasantries, so I don't mind making this quick." She pulled off her back pack and unzipping it, pulled out a wood box. "Gabriel needs your help. Only your mother knows how to break the hex Raphael is controlling him with. We have three months to fix this."

"Then why aren't you talking to my mother, and what's happening in three months?"

"The queen regent is not an easy woman to obtain an audience with." Ignoring his second question, Binah opened the box, presenting a scroll. "But I happen to have some instructions she wrote down before the whole Noah debacle."

"May I?" Luc reached for the scroll.

Binah shrugged. "Shouldn't you wear gloves or something?"

Luc rolled his eyes as he lifted it. "I believe I've handled this scroll before." He rolled it open to the first line, nodded, and placed it back in the box. "I know this document."

Binah brows furrowed. "It wasn't easy to obtain this."

"I'd be curious where you found it. You're right, it went missing along with many other of my mother's things around the time of the flood." Luc replaced the box's lid; his fingers ran over the trumpet. "Did Raphael tell you about this?"

Binah's face recovered, her lips pursing. "I'd prefer Raphael doesn't know about this."

Luc smiled. "How is the unhinged bastard?"

"If you know about this text then you know how to break Raphael's control over Gabriel."

"The heart of his enemy."

Binah's eyes swung to Wylie, narrowing on her chest.

Luc crossed back to the door, opening it again. "I think it's time for you to go."

"So, you are picking sides." She shoved the box back into her backpack.

"I'm not willing to allow either of them to come to harm."

"Why?" Binah pointed a thumb at Wylie. "She's your natural enemy."

Luc lifted his chin. "I won't ask you to leave again."

Binah tightened the straps of her backpack. "It's funny how the world starts falling apart, and the two of you are down here camping out." She brandished a middle finger at Wylie. "Lex would've wanted me to share her love." The angel projected away.

The door clicked closed.

"What just happened?" Wylie let out a breath and leaned against the wall.

"If Gabriel is under the Hex my mother added to that scroll, he's screwed. The Regent Queen couldn't reverse that hex if she wanted to, which makes me wonder what made Binah believe she could."

Wylie didn't want the world to end, but she also didn't give a shit about Gabriel and his people. A secret, dark part of her rejoiced in the idea of his suffering even though she knew she should be hurrying to get out of Hell and fix things.

"Don't look so happy. Gabriel may be a prick, but Raphael has no conscience or soul or whatever you want to call that part of every being that makes them good." Luc pulled out his phone. "I'm going to call my grandfather. We need to get back Earthside ASAP."

Chapter 6

Lex

David,

This is going to be fucking hard to believe, but here it goes: I'm a ghost! Life's a bitch and so is death. I'm writing you because Gabriel needs your help. That's not exactly true. Gabriel needs Wylie's help.

Before you delete this email, I want to remind you that they're siblings, like you and your sister. They might never figure their shit out, but with me gone Gabriel has nothing. I need him to have her and maybe even you. I know he'll always be the bad guy in your book. Maybe he is. Who fucking cares! There's a zombie fucking apocalypse happening and he's probably the most powerful angel on earth right now. He'd be good to have on your side. Think about it and get back to me . . . or not, either way I'm haunting your ass until I get a "yes."

L

She hit send and prayed, yes, *fucking prayed* that David would take her message seriously. "Zachery?" A woman in a baby-blue uniform called as Lex hit send. Weary, Lex held the tablet close to her chest as the woman walked Lex's neighbor to the exit. This left the seat beside her empty.

Carole leaned into Lex. "Where do you think they're taking him?"

Lex responded by moving the newly vacant seat. She didn't spare the pair a second fucking glance. No. She glared at Carole who glared back, her eyes promising similar violence.

"Well, I never." Carole turned away.

Lex huffed; who cared where that poor bastard was going. All she cared about was the tablet. Her eyes fell back to the screen and she scrolled through her people.

"Did you figure it out yet?" Justin collapsed into the free chair next to her. His shoulder pushed into hers as he leaned into her space.

She'd usually deck anyone who touched her, but this big guy somehow didn't feel like a threat. He was just a big marshmallow. She rolled her eyes at herself, ignoring the question, was she just about to think the guy was sweet?

"You can talk to them."

Lex's brows lifted, but she maintained her sights on her father. He'd hidden a pack of cigarettes behind his nail clippers and screwdriver in the junk drawer. So that's where he hid them. She'd caught him smoking twice now, but never saw where the old man got his smokes from. It's funny that he hid them. As if she or her mother could pop out at any moment and call him out.

"You could take those."

"What?" Lex tore her eyes from her father.

"You could take those away. You know, so he couldn't smoke them."

This guy. She didn't know why he visited her so often or why she tolerated it. But had he really waited this long to tell her this? "Are you fucking with me?"

"Do I look like someone who'd fuck with someone?" He grinned his cheeks dimpling.

She forced her lips to flatten to keep herself from smiling and shoved the tablet against his chest. "Show me." She folded her arms when he took it. She really didn't want to like this guy. That's why she never asked who he was or why he felt so familiar and for once, she was somewhere where no one could read her mind.

"Fine, what are you going to give me in return."

She rolled her eyes and the fetus kicked as if he were rolling his eyes too. "I'll name the baby after you."

He burst out laughing and everyone in the room turned to the sound. "Don't lie to me." He pinched his fingers against the screen and dragged them open, zooming in on the pack her father had peeking out of the pocket of his polo. He shook out his hand. "I'm a little out of practice." He licked his lips and then with his pointer finger rubbed the pack away, like he was using Photoshop and was just erasing part of an image. Lex couldn't believe what she just saw. She leaned forward in her seat as Justin zoomed out again, waiting for her father to notice. Was this real and some sort of mind trick? Marshmallow or not, she would punch him if he was fucking with her.

"*Damn it all to hell.*" Frank patted his chest for the second time and shook his head. "*Where did I put those bastards?*"

"Wow, he sounds a lot like you."

Lex bumped her shoulder against Justin's. "Don't be an asshole." She wasn't sure why he was helping her, but if she could contact earthside, she didn't fucking care about his reasoning. Now that there were other ways to contact David, it didn't matter if he read her email or not. She rested her hands on her belly, before she did something stupid like hug the fucker. "Now, show me how you did that."

"I told you. I want payment."

"You're fucking with me, right?"

"Here's the thing, Lex. I know that if I asked you to do something, you'd probably do the opposite. But you have morals hidden somewhere in that black heart of yours. So, if you owe me one, and I ask for a teeny-weeny favor," he shrugged. "You'd help me out."

"Teeny-weeny?" Lex cringed. "We couldn't have known each other in real life. The moment you said something like that I would've ditched your ass."

"Just tell me you owe me one."

"Fine. I fucking owe you one. Teach me."

His shoulder bumped into hers again. "See, was that so hard?"

"Fuck you."

"Here's what you need to do. Forget every movie you've ever seen about ghosts. This is not about emotions, it's about actions. You must become the change you want to see in the world."

Lex narrowed her eyes. "A Gandhi quote? Really? Are we in sixth grade social studies?"

Justin smirked. "I can't get anything past you, can I?" Justin tapped the screen and dragged the image of her father to the left. "Think about it. You're a muse. You are used to being full of power. Imagine taking everything else away. Imagine becoming that power. Let everything else fall away. Drop the emotions, the judgments, the limitations of flesh and bone and become that Scientia you were never allowed to use on your own." He pressed his finger against the door and it slammed shut.

Frank jumped. "*What the fuck?*" He glared at the door for a moment and then settled back in his chair, shaking his head.

Lex loved how her father cussed more than she did when she wasn't around. She always assumed she'd learned to cuss on her own.

"If you are nothing but Scientia, you could even project yourself like angels do." Justin closed his eyes and Lex hissed when behind her father Justin pulled back the curtain and waved. She looked from Justin on the screen to the close eyed Justin next to her. Could this place get any weirder?

Lex's father pressed his cigarette into the ashtray and slowly stood, gripping the arms of his plastic lawn chair. Shit, he was going to see Justin's dumb ass. She elbowed the man and the curtain fell closed as he opened his eyes. Frank gimped to the back door.

"He wouldn't have caught me."

"Let me try."

"Sure." He slid his finger across the screen and David appeared. The doctor unclicked his shoes and dismounted his bike. He pulled the lock off the body of his bike and knelt next to the wheel.

"Try his helmet."

All Lex had managed to do with her Scientia in the past was explode things. Now Justin challenged her to let that power out and focus it near David's head. Lex's fingers tightened around the tablet, sinking into the image like she would a good movie.

Excited and impatient, she reached out for David's helmet and grabbed air.

"It comes from inside you."

Lex side-eyed Justin. "If you Karate Kid me one more time . . ."

Justin raised his hands in mock surrender, and then proceeded to lock his mouth and throw away the key like a fucking six-year-old. Lex closed her eyes this time to help her focus. The power inside her was stiff. Unused. It didn't itch at her skin like it used to. She felt it in her forehead first. The sizzle of magic. She closed her eyes, the image of David burning into her mind and pressed the screen into her tattoo. Her Scientia reached for him and blew him from his crouch onto his ass.

David lifted his head, his hands rushing to the buckle of his helmet as he scanned the space around him.

"David." She tried again. This time her hands became his hands, their Scientia's melding. The clip unfastened, and Lex fell back into her seat, the tablet falling into her lap as the waiting room replaced the vision of David.

Justin grinned at her. "You're a quick learner." He gripped her shoulder as he leaned forward to pick up the fallen tablet. "You should rest now." He gestured at her belly. "It must take a lot of energy to be that fat."

Lex snorted, pressing the tablet into her swollen breasts with both hands. "I don't have time to rest. I have a fucking world to save."

"You sure do." He patted her back. "I have to get back to work."

Lex watched him walk away, the smile sliding from her face. What was she doing smiling? She didn't know how much longer she had before she fucking popped, so she needed to figure this out before she had a screaming baby to take care of. Her little piece of Gabriel. Her little reminder of everything she lost.

She lifted the tablet and lost track of time. She didn't notice when Carole started snoring or when another lost soul filled the seat that had emptied earlier. She was too busy switching between channels, visiting the men of her life with the intent of setting everything right. Or as right as she can fucking get it.

She started with Gabriel. Everything began and ended with him.

He'd finally fallen asleep on the ground, so she knelt next to him and practiced running her fingers through his hair without floating away. She needed to help him, but she wasn't sure how. She watched those black strands engulf her fingers. She should have felt his soft hair and the wet from his sweat, but she couldn't. She didn't feel the frost clinging to all the surfaces or the cold thickening the air. Her lungs didn't burn, her heart didn't beat. She was truly a shadow of what she'd once been. But this shadow wouldn't be useless.

Gabriel stirred, and she slipped away, glancing up from the tablet. He needed the sleep, so she let him. She swiped left in search of her father. How fucked up would it be if her mother had collected the answer to their problems? She remembered this book about the apocalypse that used to scare her when she was a kid.

"Lex?" Frank sat upright in his recliner.

Lex rushed up the stairs. Her feet barely brushed the steps as she went. She hadn't figured out how to solidify enough to touch the ground while moving. She still grabbed counters and handrails to keep from floating away.

As quickly as she could, she floated past the landing and through the door of her room. She didn't need her father catching her. Their Book of Enoch was a copy from Ethiopia and her mother put it under her bed to torture her.

Lex grabbed the bed frame, pulling herself down to her knees, just as she'd done with Gabriel. She didn't have a heart or a stomach or skin to add to the visceral experience of anxiety, but the tension made her hands less visible, and her fingers sunk into the wood, her whole body slipping upward.

Is this what astronauts feel like?

She focused, solidifying as she reached for the book. Touching it still gave her the creeps, moving it was fucking impossible. It felt as though the thing was made of fucking concrete, not paper. Shit.

"Lex?"

Double shit.

The door to her room squeaked open.

Her father wasn't a superstitious man. She didn't think he'd follow her. She closed her eyes, preparing to fade away.

"No! Don't go." *He looked around the room, searching for her.*

She froze as he walked across the room and sat on the bed.

His hand rested on the bedpost where she held tight. He sighed. "Your mother used to visit me like this. She'd leave things out, and I knew they were for you." *He rubbed his hands over his face.* "This means you're gone, doesn't it?"

"Daddy," she whispered. Lex reached for him, her hand running over his shoulder.

His eyes went to the spot, and Lex saw tears form for the first time. The man never cried. As a parent, he'd always been adamant that O'Connor's didn't cry. Especially with her brother, who was a notorious crier. But now they ran down his face freely.

She squeezed his shoulder, as he wiped his face on his sleeve and narrowed his eyes in her general direction. "Now, gal. Show me what you're here for."

First, she showed him the books, then she sent him to the attic. Now, she needed to get all of this to someone who had potential access to Gabriel. Someone she trusted.

"I'm leaving now."

Frank grunted his dismissal, and Lex went to David to follow up on her email.

Chapter 7

Gabriel

Lex sat at the edge of his bed. Gabriel knew her smell, knew her presence so well that he didn't have to open his eyes to know that she sat there.

He missed her and resented her in equal parts. She'd angered him when she'd left him. She'd chosen to leave him. And she took their child with her. She didn't give him a chance to find a solution. He'd always encourage her independence, but for this, deciding between living as a monster or leaving him forever, she should've given him the choice.

He sat up and blindly crawled down the bed until he curled around Lex. She wasn't there, but she was. He couldn't feel her against his skin, but the air lightened as his touch made her sigh. His girl was small and strong and like a live wire. That's what she'd been, a live wire, something both thrilling and deadly to hold.

She probably hated him for allowing the virus to spread. Back when she was with him, he distracted her from all his misdeeds by eating her out. He closed his eyes to all the memories they made in their short time together.

"Did you leave me because of what I am?"

"Gabriel, you're a good man."

"I am not a man and never have been."

"You don't fucking believe that, or you wouldn't have fallen in love with a human. Not once but twice."

"And look where that got me."

"Think of our baby."

"What baby? My baby is dead. You're dead. I'm arguing with a ghost."

"You're an asshole."

"You've called me that so many times, but I'm not the one that ruined everything. I'm the one left behind. We could have figured this virus out. You just had to give me more time."

"You know what would have become of me. Would you have let me suffer like that? Would you have let me become a danger to you? I had to go."

"Then go!" He wiped his hands through the silvered air where he felt Lex. "Leave me!"

The door flew open. "Sir!" His angel guard came through the door, his gun unholstered and aimed into the darkness.

Gabriel sat up; his suit rumpled from laying in it.

The angel dropped his gun. "I'm sorry, I heard raised voices."

Gabriel narrowed his eyes, imagining ripping the angel's throat out with a jagged piece of ice. "Do you think you're posted outside my door to guard me?"

"I, uhh . . ." The angel took a step back as Gabriel stood, his Scientia spilling from every pore.

"You are posted there to protect them from me." Gabriel gestured outside the room. "Now, get out."

The angel backed out of the room, shutting the door behind him. Only for a knock to sound.

"Come in." Gabriel put his gun in his holster. He didn't know why he still carried it. He sure didn't need it. All it did was press the memory of Lex's death into his back. He added his cufflinks and pulled on his jacket, ignoring the creases in his slacks and opened the door.

Binah strolled past him and flopped on the bed, her hair clicking as she got comfortable. "You look pretty as ever."

Gabriel scowled. "Don't patronize me." He checked his watch. "What did you find?"

"I spoke to the queen." Binah flicked her braids off her shoulder, the toe of her boot tapping. "She's unwilling to help us."

"Really?"

"But she offered to alter it."

Gabriel snorted. "Not good enough."

"It might be our best option."

"Ask her again. We'll support one of her sons in their political endeavors or something." Gabriel shook his head. "We're running out of time."

Chapter 8

Wylie

"No fucking way."

The sound of raised voice had Wylie's feet moving faster as she came down the steps.

Samael grunted, she'd recognize that grunt from anywhere. "It's not your choice."

"The fuck it isn't. You can't just—" Luc's mouth snapped shut as Wylie entered the room.

"What's going on?" Wylie paused at the door when realized the males in the room weren't going to include her in the conversation. Her eyes fell on Samael, and he lifted his chin. "What are you doing this time?"

The doorbell rang and Shafer shot to his feet. "I'll get it."

"Coward," Luc bit out as the demon speed walked to the door.

Shafer itched the back of his head with his middle finger, eliciting a scowl from the prince.

"He's here." Luc stood.

Wylie followed suit. "Lucifer?" She cringed inwardly as Samael used the couch arm to get to his feet. Her medical brain ran through all the human ailments that would leave him so pale and stiff.

"Yeah, Grandfather, can't you feel him?"

Wylie nodded even though she didn't actually hear what he said. *Anemia,* it was probably anemia, she reminded herself. The wounds David had stitched still seeped blood. Human wounds shouldn't bleed this long.

A large male and a female flanked Luc's grandfather as he entered the living room. Their red robes fluttered as they walked. The female's eyes pinned Wylie to the spot, but her face remained expressionless.

Luc crossed the room and the leader's arms opened wide. "Luci!" Luc pulled his grandfather close and aggressively beat on his back in that masculine way. Still grinning, Lucifer released his grandson and turned to Samael. "Big brother, it's been a long time."

Samael inclined his head. "Brother."

Lucifer turned to Wylie next. She wasn't prepared for the wave of charisma that came with the Devil's attention.

"And this must be Armageddon." Lucifer The First opened his arms to Wylie. "She's taller than I thought she'd be."

Wylie offered her hand, not quite ready to hug the Devil, but Lucifer grinned and pulled her close anyway.

"Granddaughter! Welcome to the family." He stepped back and waved at the green-eyed woman. Her hand immediately fluttered up to straighten the veil covering her hair. "This is Lady Emberlynn Grim. My future granddaughter-in-law."

Wylie turned to Luc. He raised his hands. "Not my future bride, but definitely a good friend."

The fallen angel reached over and squeezed Emberlynn's shoulder. "She's Santana's fated. Luc's little brother."

The female blushed; her eyes glued to her shoes.

"And this is Brute Hildebrandt, the Royal Tattooist." The Devil thumped the male's back.

Brute's sharp eyes also fell to the ground as he lowered his head in deference, but his hulking form made him look anything but humble. There was a tension in his stance that matched Emberlynn's, in fact static seem to flow between and around the two with an emotion that Wylie could only describe as wanting.

"They offered to escort me here, though I'm sure they only came because they were missing young Lucifer."

Luc closed his eyes, his jaw ticking.

"You've grown old," Samael said, and Wylie remembered why the King of Hell itself was there.

Lucifer laughed. "Did you just land a joke? You've certainly changed." He gestured to the couch. "We should all sit."

Wylie hung back, absorbing the energy between Emberlynn and Brute one more time. They emitted the same old, earthy Scientia that the Devils' did, but Emberlynn's felt black and sterile and Brute's felt warm and spicy. They followed Lucifer to his seat and took up residence at his back, both standing at attention. Emberlynn studied the room while Brute took up the blank stare of a guard. The two of them leaning toward each other ever so slightly.

Wylie shook her head. Why was she so entranced by this couple? She needed to get back in the game. She found her seat and studied the Devils across from her. Lucifer and his grandson sat with the same postures but that's where their similarities ended. While she considered Luc handsome—with his mahogany double-lidded eyes and black hair— he came across more like a rockstar, topped with a cowboy hat. Lucifer, on the other hand, looked more like royalty. Heavenly royalty.

Lucifer's skin gave off a golden glow, and he wore his halo like a crown. Wylie felt like a pimple on an ass sitting in the room with the male.

"I'm glad to see your health has improved, brother." Lucifer frowned. "The more Scientia you lose, the harder the recovery."

Samael nodded, and Wylie wished she could read his mind, but he'd retained his impenetrable defense of his thoughts.

"Every day is a little easier, but I know you're not here to give me well wishes."

"Indeed, I'm not. The Queen Regent asked if I'd talk to you, and I thought why not? Maybe my brother will be interested in working with me."

Samael folded his arms. "I lost my wings, not my conscious."

Lucifer waved the remark away as the two behind him shifted. "It doesn't matter, I'm just happy to have this chance to set the record straight and tell my side of the story."

"What story?" Wylie asked, her eyes bouncing between Samael and Lucifer. Who didn't the Dominion have history with?

"Of my fall."

"I was there. I know the story." Samael's jaw ticked.

"You may have been the one to cut off my wings, brother—" Lucifer sneered "—but you weren't there when it all began." His hand gracefully swept across the room, gesturing to all those present. "Here, let me show you." The room fell into darkness, and Wylie gripped Samael's forearm. She had to keep him safe.

Samael leaned into her, their shoulders touching. "It's okay. I'd never let him hurt you."

She shivered as his breath touched her ear. A stream of images projected themselves around the group, and Wylie realized she was back in Arcadia staring up at the door. Memories of Roberto's ring flooded her, and her hand slid from Samael's arm.

A golden winged Lucifer stood before the door; his forehead pressed into the wood as he pushed with all his might. "Father, I beseech you."

His Archangel wings fluttered as if to help him. He observed the dress code of the Heavenly Planes, which was nothing. The muscles of his back bunched as his feet slipped on the grass. He shook his head and checked over his shoulder as if he expected to be reprimanded at any moment. He turned back to the door and pushed again.

"I refuse to believe that you created this planet only to let it fester and rot as the humans learn sin. Adam may have taken a bite of the apple, but the solution to this beginning cannot be an end." His hand fisted. "I have a plan. I'll bring them all home to you. Father, hear me. I'll bring them all back to you." He beat against the door. "Father."

Lucifer slid to the ground, turning from the door and pulling his knees to his chest. "All I want to do is bring them home. All of them. Every one of them."

Wylie recognized the squeal of the hinges as the monstrosity slid open. The opening was four or five times larger than what Wylie had made on that fateful day she said her goodbyes to Roberto. But this time, only blinding light could be seen in the opening.

"You want to bring them all home?"

Lucifer scrambled back to his feet. "Father?"

"I ask the questions. How will you bring them all home?"

The Archangel's wings glittered as the God-light brightened. He shaded his eyes with his hands. "If, if we took their free will, they'd—"

"This is your plan?" God's voice boomed. "You want to take away what makes them different from you?"

"I—"

"Lucifer, you were made with thicker clay than most, but I didn't think you were this dense."

The Archangel's jaw dropped. Wylie imagined sarcasm had yet to be invented at this point in time.

"Think, child, what do human's need now they've discovered sin?"

"Repentance? Hope? Kindness?" Lucifer listed the words like questions.

"They have those things. I made the first angels for such menial things."

Lucifer lifted his eyes to the light. "A guide?"

"Yes. When my humans fall into darkness, and fall they will, I need someone to walk with them in that unending night. Someone to lead them through all those hateful things your siblings don't understand. Someone to wait with them for the light."

"I can do this."

"You can, son, but not alone. You must—"

"I don't believe this for one minute." Samael's voice broke through the memory and light returned to the room as the vision faded away.

"You've told your version of the story long enough." The Devil leveled his eyes on Samael. "When Adam and Eve lost their way, I came to you. You'd already spoken to the Seraphim. You reassured me that a plan was in place to recover the human destiny. I told you that you were a fool."

"I remember this conversation." Samael grumbled something in a language Wylie didn't understand and the Devil laughed. "You started your descent that day."

"No."

"Yes." A genuine smile peaked at the corner of Samael's mouth. "This argument will never end between us."

"I left our discussion angry with a new determination to speak to

God myself. I waited many years to find a time when the Seraphim were not guarding the door to Heaven. Remember the times when they'd lend their Scientia to the Thrones to build especially powerful Angels?"

Samael nodded. "The Thrones were ever trying to create what the world needed from them."

"Yes, brother, but they were not the only crafty angels to grace the Heavenly Planes. When I knocked, God answered. I've shown you what he told me."

They all sat in silence for a moment, Wylie's palms moistened with sweat.

"He told me I would need to fight for the humans—that only through sacrifice could I meet my goals. And he was right.

"Look at me now. The war, the loss of my wings, of most of my brethren was a sacrifice God intended for me to make. He promised me my own kingdom and gave me the responsibility of guiding the humans and their natural morals. The fallen understand them because we live with them. We fall with them. We draw our power from them and their world, just as they find power in us."

Samael cleared his throat. "I can't believe that God meant for a war in heaven that would lead to winners on both sides?" He closed his eyes. "I endure the pain of taking the lives and wings of too many of my siblings to believe it was part of the plan. God would never . . ." Samael rubbed his forehead, his voice drifting off.

"How could He not? He created too perfect of beings to guard his little sinners. He needed some of us to evolve into what humans can become when their humanity is worn thin. When they're hungry or desperate. You know what that's like now, don't you, Samael?"

Lucifer narrowed his eyes at Samael. "I've come to tell you that all is not lost." His lips turned up. "I can teach you to pull power from places other than heaven. You'll no longer have the burden of timeless Scientia. Water will lose its effect on you. You don't have to be an angel to fight for what you believe in. Even if what you believe is wrong."

Luc burst out laughing. "I've been telling him he's wrong for centuries. He never listened."

Samael shook his head, his pale lips forming a smile.

Wylie joined him in his grin, she couldn't let the rest bully him. "As far as I know Samael has never been wrong."

Luc clapped his knee with a snort. "You two are the perfect pair, aren't you?"

Wylie ignored him, turning her question to her grandfather. "So how does it work? This magic from the earth?"

"Simple." Lucifer stood up and raised his arms, creating a vacuum that took all breath from the room. "You take it." The King of Hell shrugged. "Brute, why don't you give us a demonstration."

Brute stepped forward, fell to a knee, and placed his palms on the ground. His arms flexed and his head bowed, shadows spreading over him, etching him into a statue. His voice rumbled in a guttural language. He dug his fingers into the ground as if gripping handfuls of dirt and tossed it into the air. The room darkened and stars sparkled along the ceiling.

Wylie rested her head back. The sudden calm of night spread over her. Samael's chest expanded next to her. He leaned into her once more.

"Brute and his family are necromancers. Their bloodline traces back to the Middle Ages. He is the fourth generation to serve the royal family." Lucifer waved his hand and light returned. "Thank you, son."

The necromancer stood and returned to his spot behind Luc. Wylie noticed how Brute intentionally stood too close to Emberlynn and then how the female's cheeks grew pink. Their shoulders touched as he straightened and her head tilted toward his. They were captivating. She was almost jealous, but wasn't Emberlynn promised to another?

"This is a lot to think about." Samael clapped his hands on his knees. "Who's to say if I'll have any potential in these arts."

"Puedes entenderme?"

Samael nodded. *"Si."*

Lucifer's smile widened. *"Watashi ga iu koto o wakarimusa ka?"*

"Hai."

Wylie recognized the first question. *Can you understand me?* The second language had to be Japanese. She'd heard it enough at work to be familiar.

"Peux-tu me comprende?"

"Oui."

"You still have the Angel Tongue then. I haven't been able to read your thoughts since I got here. You're so much more than your Scientia or a horse or whatever." He waved at Wylie as if you dismiss her. "You're the first angel. The last Dominion. You have the same potential I did when I came here. Your skills developed from something beyond the borrowed soul you feed off."

"Borrowed soul?" Wylie asked.

"His muse." Luc cracked his knuckles. "Haven't the angels taught you anything? Our muse is our soul."

Feeding on them? A flash of Wylie crawling up David's body had a cringe tightening her chest. "You guys have muses too." All heads turned to Wylie, and she had a sense that they attempted to read her mind.

"My grandfather lost his wings. Some of us, the older ones, the second and third generations were born with muses," Luc said. "But our relationships are more mutually beneficial." Luc adjusted the rings. "Our Scientia is a shared energy that flows back and forth between us."

"But that's not what you're worried about."

Wylie jumped. She'd forgotten about Shafer. Her head swung around. The demon remained standing, leaning against the wall near the entrance. Their eyes met.

"What you experienced with David during the transfer of power, gave you a taste of what it's like. Angel's need their muses because they are *weak* without them. Demons need their muses because they are *nothing* without them. They conduct and filter the power of the earth. Without them, for those of us that still have them, we're as human as Samael is now. They are our everything and until you meet your fated, David will be the most important person in your life."

"Speaking of, you should see him first when we get back Earthside. You're going to be busy once the angels get their hands on you." Luc folded his fingers together and turned to Samael. "I'm going to introduce you to my muse. She'll teach you some simple spells."

"Spells?" Samael raised his brows.

Lucifer chuckled to himself. "Oh, how far the mighty has fallen."

Samael's hands fisted.

"Mary lives in Pearl. She's a little eccentric, but a master at her craft." Luc pushed on, ignoring the King of Hell's comment.

"I don't know." Samael inched to the edge of his seat, all of his grace absent, he'd become shear will.

Luc shook his head. "There's nothing else you can do to help Wylie. Not as you are now. We can help you with that."

Samael pushed himself to his feet, and lifted his forearm to Lucifer. The Devil returned the salute from his seat, the smile never leaving those lips. "Your grandson is relentless."

"I'd like to say he got that from me—" Lucifer stood "—but I know without a shadow of a doubt that you had something to do with it."

Samael put his hand out for Wylie, and she did her best not to transfer any of her weight onto him as she stood.

"If you aren't going to take my grandson up on his offer, you could always come with me. Both of you."

A smile slipped onto Samael's lips. "Not today, Satan."

Lucifer chuckled. He closed the space between them and, pulling Samael into a proper hug this time, slapped the male on the back. "You've gotten better at telling jokes. Being human suits you."

Samael embraced the male who once had been his enemy but before then had been his brother. His face softened. *"Pro summum bonum."*

"Pro summum bonum."

Wylie's chest lightened with Lucifer's response and for the first time since Samael gave up his wing, she felt hope.

Chapter 9

Samael

"Again." Shafer clapped his hands to emphasize the syllables. He leaned against the piano in Luc's overly large sitting room, his cowboy hat a brown splotch on the instrument's black lacquer.

Samael shook his head and a bead of sweat dripped into his eye. He blinked hard, mimicking the hand movement Shafer had shown him. "*Quae magni momenti tuenda sunt.*" The Latin slid off his tongue with its usual smoothness, but the words didn't carry the same power Shafer's had.

He straightened, ready to start over again. A shock of pain stabbed him between the shoulder blades, and he remembered the smell of burnt flesh. He'd talked Luc into cauterizing the stubs of his wings again and now the stench followed him.

"Okay, I think that's enough for today." Shafer placed his hat back on his head and was several steps away before he paused. "What's Ariel's favorite candy?"

Samael wiped his brow, using all of his energy to resist collapsing onto the couch behind him. "Why don't you ask her yourself?" He couldn't read minds anymore, or smell the Archangel's scent, but he'd noticed all the half smiles and distant stares. He'd caught himself doing the same after spending time with Wylie.

Shafer raised a brow. "What makes you think that goddess would give me the time of day."

Samael didn't have the energy for this game. "She doesn't like candy. Get her a blunt or a gun or something sharp. She likes sharp things."

Shafer's laughter froze in his chest when his eyes met Samael's. "You're serious?"

"Very."

"Noted. Thank you. I'll see you tomorrow." The demon strolled away, stopping at the grand stairs and shouting. "Wylie, your ward is ready for you."

Samael glared at Shafer when he winked in his direction. *Damn that demon.* Samael straightened just in time for Wylie to project to his side.

She touched his forehead and he held his breath. "You should probably lie down." She had that curtain over her eyes. The one that so often divided them now.

He'd become a job to her.

She deliberately led him to the staircase, never touching him again. Her feet moved in slow motion, a plethora of words distracting from his weakness. "I've been thinking about the prophecy."

"What about the prophecy?"

"I'm running out of time to find my horses."

Samael grunted as he reached the landing.

"What does that mean?"

"They'll find you." He entered his room and lifted his brows when Wylie followed him in. She'd avoided his room since he began getting around on his own.

Wylie put her hands on her hips. "What's wrong?"

He passed her, wiping at yet another bead of sweat on his forehead. He was surrounded by monotony now. How is it that she couldn't see it? *Merda*, the problem was his mortal body. He sat, his teeth grinding. "Spells? Really? This is the solution to my humanity." Shame took the rest of his words from him. He thought back to Lucifer's suggestion and then to the last moments he'd spent with his brother before he fell. The glory of battle. The spray of Lucifer's blood across his face as he took everything from the Archangel. How righteous he'd been, unknowingly creating the King of Hell for God.

"You don't have to do this. You're enough on your own." Wylie's stance slackened.

He grunted a response; he'd never take to the air again. He'd never go to battle with a chest full of pride. He recognized it now. The pride. He'd fallen so low that he feared leaving tomorrow. His time with Wylie was basically over. Now, he was nothing but deadweight, mourning the time he'd stolen from the chosen one.

Wylie knelt next to him, her hand caressing the bed, inches away from his leg. "Samael." Their eyes met and those obsidian depths warmed him, blacking out the panic creeping under his skin.

She reached up and traced the black ink of his halo through his shirt. And for once the thought of it never resting on his crown was superseded by her touch. "You are more than this."

Samael shook his head, watching her fingers. Was he? Was he really? Had he made a mistake? He covered his face with his hands as despair flooded him, beating out Wylie's sweetness. She must've felt his emotions because she stood and pulled him to her, his cheek resting against her chest. He held his breath, his body wanting to crumple in on itself or pull her so close they became one person. Perhaps both at once. These feelings were not the reason he decided to donate his Scientia to Wylie, but it did make it easier. How could he regret his decision while in her arms? He fisted the blanket he sat on, not trusting what his hands wanted. He forced away the itch to run them up and down her body, the aggression of his doubts turning into an intense want. Dear Lord, how many emotions could he feel in the span of minutes? "Sunshine." He breathed, air stubbornly refusing to leave his lungs.

Her hands came to his cheeks and tilted his head up so she could devour him with her eyes again. "Can I kiss you?" The kindness softening her face said everything she didn't.

This wasn't passion, this was another treatment. Part of her nurse care plan. He'd become her patient. His eyes lowered to her lips, and his heart ached as it fluttered in his chest. He'd come to terms with being the white horse long ago, but he never realized how many times he'd break. He gripped her hands. "You don't have to." His eyes fell, shame burning his cheeks.

She stifled a nervous laugh. "I'm offering because I want to?"

He heard her words, but also the obligation that thickened them. He closed his eyes. He needed to get out of this room. "Thank you, Wylie. I'm grateful for all you've done for me, but it's time for you to focus on your destiny." His hands fell to her hips and guided her to his side before standing.

He'd forgotten how much taller he was than her. Probably because he'd 'convalesced' like a princess for so long. His mind flashed to David and the panic he'd always heard in the man's voice. Maybe the boy didn't hate him. Maybe part of it was the inadequacy that came with humanity, of knowing he would never be enough for her. Samael's hand landed on the door knob before he knew what he was doing. "I'm sorry."

"You're more than your Scientia, Sam."

He grunted before shutting the door behind him. He headed down the hall and tripped on a step, crashing into a wall. He rubbed his shoulder where a bruise formed. Shaking his head, he reached for the light switch.

The door leading to Luc's room was a different color than the others, and Samael found himself wondering why as he knocked. His hand remained in a fist, clenched in frustration. He missed projecting and sending commands with his mind. Knocking and walking down hallways were so tedious. Being human, from the wasted time in the bathroom to the wasted time in sleep, was exhausting, and simple, and no longer held any appeal to him.

Luc opened the door with only his pants, his black hair disheveled. "What?"

"I think I need a drink."

Luc lifted a brow. "What?"

Samael thought back to the minimal reaction his angel body had to alcohol and his heart raced with the promise of something more. "I need some whiskey, and maybe a beer. I'm not sure what this body can handle."

Luc grinned. "Hell, yes!" He turned back to his room. "Wait for me there. And don't move."

Samael heard a female mumble, and Luc's face hardened.

"What did you say?" The Prince asked the dark room.

"Yes, sir."

Luc turned to Samael. "Wait a moment." He retreated back into his room and a woman moaned. "I said no sounds." Heavy panting followed by a gasp and a slap. "Now, don't move an inch or you're going to be fucking yourself tonight."

Samael took a step back from the door, his face burning with what he'd come to know as embarrassment.

Luc came out of the room pulling a shirt over his head. "Sorry about that." He smirked as the door shut. "You can't be the only one getting any in this house."

Samael grunted. He didn't get it, but Luc was a demon, and Samael gave up understanding him generations ago.

"You're upset about leaving?" Luc closed his door with a click.

Samael clenched his jaw, following Luc. He felt unsettled. Unsure. Not himself. Now that he was out of the fog of healing, he'd realized that for the first time in his long life he didn't have a purpose.

Luc nodded as if reading his thoughts. "Fuck, brother. I get it, or I'm trying to get it. I remember what it was like to train under you." They made it to the wet bar next to the piano. "Let's get fucked up." He pulled out a fifth of whisky. "I've been saving this for over a century for a night like this." He cracked it open and passed the bottle. "To life."

Samael lifted it in the air. "*Prosit.*" The whisky went down smooth and smokey. "How are things looking Earthside?"

"Shittier than it did last time you saw it." Luc poured another. "That's why we're going back." He raised his glass again. "To Wylie."

"Hmph." Samael knocked the drink back. Thirty minutes of stories later and he laughed harder than he knew he could.

"And then I threw the smoke bomb in Santana's room. I swear, he screamed like a girl."

"*Devils.*" Samael shook his head.

Luc's chest puffed out with pride as he lifted his chin in acknowledgment.

Samael blew out a breath and leaned back into the couch, the world suddenly weighing him down again. "At least you know who you are. I'm nothing."

"Satan's staff, really? You're going there." Luc leaned forward in his seat, his brows lifted.

"I know I did the right thing by giving her my power, but I don't know that I should've survived. I'm useless now. You should have bled me dry."

Luc came across the room in two strides. He jerked Samael to his feet by his shirt. "You'd leave us? After all this? You'd leave me to pick up the pieces while the world fucking ends?"

Samael searched Luc's face, seeing for the thousandth time why he'd taken the boy under his wing. Hell's heir was stronger than a prince, braver than an angel, and more loyal than a friend.

Before he could speak those thoughts Luc continued. "You need to think really hard about your priorities." He pushed Samael back onto the couch. "Now, excuse me." Luc unbuttoned his collar. "I have someone waiting for me."

Samael took a few more swigs of his whiskey and then pulled his phone from his pocket. With sloppy movements he rested his head on the arm of the couch and scrolled through his contacts. Originally, he planned to call Madoc, but then realized he may or may not be able to string more than a few words together.

David.

He hit the call button before he could talk himself out of it.

"Is she okay?" The muse's worried voice broke through the static in a rush.

Samael rested his head back and stared at the ceiling. "David, David, David. Why didn't you tell me how hard it is to be you?"

"Samael?" More static. *"What's going on?"*

"I'm a mess." Samael's 'M's slurred together and his 'S's stretched out forever.

"Why did you call me?"

Samael snorted and then slapped his hand over his mouth. *What was that sound?*

"Samael." David's voice came smothered in displeasure.

"I'm human."

"Samael, pass the phone to Wylie."

"She's not here. I don't deserve her."

A silence stretched between them, and Samael finished his whisky.

"Why are you drunk dialing me?"

"Because you're the only one who knows what it's like to wait at home for her. How did you do it?" Samael pulled the phone from his ear as it crackled.

"You're sleeping with her?"

"No, David."

"Good."

Samael sat up too quickly. "It doesn't matter, I'll kill you if you ever touch her again."

"So, this is why you called me? To stake your claim?"

"I called you because I'm lost, and she hasn't left yet."

"Fine." David blew out a breath into the phone. *"You stay busy. That's the best you can do. Keep moving until there is no space left in your mind for worry. Don't forget that you are a whole person without her. You can still do good."*

Samael put his feet up on the couch and the world spun around him. "I'm so drunk."

"You are."

"David?"

"Yeah?"

"I loved your father. I loved him so much. God, I miss him."

"Good night, Samael." David clicked off.

Samael stumbled to his feet and up the stairs, leaning heavily on the handrail. He made it to his room and leaned against the doorway for a moment before entering. Wylie had fallen asleep in his bed, waiting for him. Her tawny skin cast in warm shadows by the red moonlight. She was every bit the angel he knew she'd become. He stumbled in, knelt beside her, and held onto the mattress as the spins started again. His stomach grumbled and the whisky inched up his throat. He slid to the ground, promising himself that he'd find a way to still do good.

Chapter 10

Lex

She picked up the tablet and flipped it to the next page. Gabriel sat in a lounge chair, an empty pounder in his hand, his eyes closed. Lex closed her eyes and pushed her way into his world. It felt a lot like the times she's projected with Gabriel in the past. The weird weightlessness of it. She focused, her fists clenching as she forced her projection to become solid.

She had no clue what Gabriel saw when he looked at her, but when she looked down at her hand, they were slightly transparent. She knelt in front of him.

"Lex." *His voice was gravel. His eyes remained closed.* "Why are you doing this to me?"

She tested herself, resting her hand on his thighs and then gripping them. Her fingers didn't sink into him, so she pushed the heels of her hand up his thighs until her palms rested on his abs.

His hands covered hers. "Ma petite râleuse." His lips turned down in a way they never had when she was alive. "Why did you leave me?"

She kissed his knee. "You know why."

He covered his face. "You're killing me, Lex. I wish I could've gone with you."

Her hands climbed his body, holding tight as she concentrated on staying solid.

"Lexy!" *He leaned forward, his hands taking either side of her face. It was his cold that made her whole. His Scientia and his ice turned her into more than a ghost. He took her mouth with his. He held her so tight that she wondered if he was trying to pull her through the veil.*

She returned his kiss, hungry as her tongue explored his. She moaned into him. God, she missed him more than anything. More than life or drugs. Everything, including heaven, seemed mundane next to him. Her fingers drifted to the fly of his pants and fumbled with the button. He pulled away. His eyes fell to her hands. Her fingers weren't quite solid enough to push the button through the hole.

Gabriel gripped the arms of the lounge chair, and Lex only felt more determined when she heard the shudder in his breath. She let her hands drift against the hardening outline of his cock, and her mouth watered. Gabriel's black eyes drilled into her until she won her fight with his pants. He freed his cock for her, and she wasted no time capturing it with her mouth, her tongue caressing the seams of its head.

Lex grazed her teeth along the ridges, tasting how much he wanted her. She sucked and swallowed, pulling as much of his length into her mouth as she could. She worked in a rhythm, showing him all those little attentions she'd been in too much of a rush for in life. His fingers weaved through her hair, and hers came up to settle on his, pressing them every time she took him in.

He groaned, gripped her hair tighter, and moved her head to meet his thrusts. He punished her mouth with his cock, and she opened her throat to him. He soon fisted her hair in one hand and clutched her throat with the other. "You. Did. This. To. Us." *He shoved deeper with each word.*

She gagged as her nose grazed his abs and her chin touched his balls. She swallowed and swallowed, gripping his thighs tight to keep him from shoving her off of him as he drove into her. Her knees slid on the ground, and she wound her fingers around his belt loops and pulled him to her tighter making breathing impossible.

She was dead; she didn't need to breathe.

Tears ran down her face and mixed with her spit as she hummed with ecstasy. Lightheaded with the pain and the love they shared at that moment.

"Fuck!" *he barked as his seed filled her belly.* "Fuck." *He gathered her up. More solid than ever as he wiped the tears from her face and pushed his nose into her neck, breathing her in.* "I loved you. I loved you so damn much, hellcat."

Gabriel

Lex was back, but flickering. Gabriel's phone rang, and she disappeared altogether. "Wait." He jumped to his feet, zipping his pants, and fastening his belt.

"Answer the phone."

Gabriel glanced at his desk. He didn't care about the phone.

"Answer it."

"Binah?" Gabriel put the phone to his ear.

"I think I know how we can get to Wylie."

"Fucking Binah. Tell her 'no.'"

Gabriel collapsed back in his chair, searching the room for his little live wire. When he found it empty, he closed his eyes, looking for her in the darkness there. "I will not repeat myself again. I'm desperate, not a bastard," he said through his teeth. The anger in his voice only half related to Binah's defiance. "There has to be another way."

"There is, baby."

He wanted this to be true. They sounded so true coming from her.

"Maybe. I'll keep looking, but Gabriel. We're stuck here. Right now, this is our only option."

"Bitch, shut up and get back to work."

Gabriel massaged his brow. "I said 'no.'" His thumb mashed the red button on his screen.

"Don't give up."

He pressed his forehead into the desk, the sound of her voice cutting him deeper than any blade ever had. "Lexy, I need you back. I feel like I'm going crazy." Had she really been there or was he jerking himself off?

"I'*m trying*." Something brushed against the back of his neck.

A breeze? He spun around for the millionth time that day, reaching for her presence. "Please." His lungs crowded his chest as he waited for a response. Nothing. The burgundy of the wallpaper matched the heat at his collar. Still nothing. She was gone. Or she'd never been there in the first place.

"C'est des conneries!" He threw his phone across the room. It smacked into the wall with a crunch. He yanked at his tie with both hands, fighting to free himself before tossing the thing. His jacket came next, but he still itched like he'd explode at any moment. He shoved his chair back as he stood. It smacked into the wall, and somehow the crunch of plaster gave Gabriel permission to let loose. He pulled his drawers free, turned the desk over, and shoved his bookcase onto its side. His teeth clenched against the shouts brewing in his chest. He swung around when the office door opened.

"Son?" Raphael stepped inside. His gaze slid from Gabriel's disheveled appearance to the fucking tie on the ground. "This won't do." He crossed the room, retrieving Gabriel's discarded clothing. "Did you forget you have a video conference in thirty minutes?"

Gabriel swallowed his retort, his lips flattening. The air crackled with cold as Raphael approached him. His nostrils flared. If only he were faster. He was stronger, had more power, but he couldn't risk attacking with the hex in place.

The Dominion rebuttoned the younger angel's collar and looped the tie around his neck. "Your hair is getting too long." Raphael pulled the knot a little too tight, a self-assured grin on his face. "You know, the sooner you realize I did all of this for you. The sooner things can get back to normal."

"There's no normal between us." Gabriel's skin crawled in every place where the angel had touched him. He'd kept his loathing for Raphael at bay for a week, but they both knew the truth: Gabriel stayed by Raphael's side so he'd have easier access when it came time to kill the Dominion. His father didn't seem to care.

Gabriel yanked his jacket from Raphael's hands, shrugged it on and smoothed his lapels. He strolled to the door, keeping his rage inside despite the air crackling with cold. "Touch me again, and you lose my cooperation. I'd pay to see you do a video conference with me as your puppet."

"Son."

Gabriel fisted his shirt over the side where Raphael had burned the hex into his bones.

"Don't make me hurt you." Raphael grinned, and the pain multiplied by ten. "This childishness is boring me."

Gabriel panted as he turned his back on the Dominion. With a growl he flung his door open. "Let me show you true childishness." He flung the words over his shoulder, and then pointed at Todd. "You, stay here." Gabriel waited for his father to join him before heading for the closest exit.

"Where are we going?" Raphael stayed at his heels.

"You're playing God, but not the all-knowing kind. You're more like a toddler with dolls in a sandbox." Gabriel flung the door open. "After you."

Grunts and cries met them. He gestured for his father to exit, the half-smile plastered to his face matching Raphael's.

The Dominion grimaced. "This is what I'm talking about."

"What, you don't want to look at the monsters you created?" He pointed at a subhuman who repeatedly slammed into the forcefield Raphael now maintained since Gabriel refused to.

"I'm not impressed with your theatrics."

Gabriel lifted a brow. "Are you afraid?" He stepped outside, letting the door go.

Raphael caught it.

"They really aren't that bad." The muses snarled en masse as Gabriel grew closer and the sub humans went wild, punching against the forcefield until the electrical shock dropped them, and then springing back up to compete with its neighbors for the privilege of proximity to Gabriel. "C'mon, Father." Gabriel let out a laugh. "You know, you're kind of their father too. They're basically my siblings.

You've always been good at making monsters." Gabriel tilted his head, reaching for the forcefield.

Raphael shook his head. "I hate to do this, but you need to learn a lesson." The Dominion's hand fisted and Gabriel collapsed in the grass, dirt in his mouth as he moaned in pain. He couldn't breathe.

A flash beside him had him forcing himself to roll onto his side. He saw the wall of subhumans seconds before they were upon him. Raphael had dropped the forcefield. Nails and teeth, fists and feet. The thousand cuts dealt by the beasts eclipsed the pain immobilizing him.

"Fight, baby!"

His whole body jerked as something entered him. A warmth washed over him and the agony dissipated. Whiffs of recognition settled like stones in his gut. Ice shot from his back, shredding through the subhumans, freezing them into statues of malice.

Gabriel crawled to his feet, a howl escaping his lips as Lex's Scientia left him. It had to be her. It had to. He blinked at the familiar faces of the monsters who'd attacked them. His muses, all of them. Shame and renewed loss tightened his throat.

He wiped the blood from his face, his wounds already healing. The forcefield was back up, and Raphael stood next to Todd at the door.

"I had your friend, here, bring you clothes. Change. You can't be late for your interview." The Dominion walked away, his straight back and easy gait taunting Gabriel. "Oh, and I have a new assignment for you. It's time we break this quarantine. You'll lure Wylie and her useless companions away from Earthside."

Gabriel ignored Raphael marching passed him as if he didn't exist.

"Son, I don't want to have to teach you another lesson. Let me know you're ready to get to work."

The anger that had him tearing apart his office returned. He had no choice. "Yes, Father. I'll start working on a plan today," he gritted out.

His hands shook as he entered the building, the door slamming behind him. Todd straightened handing Gabriel a hanger with a suit on it.

"Why are you here?"

"Raphael asked me to bring this."

Gabriel tore off his ripped clothes and pulled on his new suit, hating the message the Dominion sent by leaving the muse waiting for him. It would be so easy for Raphael to take more. There was always someone else his father could take from him. "What did I say to you?"

The human raised his brow. "Stay here."

The angel headed for the conference room, the muse following with heavier footballs than normal.

No one was safe around him. "I want you to be reassigned."

"What?" Todd fell a step behind.

"I want you wherever your wife is. Give me some disposable angel that's loyal to Raphael."

"But, boss—"

Gabriel stopped and Todd ran into his back. "Don't question me. Not now." The angel resumed his progress down the hall. Raphael sent just as a message by letting down the forcefield as he had by bringing Gabriel's human companion into danger.

"Yes, sir. I'll find my replacement tonight."

"No, Todd, now."

Todd footfalls stopped. "I need Dina in the conference room now," he said into his ear piece.

Gabriel pushed into the conference room to find the camera and lighting already set up. He unbuttoned his jacket and pulled up his pant legs, sitting in his leather chair with all the dignity he'd lost the moment before. He forced his mouth to lift at the corners and his forehead to smooth. The second hand of his watch ticked, tempting him to glance down, instead he lifted his head to Ken. "Ready?"

"I have a list of questions they'll ask, should I read them to you?" Ken blinked as his eyes met Gabriel's. He lifted a hand and snapped it. "Where's hair and makeup?" Ken shook his head, pointing at Gabriel's ear. "You have blood." A woman walked up with a caddy, and Ken grabbed the package of face wipes. He touched the wipe against Gabriel's face just as Gabriel's hand locked around his wrist.

"I can do it." The woman held up a mirror as Gabriel cleaned the blood and dirt from his skin. He opened his hand. "I need gel and a comb."

Silently the woman provided both.

Gabriel studied Ken and his fidgeting as he parted his hair, no wonder Lex never liked him. "I read the questions."

"Did you see that Eric Lee is interviewing you? Last time he was quite pushy."

Gabriel closed his eyes. His patience was far past gone, his mind caught between the moment he'd been attacked and the moment Lexy saved him. Because that's what she'd done. Wasn't it? "I can handle myself."

Ken nodded, his brows meeting. "You're distracted. I can reschedule this."

"Stop fussing, Ken. Just give me the countdown." Gabriel stared into the light behind the camera, the pain in his head doubling.

"Three minutes." Ken paced the length of the room. His feet dragged on the plush, red carpet. Trepidation poured out of the man. "Two minutes and thirty seconds."

"*Mon Dieu,* out." Gabriel pointed at the door, his voice coming out far too loud for his liking.

Ken stopped. "Really?"

"Out!" Gabriel never raised his voice. Never.

Ken nodded, taking a long look at Gabriel before leaving.

"You—" Gabriel pointed at the cameraman "—I want a ten-second count down." *And everyone else shut the fuck up.* The words flashed in his head as if Lex had forced them there. She would've pinched him by now or given him the one-finger salute. She would've climbed into his lap, straddling him in front of everyone as if they didn't exist and organized his curls.

And he— he would've cupped her rounded belly and listened for their little one's heartbeat. That sound would have replaced the tick of his watch. A touchstone and a promise.

"Ten, nine . . ."

He would have licked her neck, bit her collarbone, mapped the scars on her face with his fingertips.

"Two, one."

His heart. Lex had been his heart. His eyes widened with the realization.

The camera man waved and Eric appeared on the screen in front of him.

"Let's welcome Gabriel Andel. He is coming to us today from Baton Rouge, the epicenter of this threatening pandemic."

Gabriel slowed his breaths pushing the realization that Wylie's heart might actually be a person. "Thank you, Eric. It's been a while."

"Can we expect to see you at the Paranormal Response Summit in DC?"

Gabriel had no plans on attending. The humans were on their own. "I plan to attend as long as I'm able to get there."

"I'm sure you've been busy, with this virus originating in your state." Eric pointed at the top of the screen where a video of a wave of husks hit the quarantine barrier at once. Their faces slack as they slammed into the concrete until they bled.

Gabriel spared a glance. "It's been wild, but I'm used all my resources to help the people affected."

"There're some people who find this suspicious."

"In what way, Eric?" Now this was going in a different direction than the brief.

"Well, we don't know a lot about how the virus works, but somehow you do. Can you explain how you were able to respond to this illness faster than our government?"

"I have less red tape, Eric." Gabriel's smile slipped, his jaw tightening.

The man adjusted his tie, the confrontation making red splotches appear under his heavy makeup. "We have sources that say you have a lab familiar with such viruses. Is this the case?"

"We do have a high-tech medical facility on the rehabilitation center that I fund." Gabriel gestured around him.

"So, your 'medical facility' knows enough to advise the government?"

Gabriel folded his fingers together. "It's no secret that I'm an angel.

One could conclude that I would have an interest in understanding an illness that only affects muses."

"Muses?"

"Yes, Eric," Gabriel said through his teeth.

"Can you explain what those are to those watching who have never heard the term before?"

The air around Gabriel became frigid. "Of course. A muse is a human who contains an angel's energy."

"What does that mean?"

"Every angel has a human counterpart." Gabriel's knuckles whitened. "This human provides them with the energy they need to do their jobs."

"Are these humans—"

"I'm going to stop you there, Eric. We, in Louisiana, have found ourselves in a state of emergency. If you need an education in angels, I can provide you with a list of people who would happily answer your questions. People are dying. I don't have time to beat around the bush. Here's what I know. This virus only affects muses. It's not deadly but is causing major cognitive deficits. These brain injuries leave their victims unrecognizable to their families. They're violent and dangerous." Gabriel leaned forward, his mouth shrugging.

"This virus is bloodborne. If you don't know what that is, again, I'm not the one to ask. I've lost people I love to this illness. I should be mourning, but instead, I'm doing everything I can to prevent the spread of this disease." Gabriel stood, buttoning his jacket and walking off-screen. He motioned for the cameraman to cut the feed.

He had more important things to do than play politics. He had to collect his sister's heart. "I want you to leak the news that Lex is dead, and someone get me Ken. I need to plan a trip to Seattle."

Chapter 11

DAVID

David used to love Seattle. Not anymore. Now, all he heard when he went outside were sirens. The rain that once empowered him as he pushed himself to pedal faster up a hill, felt bleak, the sky constantly weeping.

He crested the hill and squinted through his glasses at Cherry Hill Hospital's sign. It shone bright red as if to spite the grey that cradled it from above and below. He rolled into the parking lot, waving at a security guard as he passed. Coming to work had become harder too, since she left. He'd come to depend on their exchange of power, even though at first, he'd resented the side effects. He hung his bike, pushing aside the image of Wylie in his mind. He needed to stop thinking of her. He shoved his gloves in a side pocket and clipped his helmet to his backpack, Lex replacing Wylie in his mind.

She started emailing him weeks ago, and since then she'd been everywhere. Standing in the corner of his vision, her eyes narrowed in a glare, she left his desk a mess after scribbling on every paper in his journal. She showed up in his dreams, demanding that he call Gabriel or visit her father. She looked exactly as he'd imagined. Short, with enough spunk to make up for her height. Her facial features unblemished and unlike what he'd glimpsed the day that he'd chosen Lex over Wylie. When he'd chosen muses over angels.

David wanted to help her. And maybe he was, by letting her haunt him, by believing in her. She seemed more solid every day, but he was busy here, and he was human. He couldn't go chasing the two most important angels in this disaster while people were suffering here.

David walked through the sliding glass doors and straight to the emergency room, his cycling shoes clicking on the beige tile. He skirted triage and went for the nurse's station. Scrub-clad men and women swarmed the area. He shook his head at the whiteboard before continuing to the doctor's lounge. It was a shit show, as usual. Life was hard enough without being haunted.

Shutting the door behind him, he unzipped his jacket. The rain he'd brought in with him splashed to the ground, and he shivered as he peeled the rest of his clothes off. The darkened room flashed with whatever news station had been left playing.

"I've lost people I love to this illness."

"That was Gabriel Andel, speaking to us from Baton Rouge."

David lifted his head and snorted when he found Lex on the screen. "You're dead and you're still the center of attention." His voice cracked with disuse as he dragged his eyes away from the screen and pulled his scrub top over his head. He had to work today. He didn't have time for her antics.

"According to our sources, Andel's girlfriend, Alexis O'Conner passed away just days ago when she was attacked by a subhuman outside her home at the Andel Compound."

David shook his head. Angeles and their lying. She'd been gone for a month now. Had she orchestrated this? David was starting to wonder what was real. A knock sounded from the door as David pulled his socks from his backpack. Ignoring the second round of knocks, he sat on the side of the bed. His brain was still stuck between the news report and the forty-five minutes of thinking he did on his commute to work.

The door groaned and then splintered. David jumped to his feet. "Hello?"

A large man stepped over the threshold and familiar black eyes connected with his. David's head fell back as the man stepped closer to him. Had he shrunk or had this angel grown taller? The last time he'd seen Gabriel, him and his buddy had threatened to throw David off a building. With his arms folded, he waited for his fate, his chest aching with the knowledge that he had no power to protect himself.

The angel smirked. "Long time no see."

David's phone buzzed in his backpack. If only he had it, but he'd never get across the room fast enough, and how would it help him to begin with? Fluorescent light spilled in through the hallway. He blew out a breath, all hope leaving him as he realized shouting for help would just put more people in danger.

"Can I put on my shoes?"

Gabriel looked down at David's bare feet. "Why?"

"You can't kill me here. My coworkers have enough shit going on."

Gabriel looked over his shoulder with a shrug. "If you insist." He leaned against the door jam, his legs crossing at the ankles, his eyes dropping to his watch. "Why do you think I'm going to kill you?" The angel asked casually.

"Why else would you be here?" David took his time lining the seam of his socks with his toes. If only he and Wylie were getting along better. Would she even answer if he called?

Gabriel cleared his throat.

"What?" David refused to take his eyes off his laces.

"Is my sister still in Hell?"

David shrugged. "That's none of your business." If the bastard wasn't going to answer his questions than why should he.

The angel raised a brow, and the air around David thinned until spots floated in his vision. "I'm not telling you anything." He dragged in a breath but he might as well be breathing through a straw. "Your sister and I aren't on the best of terms anyway."

Gabriel squatted down, his head tilting. He seemed far too interested in the David's answer. "What does that mean?"

Air rushed into David's lungs, and he shook his head as he sucked in breath after breath.

"What does that mean?" Gabriel's voice grew louder as he repeated his question.

"I'm not fucking your sister anymore. Is that what you wanted to hear?" If he was about to die, he might as well do so with some sort of dignity.

Gabriel stood, straightening his jacket. "That's disappointing."

David scoffed as he crossed the room and pulled on his wet raincoat. "Where to?"

"Stop the bullshit you guys."

Both men turned to the room's corner at once.

Solid as anyone else, Lex leaned against the wall, arms crossed and eye glaring.

Gabriel's mouth snapped shut, his smile sliding away, and David almost rolled his eyes. Of course, this meeting was Lex's doing.

"Don't act surprised."

Gabriel lifted his chin. "Did you hear that?"

"Yep."

"Yes, it's me, asshole, how many times do I have to tell you?" Smirking, Lex pushed herself off the wall. *"I don't trust the two of you unsupervised."*

Gabriel nearly stumbled toward Lex, his threatening demeanor falling away as his hands swept through the air. "Hellcat?"

Her image flashed in and out of focus as his hands passed through her. She looked up at the angel, her eyes softening as she touched his cheek. *"Stop fucking around and go to my dad."* Her image blinked away.

"Wait!" Gabriel grasped at nothing, and then his shoulder slumped, and his head bowed. He leaned into the corner, his forehead pressed into the place where the two walls met.

This was David's chance. He could run. He was a step away from freedom and with Gabriel's back to him, but something inside—maybe the doctor, or the brother in him kept him glued to his spot. *There are no words.* He said the phrase to the family member that clung to him after he gave them the news that they would never see their loved one again. It was what the policeman said when he came to his mother's hospital room to tell her that her husband had died.

David took his own advice. He leaned against the wall and waited. The angel, frozen on the other side of the room, straightened. "Why are you still here?"

"Lex told me that you needed me."

Gabriel faced David, a scowl on his face. "You're not worried I'm going to do what I came here to do?" The angel stepped toe to toe with David.

David had seen these reactions too. "If Lex trusted you, I trust you." He relaxed his body, making himself as non-threatening as possible.

"Know this. Lex's ghost can't keep you safe from me." He grabbed David's backpack and shoved it into David's gut. Gabriel pushed past

David. "I'm going to see Lexy's father, and you're coming with me." He didn't wait for an answer from him before he headed for the exit.

David looked longingly down the hallway. He should be scared. He really should be, but at some point in his short life, he realized that when he died, it would be Samael's fault. He wasn't sure if this belief was born of his hatred for the angel or if it rang of truth because it was just that. He took a breath and followed Gabriel. He wouldn't die today.

A sleek limo started its engine as the two exited the building. It was parked right off the curb where the ambulance usually sat.

A man in a suit opened the door, and David slid in after Gabriel. "You brought a limo?" David rubbed his arms as the heat in the vehicle reminded him how cold it was outside. "Can't you fly?"

"I'm not a barbarian, David."

David hugged his backpack to his chest. "Of course, you aren't."

The ride from Seattle to Tacoma took just long enough for David to really regret his decision to go with Gabriel. What was he going to tell Wylie? He was sitting across from the male who ordered her death. The angel who paid the assassins who killed her family. But he was powerless to punish Gabriel and in truth, he was a little frustrated with Wylie's judgements. Lex seemed to believe there was more to the story than Wylie knew.

The ticking of the blinker broke the silence as the limo took an exit.

"Why did you try to kill Wylie?"

Gabriel opened his eyes, his brows lifting as he searched David's face. "None of your business." He closed his eyes again, his head resting on the neck rest.

David stiffened, his face flushing with anger. "I think it is. I'm stuck in the middle here, and I need a good reason to help you."

Gabriel shifted, his legs stretching out, his face still placid with the peace of a nap. "I never asked for your help."

"But you do need it." When the angel didn't answer David pushed on. "Lex has been begging me to help you for weeks." His hands balled into fists. "I just left the hospital at the beginning of a shift with you even though you threatened to kill me. C'mon. Give me a reason to not hate you as much as Wylie does."

Gabriel shook his head. "You guys can't let it go, can you?" The angel rearranged his limbs, scooting forward until his knee touched David. "You, as a medical professional should understand better than anyone else. You pick and choose." Gabriel lifted his chin to the side, his eyes wide with a sarcastic question. "Do you ever feel guilt when you triage? When you see one patient before the other. There are rules, right? You pick the one who will die first, or the one in the most pain?" He folded his fingers together, searching David's face. "I had to make similar decisions but on a larger scale. What's more important? A sister I don't know, or the world?

"And before you tell me you'd never choose the world over your sister, I'm going to tell you that you're wrong. Every day you go to work, you choose the world over Jane."

David's hands shook. His sister's name on those lips filled him with terror.

Gabriel nodded, that ever-present smile returning. "Oh, I know you, David. I know everything about you. Down to what med school you went to, and what your GPA was your senior year of high school. I've been playing this game for a long time, but back to Jane. You chose to come to work and save lives rather than be with your sister. Even when she was at home suffering. You chose your career, your patients, you chose *you*. So, take your judgement and shove it up your ass. I've been trying to keep your girlfriend from setting this world on fire for years and somehow, I'm the bad guy. Well, no more. She can have it. Burn the place down. I'm done." Gabriel looked at his watch.

They turned a corner, and the limo rolled to a stop in front of a small two-story house. The peeling gray paint of the building blended well with the ever-stormy sky, and David rubbed his arms as a gust of wind caught the rain, smacking him in the side. The driver held the gate open for the pair as Gabriel took the lead. He'd never agree with this angel, but he'd gotten a glimpse of the passion that Lex had been drawn to.

David shivered as Gabriel pushed the doorbell. What were they even going to say? *Hey there, your dead daughter asked us to come visit you?*

"Coming." A gruff voice came from behind the front window. The TV flashed through the yellowed lace curtains. The door swung open and a grey-haired man with a belly that spilled over his pants peaked through the screen door. "What do you want?" His eyes caught David's, and the doctor quickly looked down, landing on the faded marine tattoo on the old man's forearm.

"Frank?"

"Who's asking."

"I'm Gabriel, Lex's boyfriend." Gabriel pulled off a glove and offered his hand. "And this is David—"

"Dr. Godwyn?" Frank narrowed his eyes. "Funny, Lex listed you as her emergency contact for AA, but we've never met." He ignored Gabriel's hand and took David's in a bone breaking grip.

"Yes, well, Lex and I never exactly met in person." David stretched his hand behind his back. He'd expected a man in mourning, not a wall of animosity, and then he remembered who this man's daughter was.

Frank turned back to Gabriel. "I suppose, Lexy sent you here. Wish the two of you would've made an effort to come see me before she died." The man's jaw ticked as he eyed Gabriel from his leather Oxfords to his wool jacket. "You're rich." He cleared his throat, averting his eyes for the first time. "Traveling shouldn't have been an issue."

"She talked about you often. She even told me the story of how you met Dung back in Vietnam." Gabriel squeezed his glove with both hands. "She would've come." His throat bobbed. "We would've come."

"Coulda, shoulda, woulda." Frank grunted. "C'mon in." He hobbled away.

Gabriel froze at the threshold, his nostrils flaring, his chest filling with air. Damn it, David didn't want to feel any kind of empathy for this angel.

"Several years ago, I found out my son was dead on that porch." He groaned as he sat in his recliner. "I don't like being out there longer than I need to be."

"I understand, sir." Gabriel remained standing, his lips several shades paler than his face. His eyes drinking in the place like a starving man.

David sat at the edge of the couch, watching Gabriel as intently as Frank.

"Lexy had me dig up some old boxes. She said you'd come for them." Frank cleared his throat. "Both of you."

Gabriel's eyes came back to life. "Have you seen her?"

"I'm sorry, guys, I—"

"I'm here."

Gabriel swung around, and David shot to his feet. A blur of purple floated in the shadows of the hallway.

"Lexy?" Gabriel burst forward, reaching, but the blur sped up the stairs. The angel stumbled after it.

"Go," Frank said from his chair.

David's feet dragged as he mounted the stairs. He didn't belong here, in this moment. He didn't . . .

Two hands pressed into his back. *"Fucking move faster. I'm running out of energy."*

He arrived at the landing and followed the sound of Gabriel's voice.

Lex's bed remained crumpled as if she'd jumped out of it earlier that morning. Books and notebooks lay strewn out on her dresser and desk.

"Hellcat, please. I need to see you again." Gabriel sat in Lex's bed, a shoebox in his lap.

"Shit, baby, I'm trying. It's really hard. I've been busy the last few days." She disappeared and hands pushed David's back again. *"On my desk."* She pushed harder when he didn't move. *"It's a translation of my grandmother's journal. Look at the page I marked."*

David ran his fingers over the leather cover before opening it. He scanned the words.

Forgive them for they know not what they do.

The quote leapt out at him. He lifted his head searching for an explanation from Lex. The purple cloud of Lex's hair flashed next to Gabriel. The angel lifted his hand to the apparition and it disappeared. The angel and the muse's eyes connected

A knock came from the doorway. Frank stood there, his knuckles resting against the door jam. "Do you boys want to stay for dinner?"

Chapter 12

Samael

Samael looked up at Luc's home as they climbed into his car. His head ached and his back burned from the most recent cauterization. Keeping it a secret from Wylie had become nearly impossible here. He needed to leave her to her destiny soon and go and follow his own. He'd miss it here. Even with its sharp lines and masculine balance of concrete and glass, this would always be the place where he could close his eyes and pretend the world wasn't ending.

"You can always come and visit," Luc said, their eyes connecting through the rearview mirror. "You'd learn faster on this side of the veil."

Samael looked away, answering his friend with a grunt.

"Who knows, with how fast things are going to shit, it might be the safest place for you." Luc pulled out of his driveway.

"I will not hide in hell."

"Hell's Planes."

Samael waved the conversation away, his hand falling to the empty seat between him and Wylie. His palm itched with greed, he needed to touch her. Her hand landed next to his, their skin touching, an offering. He ate up the sight, his heart squeezing with the way her cheeks turned terracotta. She wanted to touch him too. All he had to do was move it a few inches.

Wylie had mentioned once how 'giant' she felt, but her hand next to his seemed so small. Everything about her was both delicate and sturdy. Her tiny shoulders, thrown back with a confidence born of her angel powers. The way her thick thighs tapered to the point of her knees. Her little foot tapped to the beat of his heart.

"Where are you going once we're Earthside?" Wylie asked.

Luc stopped at a stop sign and waved at a woman who walked the crosswalk with a toddler tethered at her side. "The Pride and I will go back to Pearl."

"Where's that?" Her hand went back to her lap and Samael didn't have to read emotions to feel her disappointment. She'd waited for him and he failed. He'd have to fail her in this if he was going to succeed in regaining enough power to yet again be a tool of God.

"Pearl Falls, Tennessee." Luc pulled forward.

"How'd you guys end up there?"

"It's the closest town to the hole my little brother, Santana, tore in the veil between Hell's Planes and Earth."

"He tore a hole?" Wylie scooted to the edge of her seat. She sounded far too excited to hear of another angel who could manipulate the planes.

"Yes, that's where we're heading."

"Who'll be waiting for us on the other side?"

"Samael's two favorite angels. Twiddle-dee will take you to see Dumah and twiddle-dumb will drive Samael. You should probably go see your boyfriend soon."

"He's not my ..." That terracotta returned to her cheeks and Samael didn't know if he should thank Luc for bringing this pretty color to her face or punch David for causing her to have that reaction. He settled for turning away, it wasn't for him, he didn't deserve her blushes.

"Shafer said you and the good doctor looked pretty cozy." Luc took a left and the tear in the planes became visible just over the tops of the city's buildings.

Samael ducked his head and pointed, ready to change the subject. "Do you see it, Wylie."

Her eye's rounded, her jaw dropping when she saw the tip of the bright red scar in the sky. "How long has that been there?"

"What was it, Samael? Maybe a little under half a century ago?" Luc asked.

"So, the 80s?" Wonder brightening her face as they grew closer.

"Yeah, why do you think there were so many assholes born that decade?"

Wylie snorted and again Samael was torn between gratefulness and violence. Some foreign part of his brain only wanted her to smile for him and him alone. He shook his head. What was wrong with him?

The tear loomed large in the sky, and Samael's jaw clenched. The loss of the cocoon Wylie had built for him as he recovered was an emptiness in his gut. Like he was hungry, but his mind knew he'd never eat again. They pulled up to the stoplight directly in front of the hole. A one lane road ran into the unknown. The neon pink reflected off her face, highlighting her frown.

The light turned green and the car rolled forward. "This will only hurt for a minute." Luc shoved his foot on the gas, and the engine roared.

Wylie stiffened, drawing in a deep breath as if they were going underwater.

The light engulfed them and soon they were on the other side. The air thinned, filling his lungs easily. The landscape went from desert to wooded forest in an instant. Luc slapped his thigh, his laughter becoming wild. "You should have seen your face."

Wylie's eyes narrowed. "You!" She smacked his shoulder. "You're an asshole!"

"You know it." Luc winked at Wylie

They turned into a rest stop where several cars sat surrounded by old-growth cypress and pines. Madoc pulled open Samael's door before they came to a stop. The Archangel hungrily searched Samael's face. His blond brows lowered as his hand fisted Samael's sleeve. "It's true." The color left the angel's face as he leaned against the car.

The lost look in Madoc's eyes woke Samael up in a way nothing else had. He forced his way out of the car, standing toe to toe with Madoc. "Stand down."

Madoc shook his head. "How could you?"

"Stand down." Samael's voice rumbled in his chest, and he heard the other doors open and close.

Madoc stepped back, his head still bowed, his eyes leveling with Wylie who came around the back of the car. "I knew you'd figure out a way to fuck everything up." His wings appeared, opening wide with a threat.

The calm of leadership filled Samael. He stepped into Madoc's line of sight. They straightened, jaws setting, hands fisting, and then Ariel smacked the back of Madoc's head.

"This couldn't wait for us to get home?"

"But he—"

"Just shut up, Madoc."

"*Pro summum bonum.*" Samael held up a hand as Madoc opened his mouth. "I am the white horse. This has always been my destiny. Do not belittle my sacrifice because you aren't willing to do the same in the name of God."

Madoc's mouth snapped shut, the challenge in his posture loosening into the hopelessness he'd shown when the Archangel first opened the car door. He turned away. "More like you took the coward's way out."

The words barely reached Samael's ear before Luc was behind Madoc with a forearm to his throat and a hand in his hair. "What the fuck did you say?"

Madoc's face turned red, his eyes leveling on Samael. "He's a coward."

"Apologize!" Luc kicked the back of Madoc's leg, and he fell to his knees.

Samael's hand fell to Luc's shoulder. "Brother, let go."

Luc blew out a breath, shoved the angel, and backed away his hands in the air.

Madoc wiped spit from his lips with his tattooed forearm.

"Thank you," Samael said. "Madoc, I want you to look at Wylie." He waved to the spot where he felt her standing behind him. "You've punished her enough. The end days are here, and it's time for you to give her your loyalty she deserves."

Madoc folded his arms, his "fuck" and "off" stacking on top of each other, his mouth flatlined as he studied Wylie. "I don't understand. Why her?"

Samael's brows rose. "You've never felt it, have you?"

Madoc's jaw ticked in response.

Samael turned to Wylie reaching for her. His sunshine's hand found his. He'd never asked this of her. He wasn't even sure if she'd tried it on her own, but he'd always felt her from the first moment he laid eyes on her until the moment he gave her his power. "Don't hold back. Show us your Scientia. Show us everything."

She gave him a nod, tangled her fingers with his and let loose.

Samael didn't feel it. He couldn't anymore. But he saw it. Like a gust of wind, it came from her. The angels around her fell to their knees with tears in their eyes, the trees bowed, and the sun somehow brightened as if it decided to shine for her and her alone. She was a goddess. Samael knew it, and now everyone else knew it too. The sun could shine for her, but it would have to get in line.

Chapter 13

Wylie

The car door slammed shut and Wylie watched the back of Samael's head as Ariel pulled out of the parking lot.

"Ready?" Madoc gripped her shoulder and projected without waiting for an answer. They arrived on a grand porch with white columns and red brick. Without a word, the Archangel yanked the door open and stalked away. Wylie swallowed the nervousness crawling around in her belly and peeked inside. She hadn't expected to arrive at a mansion. Mahogany furniture dripped with cream-colored silks, all perfectly placed like a movie set. She stepped inside. "Dumah?"

"Baby girl!" The Virtue's rich voice came from somewhere in the house, the southern twang taming Wylie's anxiety. "I'm in the kitchen, baby. Shut the door behind you and come join me."

The door clicked shut behind her, and Wylie checked her shoes for dirt before following the white carpet after Dumah's voice.

"Look at you," Dumah said as she shrugged something into her pocket. "You're back and just in time." She came around the island, her heels clicking gracefully.

Dumah pulled Wylie into a hug. She didn't realize how much she needed it. She'd been stuck in a sort of purgatory with Samael. The room became a blur as her arms wrapped around Dumah. She buried her face in the angel's shoulder and sniffled before she could stop herself. Dumah's accent always reminded her of her mother.

"It's been too long."

Wylie nodded, unable to end the hug.

Dumah patted her hair. "This is just the beginning."

"I know. I'm ready." Wylie pulled back. "I don't have a choice." The awe in Madoc's eyes as he fell to his knees had done something to her that Samael's reassurance never could. His reluctant belief in her sparked a fledgling confidence she'd never felt as an angel.

"Good, because we have two weeks until you have to prove it to the world." Dumah brushed a tear from Wylie's cheek.

"Are you talking about the Summit?"

"Yes. Mariam's on her way here. Our last Throne will be here in a few days. You need to get to know your angels if you're going to stand in front of the world and speak for them."

"You're not helping."

"I'm not here to help you. I'm here to shape you, but before we get into the politics, let's discuss the prophecy." Dumah pulled a deck of cards from her pocket and handed them to Wylie. "Here, hold these." She handed them to Wylie, before heading back to the barstool where she'd been when Wylie arrived. "Do you know who your horsemen are?"

Wylie joined Dumah, studying the deck in her hands with the hope that Dumah would forget she asked the question.

"I'm guessing that's a 'no.'" Dumah leaned onto the island with her elbows. "What do you think of my cards?"

Wylie shuffled through them. She assumed they were tarot cards. The backs had prints of wings and roses. She ran her thumb over the feathers. "They're beautiful."

"Can you pick the ones that make you think of your horsemen?"

Wylie turned the deck over and immediately smiled when she saw a man in red robes that reminded her how she'd thought of angels before she met Samael. "What are we doing here?" She asked picking out three more for no other reason than the images reminded her of what she wasn't. Like if they represented her horsemen then they'd need to represent what she felt she needed.

"Lay them out. Put one here, here, here, and here in no particular order. Just do whatever feels right." She pointed to four spots.

Wylie followed her directions.

"I once had a muse named Marie Lenormand." Dumah opened her hand expectantly and Wylie handed over the rest of the deck. "She used to read cards for Napoleon."

Wylie raised her brows. Lucifer had shown them that there was more magic than Scientia in the world, but she hadn't thought of humans using it. If these were real how much of her paranormal romance collection was real too?

"You chose The Hermit, The Emperor, The Hierophant, and The Devil." She lifted the card with the robed man, squinting at it as if she were reading script Wylie couldn't see.

"I have to ask. Why would an angel read tarot cards?"

"It started as a joke. When I visited, she'd read me by handing over the cards just like I did to you. I'd always known she was different. Her mother had been strange too, but nothing like Melle." She held the cards in both hands, the umber of her knuckles turning tawny as she gripped them. "Anyway, I see it as a form of prayer, and with the Seraphim gone, any connection with God is vital." Her eyes lifted to Wylie's. "This isn't going to give you the answers, but hopefully it will help you know what to look for."

Wylie nodded. The prophecy didn't give her much to go off of, and if Dumah thought this would work, it was worth a try. She turned back to the cards. "Right, so the only horseman I know for sure is Samael because he flat out told me. but I have some guesses at who the others could be."

Dumah picked up The Hermit card. "This person helps you better understand yourself. They give you security and time." The Virtue continued weaving words in a way that Wylie had never heard before. It reminded her of the days when she and her husband went to slam poetry events in dirty bars that weren't much more than four walls and a stage. The cadence of her usual speech took on this lyrical edge, and Wylie knew exactly who this card belonged to.

"It's David. That's definitely David."

"But which horse?"

"Samael's the one who found me." She swallowed, knowing what she'd done in return. "Then there's the one who betrays me, the one who wakes me, and the one who protects me. I think Gabriel is the one who woke me, when he . . ." Wylie shakes her head and points at The Emperor, changing the subject before the flashes of Dean limp in Roberto's arms took over her concentration. "That guy looks arrogant enough to be Gabriel." She clears her voice, her finger sliding over The Devil. "This couldn't be Luc. It's too obvious."

"Wylie!" Hands clapped and Wylie lifted her head to find Mariam standing on the other side of the island with open arms and a smile on her face.

Wylie nearly tripped as she rushed to her mentor.

The nun squeezed her once and then pulled her away, her eyes bouncing around Wylie's face. "You feel depleted."

"I'm fine." Wylie shrugged. She hadn't seen David in a while, but she thought that had something to do with Samael's Scientia. She couldn't feel hers anymore, just his. It buzzed around her, always busy assessing the world as if it were a living thing.

Mariam's soft hand took Wylie's, pulling her to her side. "Sister, she needs to see her muse."

"She will. Once we've—"

"No. Now." Mariam straightened, pulling Wylie against her. "What if the world went to hell this very moment? We'd have a half-cocked weapon and no backup. We can't take any risks with Samael gone."

Wylie stiffened, her eyes dropping as the two female's wings appeared. Were they planning to duke it out in Dumah's fancy kitchen. "Hold on." Wylie stepped between them. "Dumah, she's right. I need to see David. Maybe now that I've seen his card, I'll be able to figure out who he is in the prophecy."

Dumah's hands fell to her hips. "Fine, side with the nun."

Mariam started laughing first, and by the time Wylie left, the two were reminiscing about their escapades in Mesopotamia. She projected to Seattle, arriving on the roof of David's apartment. The sky thundered, reflecting her inner turmoil.

The clouds churned like concrete, and the rain drenched Wylie in seconds. She projected outside David's apartment and hesitated before pushing the doorbell. She shoved down the guilt that came with the attraction she now acknowledged she had for Samael. Her finger pressed down. Shortly after, Emily opened the door. The dark circles around her eyes had grown darker since Wylie last saw her.

"Oh, it's you." She opened the door wider. "They've been waiting for you."

Stunned, Wylie's brows raised, but the flat affect remained on Emily's face.

"Are you coming?"

Wylie closed the door behind her before following Emily into the apartment.

David stood from the kitchen island, his eyes wide, his body frozen in place. He'd grown out his hair everywhere, the top of his head, his chin, his lip. There was a red tint to his hair that Wylie didn't know he had. She almost didn't recognize him. His honey eyes and the way his muse magic immediately crawled under her skin, gave him away. Neither angel nor muse spoke, but he cringed as he shoved his hands into his pockets as if keeping them to himself physically hurt him.

"Hi." She flushed with the memory of the last time she'd been there. She'd stormed out after yelling at her muse.

David blew out a breath. He leaned into the island, his arms and shoulders tensed, straining against his cycling jersey. His eyes lifted, landing on something behind her. Jane hit Wylie from the side in a bear hug that didn't match her petite frame. "Wylie!"

Wylie peeled Jane's arms away and turned to the girl. Jane wiped her cheeks. "You left so mad last time. I didn't think you'd come back."

"Sorry, I . . ." Wylie had a hundred excuses, but suddenly none of them felt good enough. "Sorry."

Jane hugged Wylie again. "Where have you been?"

"Louisiana."

David let out a puff of air from the kitchen as Wylie sized up Jane. Her hands gripped Jane's shoulders, ignoring the way David's eyes felt on her back. "You've grown."

"You look different too."

"How?"

"I don't know. More badass." Jane pulled Wylie's sleeve. "Have you been working out?" She took Wylie's hand and pulled, heading for her room. "I get first dibs," she said over her shoulder. "I don't want David to piss you off before we get a chance to talk."

Wylie glanced over her shoulder to find David gripping the kitchen counter. She wanted to comfort him. The storm going on in his head was intoxicating, but she couldn't be everything to everyone and her muse deserved someone who gave him their whole selves.

Jane pulled Wylie inside and shut the door, jumping on the bed. "Sit." Her one word carried the same authority David often used.

Wylie sat at the foot of the bed, ready to take whatever Jane had to dish out. The teenager had never been this commanding with her, and Wylie couldn't pick out which of the girls swell of emotions was focused on her.

"Spill." Jane folded her arms.

Wylie searched the teenager's eyes. "What do you know?"

"You're an angel?"

Wylie nodded. This was not the direction she thought this conversation would take. She smoothed the bedcover. David had the same one on his bed. "I am."

"And David had a problem with that."

Wylie lifted her head. Jane frowned, her face stark white against her flaming hair, her posture so much like her brothers. She looked so strong with her chin jutting out, as if she'd take on the world, let alone her brother, to protect Wylie. If only the girl knew, Wylie was willing to do the same.

"It has nothing to do with me being an angel. Sometimes adults don't get along."

"I'm not a baby. I know you and my brother were sleeping together, even if neither of you admitted it." She huffed out a breath, leaning against the head of the bed.

"I'm sorry we kept it a secret." Wylie closed her eyes. "David is very protective of you. As he should be." She cleared her throat. "It was just a fling."

"Wylie, he's messed up. You saw him. Something happened."

"I would never hurt your brother." *I love him*. He was her soul, after all. She almost said but held it back. What did Jane know about muses? Would she understand? In that moment she wanted to tell the teen everything, but she didn't need another fight with David. "We weren't right for each other."

"Don't bullshit me."

Wylie lifted her brows, studying the girl she'd healed. "You're angry with me."

"You just disappeared."

Wylie scooted up the bed and pulled the girl into a hug. "I'm doing the best I can."

Jane's shoulders bounced as Wylie squeezed. "You can breakup with my brother, but you can't breakup with me."

"Jane, I will always be here for you, but things can't be like they used to be."

The girl pulled away. "Why?"

She had to tell her. "What do you know about muses?"

"Muses?" Jane blinked up at Wylie. "Like the humans on the commercials that are tied to an angel?"

Wylie nodded. "David's my muse." Wylie rubbed Jane's arms.

"Your muse?"

"David and I were confused. We thought our connection as angel and muse was something different. We were wrong. This is why we didn't tell you. We didn't want you to be sad if things didn't work out." But it was true. Even now, Wylie couldn't separate her need for David from the way his muse magic brought her peace. Wylie pushed Jane's strawberry locks from her face.

"And David knows he's your muse? Because he's just so messed up right now."

Wylie pulled Jane close again. David lost Lex and Wylie at the same time. She couldn't blame the man for having a hard time. "I'll talk to him."

Jane nodded, her hands coming up to wipe her face, her tears glistening under the light that snuck threw the dissipating clouds outside. "I'm so worried about my brother."

Wylie helped wipe Jane's face and kissed her cheek. "Let me go talk to him."

Jane nodded. "Okay. But promise me that you'll never leave me hanging again."

"I promise." Wylie stood.

"Good." Jane folded her arms again. "Go fix my brother."

Well, that was a lot of pressure. Wylie smoothed Jane's hair one more time and headed back to the living room. David sat at the island, now wearing scrubs. He stood and their eyes locked. The pair met each other in the middle of the room.

"Do you want to walk with me? I have to go to work soon."

The invitation was an act of kindness. David wanted to have this conversation on neutral ground, not in his apartment. Wylie read it in his body language and his emotions.

On the way through the floor's common area, David's hand floated between them as if he wanted to take hers. She folded her arms, ashamed of the temptation to selfishly take it and soak up his comfort. They didn't speak until they were in front of a fireplace. David turned up the gas flames, and Wylie settled on an ottoman, her back straight. This was just so awkward.

David combed his fingers through his hair as he sat. The news played across a TV screen behind him, the shadows danced in the hallows of his face. "Thank you for stopping by." He frowned, his whole-body stiffening, his honey-colored eyes beseeching. "How's Samael?"

Wylie suppressed the urge to read his mind. What did he know? It would be so much easier than having this conversation. She wanted to squirm, like he was the one looking into her head, like he could see through the darkness of that night when she'd given into Samael's infatuation with her. "He's doing better."

"Hmm." He took a seat across from her, his head turned to the fire. "That's good. That's good."

Wylie watched the flames dance until David cleared his throat.

His eyes were back on her. "I need to confess something."

Wylie raised a brow. "A confession?"

David nodded; his face emotionless. “I met Gabriel the other day.”

Wylie surged forward, her hand wrapping around David’s wrist as she searched his body for any signs of abuse. “Did he hurt you?”

“No.” David rested his free hand on Wylie’s, removing it only when her attention returned to his face. “I think the two of you want the same thing.”

He might as well have slapped her in the face. “What did you say?” It came out as a whisper as all of her empathy for the man drained away.

“If you worked with Gabriel, the two of you—”

“David, he killed my family.” Tears filled her eyes. “I can’t believe that you talked to him.”

“I’m not saying you have to be friends. I’m just saying you cou—”

Wylie stood. “He killed my family! Whose side are you on?”

“The humans’ side.”

This wasn’t the first time she’d asked David this question, but his answer had changed. “I thought you were on my side, ‘always.’”

“I didn’t think you were on opposing sides with us humans. I expected more from you.”

Wylie turned away, her heart threatening to choke her as the image of Gabriel and David shaking hands. She couldn’t be sure if it came from her imagination or from his memories. She wandered to the fireplace and gripped the mantle. “I can’t believe you talked to Gabriel.”

“Don’t you think you’re being a little childish?”

She closed her eyes, cringing inwardly as her hand itched to strike him. She’d been away from humans for too long.

David became a wall of disappointment behind her. “Think about it. I need to go to work.”

She listened to him leave. She wouldn’t let this conversation ruin her next stop. Wylie pressed her forehead into the marble. She’d have to speak to Dumah and Mariam about this. They’d know what to do. With a cleansing breath, Wylie let go of the tension in her muscles and projected to the Hernandez house. She needed her family to remind her why she was sacrificing so much.

Chapter 14

Lex

Gabriel marched through the hall. Muses and angels cleared the path. Once in their rooms he yanked off his suit. His sculpted body rippling as he lowered himself to the ground. Taking up a plank position, he started pushups.

Snow fell from the ceiling. Frost covering the walls and the bedcover that they once shared.

"I know you're watching me. I feel you watching me," *he said to the ground. His curls bounced every time his arms straightened. His breaths became heavy as he increased his speed.* "Come back to me, hellcat. Come back."

"I'm here." She pushed her Scientia around him, surrounding him.

Gabriel fell to his chest and rolled onto his back, reaching for her as if she were there. His hand closed and the bones of her wrist creaked.

She gasped as she solidified under his touch.

"Lexy." *He sucked in a breath, pulling her against him. He pressed his lips into her neck. He pulled back and his thumb drew a line down her face.* "Your scar?" *The ebony of his eyes ate her up, tears formed and froze.*

Lex's heart stumbled. She stretched her fingers, watching them move. They were real. She curled them in Gabriel's hair. There weren't any words for this moment.

His hands roamed over her until they found her belly and gasped. He sat up, rearranging her in his arms. "This can't be real." *He shook his head at her and the baby kicked in response.*

She squealed as he lifted her, his face burying into her belly.

"This can't be real." *Their baby muffled his voice as Gabriel's nose nestled into the little one.* "You shouldn't be this far along."

She allowed him silence with his kicking child before explaining. "Time goes by faster up there."

He gently lowered her to her bottom and knelt before her, his fingers gripping her all the while. His hand went to her throat, and he stared up at her through his dark fringe of lashes. "Your voice."

"My voice." She smiled; it was her turn to touch. He'd lost some weight, the softness replaced by more muscle. Otherwise, he felt the same under her foreign fingers. She cupped his face, kissed each cheek, his nose, his forehead, and then took his mouth. He tasted the same.

He allowed her control as she explored his mouth, but the moment her hand wandered to his cock, he lowered her to her back, pushing her legs apart with his knee. Suddenly, they were laying in the grass again, the stars stretching out above them. Their hips rolled with each other. "I love you." *There, she fucking said it.*

He pulled away, bracing himself with his hands on either side of her head. Their eyes met and … She was back in the waiting room, Gabriel on the screen, alone, kneeling on the carpet. She shook her head, *no,* and forced her Scientia back into the screen.

This time he'd caught a hold of her by the shoulders. She lay beneath him, his wild eyes staring through her. It must be him that made her solid.

"You disappeared."

"I'm a fucking ghost, I do that shit."

"You just blinked away." *He rested his forehead on her chest his voice becoming serious.* "Don't ever do that again." *His breathing slowed with the rise and fall of her chest.*

"I think I can stay here as long as you hold on to me."

His grip tightened. "I'll never let you go, râleuse."

"Kiss me."

This time he went slower, his eyes jumping to his hands as if they'd betray him and stray off her skin. Cheek to cheek, and pause. He breathed her in, his nose running from her ear to her collarbone. "I've missed you," *he growled into her skin.* "But everything about you is different." *He palmed her breasts.* "These are different too." *He took her nipple between his teeth.* "Mmm, you taste the same," *he said with a full mouth.*

"Fuck, Gabriel." She arched into his mouth, as his hand slipped into her pants.

"How long?"

"How long, what?"

"How long can I have you?" *His middle finger slid between her folds.* "If these are our last moments, if I'm getting a redo, I can't just give you pleasure. I have to make sure you know that you and my child are the world to me. That I love you more than life." *His finger slipped inside her.* "You need to know that your body, your face, covered in the evidence of your bravery or not, are what my dreams are made of." *She rocked into the emptiness his hand left as he struggled to remove his pants. His free hand desperately gripped her hip. She fought with the scrub pants that so reminded her of her times as an inpatient.* "You're my heaven. God wrote my name when he created you. That's why you came first, because he couldn't coax me into a world without you. If I was born to end the world. You were born to give me a reason not to."

She reached for him, pulling him close and holding onto him like her existence depended on it, and maybe it did. "Gabriel, please."

He lined his cock with her entrance and locked eyes with her before rocking into her. Tears dripped down her face as he filled her. "God, I love you. I love you." *It became his chant as he thrust. She couldn't look away from him, she had to memorize the shadows on his face. The tears in his eyes. The feel of him moving inside her. She tangled her finger in his curls and pulled his mouth to hers, moaning into their kiss.*

He pulled away. "I need to see all of you." *He lifted her to her knees and guided her arms to the bed. He traced her back with his lips then, pulling her ass cheeks apart he licked from her clit to her cunt. She collapsed forward as he tasted her, using the bed to muffle her cries and just when she came up to breathe, he lined his body against hers, pushing into her as he kissed her neck.* "Please, please, please."

She never heard Gabriel beg before, but he was on his knees and she knew what he was asking for. If only she could give it to him. For once she felt grateful to a higher power, one she wasn't sure she believed in, that she could be here with him one last time. She braced the bed as Gabriel lifted her from her knees with each thrust, one hand bracing her hip, the other cradling her belly. Soon, they ran over her ass, down her thighs, her calf, and then gripped her feet, forcing her to bow backwards, and his cock drove ever deeper into her.

Her breasts bounced and swayed as he used his body to show his love. To say the things words never fucking could. She opened her mouth to say that very thing, but her voice was stolen by a pain that threatened to break every bone in her body. Gabriel froze behind her. "Fuck." The word fell out with relief.

"What's wrong?" *Gabriel slid out of her, his eyes widening as he helped her sit on her ass.*

Again, she tried to answer, but her breath was stolen from her. She groaned, curling around her baby who fought against her tightening muscles as much as she did. The world closed in on them. "Mother fucker!" The words came and so did a gush of hot fluid. Two short breaths and her lungs were tightening. She roared, her legs kicking out.

Only Gabriel holding her up kept her from crumbling onto her side. "Lexy, what should I do?" *he said in the silence between the pain.*

"Don't fucking touch me!"

His hands jerked away, and then he disappeared.

Lex blinked against the harsh light of The Grand Queue barely realizing she leaned against Carole before another contraction took her. "Holy shit, mother fucking fuck!" She squealed. Tears came, real-ass tears, she was alone again. She was going to have to push this fucking baby out, and she was going to have to do it on her own. "No. Gabriel. Come back." She clung to Carole even as the woman stood.

"Help! Somebody, help! Her water just broke!" Carole shouted like a sergeant. Their otherwise stationary line companions stood. Carole's head dipped as she turned to Lex, their eyes connecting. "You'll feel better if you stand up."

Mesmerized, Lex nodded. One hand crawled up the woman as she got to her feet, while the other held the tablet close to her chest. The cramp started again and turned into tiger claws drawing lines across her middle. The slapping of a pair of boots against the tile punctuated the scream that clawed through her throat. Carole spoke, but Lex couldn't comprehend, instead she dipped her head in consent, just wanting the woman to stop talking. The muse moaned as the woman pressed the heel of her palm into her lower back. It was like the woman had pressed the button that opened up Lex's lungs.

Justin's familiar presence towered over Lex as she caught her breath. "Lexy, I'm going to pick you up."

Another contraction took Lex, and she punctuated her howl with a grunt.

"That was a push. She's going to birth in front of all of these people if we don't move now." Carole rubbed Lex's back as the fog of pain receded.

"What's wrong with me? This isn't right. This isn't right," Lex chanted.

"You've got great genes, mama." Other than Gabriel, Lex had never felt so reassured by touch as she had by Carole's firm touch. "Now, let's go have a baby."

She gripped Carole's arm. "Don't leave me."

"I've got you. We've got you."

Lex's tablet fell to the ground as Justin lifted her. She held her breath and clung to Justin's neck.

"You've got this. Breathe. Your baby needs oxygen," Carole said from behind them.

Her baby needed oxygen. Her baby needed oxygen. Somehow each breath she took, she took for Gabriel, for Gabriel's child, *their baby*. Tears filled her eyes as she was rushed down the aisle, the voice coaching her to do the one thing her body had always known to do.

"There you go. Nice and slow. Touch baby with your lungs."

The breaths came in slow ragged gasps as they passed through double doors that lead to the sterile halls and white tile of a hospital. She cried out and, a hand gripped her shoulder.

"I've got you. Just breathe." The female's voice lost its calm tone and grew distant. "They're coming on fast, and she's not getting any breaks."

"Thank you, Carole. You can get back in line."

"But she's going so fast, her family won't make it. I can stay with her."

"Carole, you have other things to focus on. She'll be safe with us."

"No!" Lex stumbled out of the wheelchair and grabbed the older lady's arm. "I can't do this without her." Lex gritted her teeth. "Ow, ow, ow!"

Curtains were drawn around them. A sterile bed stared at her with the promise of pain.

"Turn to me."

Lex did as told.

"Rest your hands on my shoulders."

Lex leaned into the woman.

"Now dance with me."

They rocked back and forth, breathing together. In the stolen seconds in between, Lex rested her head on the stranger's shoulder until the contractions worsened to a point that Lex needed to escape. "I can't anymore." Lex ripped at her clothes, pulling them off and climbing on the bed where she rocked on her hands and knees.

"She's pushing," Carole called out.

Lex didn't care as the curtain pulled back, and a chorus of footsteps filled the space.

"Okay, Lex, next time you push, hold it longer." Carole's voice became Lex's constant, and when her demands were replaced with the sound of a screaming infant, a wet wiggly baby was placed on her back.

Lex was directed to her back and a screaming baby boy was placed in her arm. Her baby. Her fucking baby. She pulled the little one close, her lips grazing the infant's forehead. Nothing else mattered. Nothing but those curling fingers and gaping mouth. In that moment she promised herself that she would not waste this second chance. She'd spend the rest of her existence trying to be worthy of this infant. Of this little guy that represented the culmination of Gabriel and her love.

Gabriel. Her breath shuttered as she pulled the baby to her face. Gabriel.

Lex wasn't how long she sat there lost in loss and gratitude. The room had emptied, only Justin sat beside her. Lex lifted her eyes to look for the woman who carried her through the labor. "Where did Carole go?"

"Heaven."

"Heaven?"

"She stopped hurting."

Lex bounced the bundle against her chest. "Heaven. That's where we're going." The now silent infant grabbed her hair. "Somewhere, your father can never go."

Chapter 15

Wylie

DAVID:

I'm sorry about walking out on you.

We need to talk this out though.

WYLIE:

There's nothing to talk about.

Wylie

No, David. The answer is no.

Mariam pulled the phone from Wylie's hand. "Stop texting and tell us what you think?"

Wylie's eyes lifted to the mirror. The *dress* Mariam brought Wylie had slits that were illegal in most states. The damn nun should've been a nudist with how much skin she encouraged Wylie to show. Wylie snatched back her phone. "Where am I going to put my weapons?" She asked Ariel, her eyes pleading for the warrior's help.

The archangel grinned from where she leaned on the door frame. "That's what your halo is for." She walked up to Wylie, swirling her finger in the air, directing her to turn back to the mirror. "The thing about the dress is . . ." Their eyes connected through the mirror and Ariel's rare smile turned evil. "No human is going to argue with you at this Summit."

The Summit would bring human leaders and Angel leaders

together. Gabriel would be there, though he'd have to push through the growing horde of Scientia Eaters that was Baton Rouge.

Wylie smirked back; she did feel fierce in the satin, but the thing was overtly sexual. The crimson fabric draped across her torso in a way that accentuated the width of her hips, the bust a little too tight. Men that wouldn't have looked at Wylie twice in her scrubs would break their necks to see the place between the two slits in her dress. She imagined Samael's hands resting in the tightest spots. Her face flushed, the sexual tension between the two was palpable, maybe this was all he needed to tilt the scales. She couldn't wait to show him the dress.

"Whoa, whoa, whoa." Ariel jerked away, her cheeks flushing. "Keep those thoughts to yourself."

The comment immediately squashed Wylie's dirty thoughts. Ariel was blushing. The female was a weapon, she didn't blush. In fact, she hadn't acted right since Wylie got home. "You're not the same since I've been back, what's up?"

"I'm not the same." Ariel went to the window, her unmatched eyes glossing over. "You saw, he carved out my eye . . . took my wing. I . . ." She shook her head. "I'll never be the same."

Wylie stiffened. She suddenly hated the dress and the smile that was still slipping from her face. "I'm sorry."

"Can we just drop it."

Ariel confused Wylie, but this had always been the case. One on one, the female never stopped talking, always sharing too much and saying inappropriate things. In groups she stayed silent, playing with her weapons, and only opening her mouth to correct Madoc.

Mariam stepped behind Ariel, her hand resting on the small of her back. The age spots standing out next to Ariel's youthful skin. "You don't have to talk about it." Mariam tucked one of Ariel's curls behind her ear, the strands glowing orange in the sunlight. "We just want you to find peace."

Ariel leaned away from Mariam. "Peace is not a gift God gave the angels." She turned back to Wylie. "Wear the fucking dress, Wylie. You look hot as sin." With that, Ariel's combat boot announced her exit.

Wylie reached for the zipper of her dress. "I didn't know she was having such a hard time."

Mariam helped her pull it down. "I think having one of her wings removed changed her. She knows it. She isn't just an angel anymore."

Wylie shook her head stepping out of the fabric and pulling back on her running tights and t-shirt. "Does the wing I made her work?"

"No one knows. No one has seen it." Mariam hung the dress.

A knock sounded from the door. "Wylie?" The door handle jiggled, but Samael didn't enter.

"Come in." Mariam double checked her wimple in the mirror and then slid around Samael. "I'll let you two know when Ophanim gets here. Everyone is excited to speak to you." She shut the door behind her.

Samael and Wylie hadn't been alone since they arrived at Dumah's home. They hadn't slept either, catching a few minutes of sleep here and there when the conversations lolled. Wylie had learned a lot. Either from Dumah or Mariam or Samael himself. In the meantime, angels came to her for council. She quickly realized that angels as a whole needed an update.

They'd been left without any way to contact God, and the last Dominion was not faithful to heaven. Wylie was expected to fill Samael's shoes, and his feet were huge. She remembered back to the times when he'd visit her and brush her hair. How did he work that into his busy schedule?

"We need to talk." Samael stood by the door. His fingers stretched and curled, stretched and curled. Those moss green eyes looking past all the confidence she'd dressed herself in since coming back Earthside.

Why had his familiarity dissipated since they left hell? Their time together was limited to learning opportunities. She closed the space between them and took hold of his hands, instantly bringing his movement to a stop. Her chest ached with the sliver of doubt. "Sam, what's wrong?"

His head tilted. "Nothing's wrong."

She squeezed his hands before letting go. Her eyes lingered on

Samael's lips. Her facade wasn't strong enough to withstand another rejection. "You're distant."

"Wait." His hand landed on her shoulder. "I'm going to Pearl. You're in good hands, and I need to study if I want to be of use in the last days."

She let go, turning away as her vision blurred. The last time she'd cried in front of him, the rain hid how many tears fell. She still couldn't stand to see him in pain, but it was the longing that hurt the most. Had she thrown away her one chance? Had she guarded herself so well that even God's first angel refused to breach the walls she'd built?

Wylie closed her eyes. She didn't want him to go. Her lashes fluttered when he gripped her other shoulder and pulled her to his chest.

His cheek rested on the top of her head, his arms tightening around her, his breath lifting one of her curls.

Wylie shifted, her arms locked at her side with shock.

"Let me hold you for a few more minutes." His lips pressed into her hair, turning down into a frown. The ever-present hesitancy permeating off him intensified.

"Samael?"

He blew out a breath, leaning down until his stubble brushed her cheek. "I'm only human," he whispered, his lips brushing her ear.

Wylie wasn't anymore, but all the heavenly hosts couldn't stop her from wanting this. She closed her eyes, breathing in deep as his nose found her neck. Her whole body rocked into him when he nuzzled the tender skin.

Samael's emotions crescendoed around them and his warmth suddenly left Wylie. He was pulling away.

Her eyes snapped open, indignation turning her hands into fists. She wouldn't take one more rejection from this man. "You're killing m—"

His lips came crashing into hers before she could finish her thought. His fingers wound through her hair and Wylie forgot how to breathe. How to think. Samael's curious lips coaxed hers to part and when their tongues finally touched, the only thing keeping her on her feet was the man she clung to. She'd never had a kiss like this.

Chapter 16

Samael

Samael hadn't realized he was walking backward until his back hit the door. Wylie fisted his shirt and an involuntary sound grumbled in his throat. She could have him. All of him. He was hers. He was made for her. He surrendered completely to the need to grip the curves he'd so often imagined touching, his hands sliding to her hips. Her body pressed into him in response and the ache between his legs returned. That tool of his hardening to the point of bursting.

How long had he wanted to taste her? Last time had been unreal, a fever dream. But this time . . . How fast could a human's heart beat before they died? Before the organ beat right out of their chest?

Samael froze as a knock sounded just behind him, but Wylie braced his cheeks the instruction of her tongue continuing.

"Ophanim's here," Madoc barked, hammering on the door.

Wylie's hands dropped. Their lips parted and Samael's foggy mind couldn't think of a greater loss.

More knocking. "Everyone is waiting!"

"We heard you, brother." Samael's chest rumbled as he spoke, his racing heart skipping a beat before trudging ahead into a darker place.

"Then hurry."

Samael teeth set as he guided Wylie backward. He couldn't tolerate this insolence. Samael the angel hadn't, why should Samael the human? He yanked the door open and marched straight into Madoc, plowing him into the wall. "Is this how it's going to be between us?" Samael grabbed Madoc's nape. "Are all of our years together dust now my wings are gone?"

Samael didn't need Scientia to sound dangerous. He didn't need wings to stare his brother in the eye until the male had to look away. Samael shook the Archangel as his gaze dropped. "All the blood we lost together is nothing to you now?"

Madoc lowered his head, averting his eyes. "It meant nothing to you."

He shook the angel again. "What? Is that really what you believe?"

"I refuse to go to blows with you. I'd break you. You gave up being my brother when you cut off your wings."

Samael's hands dropped with his jaw, too shocked to respond when Madoc shouldered his way past him. "I'll tell everyone you're on your way," the angel said over his shoulder.

Samael's shoulders bunched. The kiss and then this had his breath coming in gasps. This had to be the worst part of humanity. The emotions. Good or bad, his body didn't care, it responded the same way.

Wylie came behind him. Her hand rested on the scars where his wings had been. "He's wrong."

Samael shook his head. "I knew I was giving up more than my position and my power." He held his breath, hoping it would help him regain his composure and when it didn't, he turned to her. His why for all of this. Those black eyes set a warmth blooming in his chest, his lungs finally opening for the oxygen he needed. He took her hand. "Never doubt this, Wylie. No heavenly sibling, no divine calling, could've stopped me from making this sacrifice. I have faith in you above all else."

She stroked his face, as she entwined her fingers with his. "Let's go see Ophanim."

Wylie and Samael were the last to enter Dumah's living room. The walls creaked and Samael knew it was from trying to contain the Scientia coming from the most powerful being on earth. Ophanim's ethereal glow felt like sunshine, and the angels sitting closest to her leaned in her direction.

All heads turned their direction, and though the Wylie froze midstep, her face remained the mask she wore for all angels. Dumah smiled encouragingly, Madoc openly glared, and Ophanim stared at Samael with her milky white eyes. Mariam sat next to Ariel, her brows lifted, her head nodding as if she were waiting for Wylie to say the punch line to a joke.

Wylie took a deep breath and lifted her chin. "Thank you all for coming. We're here to prepare for the Summit in DC. I've prepared some talking points and want to verify with you all that I've covered the concerns of God's Angels as a whole."

"We're ready to hear your thoughts, but first let me introduce Mebahiah and Vehuel." Dumah waved at the two males in the far corner of the packed room, and Wylie's eyes bulge with recognition.

"Vice president Mendez?" She swallowed hard, her hand coming to her chest. "Robin Williams?" Tears filled her eyes. "I thought you were dead."

"I've come and gone so many times." His trademark smirk was framed by smile lines. "This last time was difficult. I left in a way that reminded millions the importance of staying."

"Erm," Wylie's eyes skipped around the room. "Can I give you a hug?"

"We're glad to have you here, Armageddon." Mebahiah patted Wylie's back as she pulled away. "We've all waited so long to meet you. I was at your Catharsis and was so impressed by your endurance and bravery."

Wylie's cheeks grew terracotta. "It feels like so long ago."

"But it wasn't, and you've come so far. You should be proud."

Wylie back straightened and she turned back to the crowd. "I've spoken to a handful of Archangels with loud opinions over the last few days—" Wylie glared at Madoc "—and the Virtues who have together filled some of the roles of the Dominions we lost. I think, with the guidance of the angels in this room, I can speak for God." Again, Wylie's cheeks burned red.

Lex

John showed up soon after, a huge smile on his face. “Lexy!” He wrapped his long arms around her and the babe. “I’ve missed you.”

“Johnny.” The name was a memory on her tongue. This is not how reunions should happen. With her sitting in a puddle of her own bodily fluids and a bastard of a baby in her arms.

“It’s okay, sis.” His hands settled on her shoulders and he bent in half so his eyes could connect with hers. “There’s nothing the two of us can’t do. Remember?”

She remembered believing this before he died. A part of her had died with him. She’d found those pieces in the arms of Gabriel. She loved her brother and had missed him more than she’d ever try to explain, but she needed different man right now.

The plastic chair beside her creaked as Justin stood and reached out his hand for Johnny’s. With his other he held the tablet against his chest. “It’s good to see you again.”

“I’m just so honored you’ll be spending time with us,” her brother said.

They continued talking but Lex’s eyes were on the tablet. She wanted it. Wanted to tell Gabriel she survived it. Wanted to show him what they’d made. A perfect little raven haired boy, with lashes for miles and hair on the backs of his ears. She wanted to see them together. The way Gabriel’s face would light up with the baby curled up against him.

She leaned back in the bed, when she realized both men stared at her. Had someone asked her a question. She lifted her brows. “Hmm?”

“What’s his name?”

Lex run over her little one’s cheek. “Persius.”

“Can I hold Persius?”

She nodded, totally numb from her lips to her toes. For the first time in heaven she thought about sticking a needle in her arm. Thought about laying back and enjoying the ride. Her brother took her son. And something about the two together brought her back to her senses. "You two look a lot alike."

"Yeah, he's just more handsome." Johnny rubbed his cheek against the baby's hair. "He's so squishy."

Lex resisting the urge to smile. "So, you've come for me?"

"Of course I have." His eyes never left the baby. "What a great opportunity, right. My little sis and my nephew have to stay with us until they get all settled. Gary can't wait to meet you guys."

"Your husband?"

"Yes." he said in a sing songy voice. "My husband, Lexy. I'm gay."

Little Persius blinked up at his uncle, his tiny eyes full of wonder.

"I knew that."

"Ha! Well, I didn't." John lifted his head.

"I was so sad that you never got to come out of the closet."

"I was too. I ended up in the waited for a long time to get over that pain before I could enter heaven."

"But they're going to just let me in?"

"You're special."

"How so."

"I'm not really in the know. I've been told that it's my job to help you threw this. That you would stay with me until you're healed enough to live on your own." He kisses his nephews forehead. "It's more like I volunteered."

"Thank you." Lex covered her face.

"It will get better. I promise. Now, I'm going to call a nurse so you can get ready to leave."

"Where's mom?"

"Mom will see you when we get home."

"Is she still, you know, her?"

John laughed. "You'll have to see for yourself. I've been with her up here for so long that I don't really remember. I can tell you one thing. Everything is better up here, you'll see."

He rang the nurse and Justin helped Johny figure out the car seat as Lex breastfed for the first time. Her heart slowed and she actually sighed as Persius latched. This is what she needed. She relaxed into the bed. This was the closest thing to being high she'd experienced since Abaddon. When she was done John put the baby in the carseat and Justin helped her into the wheelchaired. John's first car sat at the curb waiting. "So we are just going to drive there?"

"You'll see." John strapped the car seat in and Lex sat beside Persius. She couldn't sit in the font seat. She didn't think she could tolerate sitting so far away form the little guy. Justin shut her door and climbed into the front passenger seat.

"Johnny."

"Hmm?"

"Thank you."

They pulled out of the parking lot and directly onto a freeway where they met the biggest traffic jam Lex had ever seen. John jumped over to the toll lane traffic was moving quite fast.

"What's up with this traffic," Lex asked as she studied the cars they passed.

Justin turned his whole boy in his seat, looking directly into Lex's eyes. "They are waiting too. A lot of them died by car. Some of them loved their cars more than anything else. They all have their reasons. Everyone gets in, it's just 'when' that's the question."

"Everyone but the angels."

Justin's eyes dropped and Johnny ended up answering. "We don't need angels, Lexy. It is a beautiful place."

Lex resented any place that didn't want angels. She studied her brother in the review mirror. He'd aged. She hadn't noticed before now. He had to be in his mid fifties at least. They still had matching eyes and lips. He had dad's chin and square jaw. She has mom's round one. They shared the inbetween nose. That lay right in the middle of their Irish father's and Vietnamese mother's genetics.

The drive was a blur of trees and smooth suburban roads. Just right for a woman with a sore bottom and a heavy heart. Gary met them in the driveway. The house looked beautiful. Not too big, not too small. Modern with huge windows facing the drive.

"Can I hug you?" Gary asked as he wrapped his arms around Lex. "Sorry, I'm a hugger and we've been waiting for you for so long."

Lex's body locked up. "I'm happy John is happy."

Gary carried Lex's bag and Justin took the carseat as John rushed forward to open the door.

"Just wait, Lexy. You're going to love it here."

Justin and Lex followed Johnny to a spare room decorated in browns and grays. The big man settled the carseat next to the bed. "Hey John, I needed to talk to you."

Johnny nodded. "Do you need anything Lexy?"

Just one thing. "No."

"Okay, sis, come find me if you need anything."

Justin paused next to Lex and dug into his lab coat pocket producing he tablet. "I thought you might want this."

Lex snatched it from his hands, gingerly sitting on the bed and powering it on. "Justin," Lex said as he made it to the door. "Thank you."

Justin paused, his shoulders shrugging. "Of course, babe."

Lex rolled her eyes like she always did when it came to him and swiped the screen.

Gabriel stood in the foyer in tactical gear, Binah at his side and a male Lex didn't recognize at the other. Gabriel stared his father down, his jaw ticking.

"I'm not asking for a lot. I just want a good distraction. It's really up to you how you do it. I just need some time without the angel demon power team breathing down my neck."

"I will not help you spread this virus."

"Let's be honest with each other, son. You aren't here to help me. You are here to follow my commands."

Gabriel blew out a breath and turned his back. "Let's go."

"You will not ignore me."

Binah opened the door and Gabriel fell to a knee his hands gripping his side.

"Binah, shut that door. My son needs to show me some respect before he

leaves." Raphael straightened his lapels, his mad smirk curving one side of his mouth.

Binah froze, her hand shaking on the door knob but the door didn't close.

"Binah, I said close that door."

Binah's hand fell as she turned to Gabriel. "Get up." She grabbed his jacket sleeve and pulled him to his feet.

Raphael's smile fell as Gabriel stood. "Gabriel. I gave you an order."

Gabriel cringed as he stepped over the threshold.

"Son! You will no–"

Gabriel stepped out of the compound the door shutting behind him.

"Well that was dumb of you." Binah said, folding her arms around her middle, he face paling further as she looked around them. The sound of thudding feet suddenly drowning out the sound of Gabriel painful pants as a hoard of Husks stormed toward them from every angle. "Why did you drop your forcefield?" Binah yelled, not sparing Gabriel a glance as she opened fire. She and the male angel pulled out their Glocks at the same time.

Gabriel shook his head as if he could shake off the pain. "You try holding it up while your ribs are burning from the inside out." He lifted his arms. "Hold your fire." The closest subhumans ran into an invisible wall. The angels hurried into the armored limo parked at the bottom of the front steps as Gabriel held the monsters at bay. He dropped his hands when his team entered the limo. The creatures mere feet away when he closed the door behind him.

"Ya'll I think I just shit myself a little." Binah started the car, her voice a higher pitch than Lex had ever heard it.

Gabriel's eyes closed, his head resting against the hearest. "Did you recognize any of them? We used to share meals with some of those muses."

"And now we're the meal, brother." The car pulled forward. Three bodies in rapid succession crashed into the windshield and flew over the top of the hood.

Gabriel rolled up the divider and stretched out his legs.

Lex settled into the seat next to Gabriel. The exhaustion hit her all at once.

He shivered and paused. "Hell cat?" He reached for her, and soon he gathered her in his arms, his forehead rested on her as his breaths slowed.

"We had a boy." Her arms, barely visible, snaked around Gabriel's neck. "We had a boy. I named him Persius."

"You. . ." One of Gabriel's tears fell on Lex's cheek. "You are. . ."

Lex didn't wait for his words. She was too tired for his words. She knew what he wanted to say. "Gabriel. I need you to listen to me. You need to talk to your sister." She felt her energy draining. She didn't need eyes to know she was disappearing. "Promise me you'll talk to your sister." And then she was back in Johnny's guestroom, falling back on the mattress. The glitter on the ceiling blinking down at her.

Chapter 17

Lex

Her hospital room crowded her with its white and teals. Justin snored in the chair next to her as if he'd been the one to push a baby out. She grounded herself with the sound, grinding her teeth against the need to lose her shit.

The door swung open and the male version of Lex froze in the doorway. "Lexy?" He wiped at the tears streaming down his face. "You're here." He crossed the room in four long strides gathering her and the babe in his long arms. "I've missed you."

"Johnny." The name was a memory on her tongue. This is not how reunions should happen. With her sitting in a puddle of her own bodily fluids and a bastard of a baby in her arms, but she needed this. Needed something familiar right at that moment. She pressed her face into her brother's chest. "I can't do this." She meant the baby and heaven and a life without Gabriel.

"It's okay, sis." His hands settled on her shoulders and he bent in half so his eyes could connect with hers. "There's nothing we can't do. Remember?"

She remembered believing this before he died. A part of her had died with him then. But she'd found those pieces in the arms of Gabriel. She loved her brother and had missed him more than she'd ever try to explain, but he was wrong. So wrong.

The plastic chair beside her creaked as Justin stood and reached out his hand for Johnny's. With his other he held the tablet against his chest. "It's good to see you again."

"I'm so honored you'll be spending time with us," her brother said.

They continued talking, but Lex's eyes were on the tablet. She wanted it. Wanted to tell Gabriel she survived. Wanted to show him what they'd made. A perfect little raven-haired boy, with lashes for miles and hair on the backs of his ears. She wanted to see them together. The way Gabriel's face would light up with the baby curled up against him.

She leaned back in the bed, when she realized both men stared at her. Had someone asked her a question. She lifted her brows. "Hmm?"

"What's his name?"

Lex's finger ran over her little one's cheek. "Persius."

"Can I hold Persius?"

She nodded, totally numb from her lips to her toes. For the first time in heaven, she thought about sticking a needle in her arm. Thought about laying back and enjoying the ride. Her brother took her son, and something about the two together brought her back to her senses. "You two look a lot alike."

"Yeah, he's just more handsome." Johnny rubbed his cheek against the baby's hair. "He's so squishy."

Lex resisted the urge to smile. "So, you've come for me?"

"Of course, I have." His eyes never left the baby. "What a great opportunity, right. My little sis and my nephew have to stay with us until they get all settled. Gary can't wait to meet you guys."

"Your husband?"

"Yes." he said in a sing song voice. "My husband, Lexy. I'm gay."

Little Persius blinked up at his uncle, his tiny eyes full of wonder.

"I knew that."

"Ha! Well, I didn't." John lifted his head.

"I was so sad that you never got to come out of the closet."

"I was too. I ended up in the waited for a long time to get over that pain before I could enter heaven."

"But they're going to just let me in?"

"You're special."

"How so."

"I'm not really in the know. I've been told that it's my job to help you through this. That you'd stay with me until you're healed enough to live on your own." He kisses his nephew's forehead. "It's more like I volunteered."

"Thank you." Lex covered her face.

"It will get better. I promise. Now, I'm going to call a nurse so you can get ready to leave."

"Where's Mom?"

"Mom will see you when we get home."

"Is she still ... you know, her?"

John laughed. "You'll have to see for yourself. I've been with her up here for so long that I don't really remember. I can tell you one thing. Everything is better up here, you'll see."

He rang the nurse, and Justin helped Johny figure out the car seat as Lex breastfed for the first time. Her heart slowed, and she actually sighed as Persius latched. This is what she needed. She relaxed into the bed. This was the closest thing to being high she'd experienced since Abaddon. When she was done, John put the baby in the car seat and Justin helped her into the wheelchair. John's first car sat at the curb waiting. "So, we're going to drive there?"

"You'll see." John strapped the car seat in, and Lex sat beside Persius. She couldn't sit in the front seat. She didn't think she could tolerate sitting so far away from the little guy. Justin shut her door and climbed into the front passenger seat.

"Johnny."

"Hmm?"

"Thank you."

They pulled out of the parking lot and directly onto a freeway where they met the biggest traffic jam Lex had ever seen. John jumped over to the toll lane, traffic moved quite fast there.

"What's up with this traffic," Lex asked as she studied the cars they passed.

Justin turned his whole boy in his seat, looking directly into Lex's eyes. "They're waiting too. A lot of them died by car. Some of them loved their cars more than anything else. They all have their reasons. Everyone gets in, it's just 'when' that's the question."

"Everyone but the angels."

Justin's eyes dropped and Johnny ended up answering. "We don't need angels, Lexy. It is a beautiful place."

Lex resented any place that didn't want angels. She studied her brother in the rearview mirror. He'd aged. She hadn't noticed before now. He had to be in his mid-fifties at least. They still had matching eyes and lips. He had their father's chin and square jaw. She had mom's round one. They shared the in between nose that lay right in the middle of their Irish father's and Vietnamese mother's genetics.

The drive was a blur of trees and smooth suburban roads. Just right for a woman with a sore bottom and a heavy heart. Gary met them in the driveway. The house looked beautiful. Not too big, not too small. Modern with huge windows facing the drive.

"Can I hug you?" Gary asked as he wrapped his arms around Lex. "Sorry, I'm a hugger, and we've been waiting for you for so long."

Lex's body locked up. "I'm happy Johnny is happy."

Gary carried Lex's bag and Justin took the car seat as John rushed forward to open the door.

"Just wait, Lexy. You're going to love it here."

Justin and Lex followed Johnny to a spare room decorated in browns and grays. The big man settled the car seat next to the bed. "Hey Johnny, I needed to talk to you."

Johnny nodded. "Do you need anything Lexy?"

Just one thing. "No."

"Okay, sis, come find me if you need anything."

Shit, everyone should have a brother like Johnny.

Justin paused next to Lex and dug into his lab coat producing the tablet. "Siblings are truly a blessing, aren't they?"

Lex snatched it from his hands, gingerly sitting on the bed and powering it on, annoyed that the male might have just read her mind.

"The world would be a better place if we all had a sibling like yours." The male turned from her, but his voice carried that tone that meant he was saying multiple things at once.

Lex looked up at his back, her brows dropping. "I'm too tired to fuck around right now, just say what you want to say."

"Gabriel has a sibling too." It was the first time Justin had spoken

Gabriel's name, and it made Lex's palms sweat. "He doesn't have to do this on his own either."

Lex nodded to herself. He was right. Gabriel and Wylie working together may be the world's only hope of stopping Rapheal. "Justin," Lex said as he made it to the door, "thank you."

Justin paused, his shoulders shrugging. "Of course, babe."

Lex rolled her eyes like she always did when it came to him and swiped the screen.

Gabriel stood in the foyer in tactical gear, Binah at his side and a male Lex didn't recognize at the other. Gabriel stared his father down, his jaw ticking.

"I'm not asking for a lot. I just want a good distraction. It's really up to you how you do it. I just need some time without the angel-demon power team breathing down my neck."

"I will not help you spread this virus."

"Let's be honest with each other, son. You aren't here to help me. You're here to follow my commands."

Gabriel blew out a breath and turned his back. "Let's go."

"You will not ignore me."

Binah opened the door, and Gabriel fell to a knee his hands gripping his side.

"Binah, shut that door. My son needs to show me some respect before he leaves." Raphael straightened his lapels, his mad smirk curving one side of his mouth.

Binah froze, her hand shaking on the door knob, but the door didn't close.

"Binah, I said close that door."

Binah's hand fell as she turned to Gabriel. "Get up." She grabbed his jacket sleeve and pulled him to his feet.

Raphael's smile fell as Gabriel stood. "Gabriel, I gave you an order."

Gabriel cringed as he stepped over the threshold.

"Son! You will no—"

Gabriel stepped out of the compound door, shutting it behind him.

"Well, that was dumb of us." Binah said, folding her arms around her middle, her face paling further as she looked around them. The sound of thudding feet suddenly drowning out the sound of Gabriel painful pants as a

hoard of husks stormed toward them from every angle. "Why did you drop your forcefield?!" Binah yelled, as his men pulled out their Glocks at the same time.

"I didn't." Gabriel lifted his arms. "Hold your fire." The closest subhumans ran into an invisible wall. The angels hurried into the armored limo parked at the bottom of the front steps as Gabriel held the monsters at bay. He dropped his hands when his team entered the limo. The creatures, mere feet away when he closed the door behind him.

"Ya'll, I think I just shit myself a little." Binah started the car, her voice a higher pitch than Lex had ever heard it.

Gabriel's eyes closed, his head resting against the headrest. "Did you recognize any of them? We used to share meals with some of those muses."

"And now we are the meal, brother." The car pulled forward. Three bodies in rapid succession crashed into the windshield and flew over the top of the hood.

Gabriel rolled up the divider and stretched out his legs.

Lex settled into the seat next to Gabriel. The exhaustion hit her all at once.

He shivered and paused. "Hellcat?" *He reached for her, and soon he gathered her in his arms, his forehead rested on her as his breaths slowed.*

"We had a boy." Her arms, barely visible, snaked around Gabriel's neck. "We had a boy. I named him Persius."

"You . . ." *One of Gabriel's tears fell on Lex's cheek.* "You're . . ."

Lex didn't wait for his words. She's wanted to see him for herself, but now that she'd drank her fill of his handsome face, she needed to give him a message. "Gabriel, I need you to listen to me." She gripped his arm. "You can't do this alone and I can't help you, but you're not alone. You need to talk to your fucking sister." She felt her energy draining. She didn't need eyes to know she was disappearing. "Promise me you'll talk to your sister."

And then she was back in Johnny's guestroom, falling back on the mattress. The glitter on the ceiling blinking down at her.

Chapter 18

Samael

When Samael entered the sitting room Mary, Luc's Muse, stood in front of the brick fireplace with her crimson lipstick pressed into her bottom lip, her purse tucked under her arm. Her ice-blue eyes connected with his through the grand mirror.

Samael grunted when she raised her brows. His low expectations for the day met his apprehension that learning from a muse would be useful.

"Is this how you introduce yourself to everyone?" She turned, returning the tube of lipstick to the purse before putting out a hand. "Luc said you'd be a difficult student." Her grip was tighter than he'd expect. "He said I might have to put you in your place." She dropped his hand and sat. "I hope it won't have to be like that. I traveled a long way to help you." She shrugged. "And usually, the men I put in their place want to be put there. So, I don't have a high tolerance for brats."

"Brats?" Samael looked around the room, was this really happening?

"Yes, people that aren't good at following commands." Their eyes connected again and he shivered. He'd met queens that were less regal. "Are you good at following commands?"

"It depends on who is issuing the command."

"You mean God, right? You take commands from God?" She pursed her lips. "Today, I'm your God. Sit." She gestured at the seat across from her. "This is your last chance to train before the Summit.

You need to perfect what you've learned, and your arrogance isn't going to help."

Samael sat, folding his arms across his chest, suddenly understanding the indignation that had Madoc making the same gesture.

"Why did you agree to do this?"

"Because I cannot be powerless." He rested his hands on his knees. He'd protect Wylie in whatever way he could. "Not now, not ever."

"And what makes you powerless?"

"Being human."

Mary's purse crashed to the ground as the woman slid to the edge of her seat. "That will be the last time you insult my kind." She snapped her fingers when Samael's eyes lingered on her purse. "We have great power, many of us don't know how to harness, but there are those of us who do it innately or who practice until we get it right." She pulled a pin from her hair. "Watch." She drew an angry red pattern on the back on her hand. She slapped Samael's knee. "Now, try to move."

His muscles bunched, but his body wouldn't follow his directions. "How are you doing that?" His hands were glued to his knees, his mind racing as he remembered doing this with his Scientia, but he hadn't been able to detect Scientia since he'd lost his wings.

"I could hold Luc for a day with this spell and he's the heir to hell. Now, tell me humans are weak."

Samael grunted, pushing against the magic again.

"Are you paying attention?" Mary snapped her fingers again. "You can't break through this spell."

"I see your point."

The woman dropped her hand, and Samael's muscles loosened.

"How long has it been since you were a student?"

"How old is this planet?" He asked the question absently, but the woman's eyes narrowed in annoyance.

"Fuck, why did Luc think this was a good idea." Mary's red lips lowered into a frown.

"Because I'm human now, therefore, I should learn from a human."

He let his arms drop to his side, summoning the humbling he'd learned while absent of Scientia.

"And he told you how I gather my power."

Samael's cheeks warmed. Luc had told him that Mary used sexual energy. She'd trained under a succubus, and was known as a witch of great power.

"Ha, I love a blush on a big man." She settled back into her seat, arranging her black velvet skirt on her creamy legs. "Do you think you can handle this?"

Samael had come to terms with how uncomfortable this would make him. He didn't understand sexuality yet, but he knew the power it had over him. "As long as you know I'm mated and have no interest in another."

She smiled. "Mated?"

"What else do you call it when you wish to bed only one woman."

Her smile grew. "Dating?"

"Dating?" Samael shook his head. "We have something deeper than that."

"I see. This will be in your favor." Mary waved her hand at Samael dismissively. "Close your eyes and imagine her."

Samael folded his arms, his eyes closing. He could draw a picture in his head that included every freckle on her body.

"Do you know the power of worship? Have you paid attention to humans as they use it?"

He nodded; his eyes still closed. "I have."

"Then get on your knees."

Samael's eyes opened wide. He'd only ever knelt for God.

"I can see what you're thinking." Mary's red lips pressed together. "You're thinking of your God."

Samael grunted an affirmative.

"Then try it, close your eyes and picture your God."

Samael slid to his knees, bowed his head and conjured God's image in his head.

"You can't because you've never seen him." Mary leaned forward and poked his nose.

He jerked away.

"Now, picture Wylie again. And tell me that what you feel isn't stronger."

It shamed him, but he didn't have to follow her directions to know she was right.

"Love is the closest a human can get to God."

His heart raced as the truth of it hit him. "But, God . . ."

"Left more of himself here than you can imagine." She cleared her throat. "Now, close your eyes and use what he gave you. We've got twelve hours."

Guards met Wylie, Luc, and Samael at the entrance and escorted them to the map room, where Ariel and Madoc waited on one side, and Shafer on the other, a grin on the latter's face. Madoc stood immediately. "It doesn't make sense why we have to work with this filth." He pointed at Shafer, and Ariel's face grew beat red.

Luc strolled to his seat. "Aren't you a little old for name calling?"

"Their presence—" Madoc waved at the demons "—the fact that you take council from the Prince of Darkness after he took our last Dominion from us, it's an insult." Madoc's eyes narrowed on Wylie.

"We're lucky to have Wylie here to act as a bridge between angels and the fallen. I have faith in her performance today," Samael said, his chin lifting.

"I do, too," Luc said from his chair, his cowboy hat sitting in his lap. "Isn't it funny that my cousin is your humans' savior?"

A knock came from the door, interrupting Madoc as his mouth dropped open.

Wylie lifted her head as the door creaked open and a Scientia as familiar as her own entered the room. Every angel in the room stood as Wylie's twin marched past her to stand toe to toe with Luc.

"Why is she here?" Gabriel straightened his shoulders, rage rolling off of him.

"Are you talking about me?" The temperature in the room fluctuated from hot to cold in flashes as Wylie took a step toward her brother. She'd never forgive him. Even if now, he could understand her pain.

He held up his hand, ignoring her, his eyes trained on the Devil's smirk."

"She's supposed to be in hell. You were supposed to protect her. We had a pact."

"I am protecting her."

"Really?"

Wylie flew backward as Gabriel spat out the words. She slammed into the wall, her breath catching in her chest. Samael's Scientia surrounded her before she could think to react and with it and its foresight. Flame met the next wave of Gabriel's Scientia and steam filled the room.

"Enough!" The room darkened and total hopelessness squeezed Wylie's lungs. Blackness swirled around Luc as he stood. "Ask your 'father' why your pact was dismissed."

Gabriel blew out a breath. "Demons." He turned to Wylie. "You'll regret coming back here."

Again, the room cooled, and she stole a glance at Samael. He was the only human present, and she needed to know he was safe.

Gabriel's eyes slid from Wylie to Samael and back again, his brow lifting. "I see." And without explanation, he exited, a million indecipherable thoughts running across his face.

A man in a plain suit and an ear piece stepped into the doorway, filling the empty spot Gabriel had left behind. "Excuse me, we'll start in ten minutes." He followed the path Gabriel had taken, the door shutting silently behind him.

Wylie smoothed her dress, the crimson silk sliding under her palms. Wylie pulled her halo from her wrist and placed it on her head. "Let's go."

"Yes, go ahead. We can't be seen together from here on out. Don't let the politicians intimidate you," Luc said, placing his hat back on his head.

She nodded, and they shared a smile before she turned her back on her cousin and headed for the exit. Samael fell in line behind her as Madoc opened the door, a mask of indifference on his face. Wylie stepped into the hall, forcing a smile. She'd worked with old men in the ED enough times to know what this lot would expect from her.

"You're here." A man with his hand on his earpiece waved Wylie forward. He opened the door for her, and she walked out onto a balcony flanked by Madoc and Samael. Ariel followed, her confidence in Wylie a comforting presence.

Wylie sat down in a red theater seat, and a man approached with a small microphone. "May I?" He gestured at the shoulder of her dress.

Madoc stood and lifted his hand, palm up. "I'll do it." He waited for the man to walk away before pinning it to the thin strap of Wylie's dress. "Dumb humans, didn't do any research," he grumbled. The fact was, she didn't need such a system. With her angel ears, she'd hear everything said in the room, whether magnified or not. She'd also discovered she had an uncanny ability to project her voice as well.

Madoc's hands dropped, but he made no move to sit. "I might hate your guts, but I do believe you were chosen. So, do me a favor and don't fuck this up."

Wylie forced herself to keep a straight face. She wished she hated the bastard as much as he hated her. Samael and his team's presence legitimized Wylie's place more than anything else could, so she'd deal with his childishness. She forced her anger down and stepping forward, leaned against the railing and studied the humans around her. She'd been led to believe that this would be more of an intimate meeting. Only a few representatives should be present. It looked like there were a few representatives, it was true, but a few for every country. She knew they all had questions, and that they either learned what they knew from their religion of choice or Gabriel's infomercials.

Gabriel entered the balcony next to Luc's. Their eyes met and he forced a thought into her mind. *Are you ready, fragine?* He smoothed his bespoke suit.

Wylie averted her eyes, pretending she didn't get the message and returned to her seat.

"Humans, paranormals," a man at a podium said as a means of gaining their attention.

Wylie stood, wondering why she'd sat in the first place. "Angels, we're all angels."

"But ..." the man lifted his eyes to Luc's balcony.

"They're part of angel kind, just distant relatives."

The man cleared his throat. "Humans and angels."

Wylie sat at these words.

"We've gathered at this Summit to discuss the state of the world." His hands flattened on the podium, and he leaned forward. "We were warned that the world would end. We're not as ready as the angels are to accept this fate."

Wylie stood again. "Sir, it sounds like you are referring to God's Angels."

The man visibly shivered at the word 'God.' "No one here wants to argue with the word of God. But it is my understanding that the angels lost communication with God months ago."

"This does not change his plan." Wylie used her angel voice the way Dumah taught her to. It was a step less than compulsion, more like charisma, and she saw the changes on the humans' faces, how they softened as their eyes widened.

An unwelcomed voice chimed in. "The plan you speak of was concocted before the first human was born. It's antiquated at this point. The world, no, humans have become great enough to rule themselves. They don't need invisible hands shoving them in all directions. I mean, look at who the second most powerful person in the United States is. Your vice president is an angel, planted there to control you. And look he sits behind her instead of your president." Gabriel steepled his fingers as he spoke, the male hadn't bothered to stand. "We're as tired as you are of this underhandedness. We wish to rule ourselves and I'm sure you feel the same."

A man's laughter filled the silent room at the wake of Gabriel's announcement. Luc took off his hat and put it to his chest as he tilted his head back in mirth. "Says the man who created zombies." He fanned himself. "You expect us to believe that you will leave the humans to their own devices?"

"That accusation is an unfair one." Gabriel smirked as if he were in on the joke. "And we don't plan to leave humans unprotected from your kind."

"Excuse me, but it seems as though you forgot we were here," said the human man. All eyes returned to him. "We brought you here for an announcement." He waved at the humans who filled the lower level of the room. "We've taken it upon ourselves to police the comings and goings of angel kind. Together we have created an international governing body called the Paranormal Protection League or PPL. We all have our myths and legends regarding your kind, and though worship has been involved in the past, we believe we will be led by God to trust those of you he truly favors. For now, I'd like to welcome Garret Palmer to the podium."

The man who stood and made his way forward was a mass of muscle and scars. He prowled more than walked and wore lines on his face that spoke of a permanent scowl.

Madoc cursed under his breath. Wylie settled into her seat. Every angel around her began pushing thoughts into her mind. Apparently, they forgot to tell her about Mr. Palmer, and no one had anything nice to say.

"This man will lead PPL into the future of a safe humanity. Please welcome General Garret Palmer. He has protected and served this country forty years and was a first responder when heaven fell to earth, creating this unit that is now becoming its international equivalent." The man stepped aside, and Garret took his place in front of the microphone.

"We don't trust you." He lifted his head, his eyes leveling on Wylie. "We haven't forgotten what you did to those protesters. You're not in control of this planet. If you and your kind plan to end the world, you will end it in a hell storm of human defense. Now, I demand that you fix the problem y'all made in Louisiana and go back to where you came from."

This time Gabriel stood. "We were here before God dreamed you into existence."

"You, sir, weren't here when I was born. I've done my research."

Luc stood. "Garret has worked against my people for a long time. It is an insult having him here."

Garret smiled, and it was a wicked thing to behold perfectly straight and either pearly white or silver. "Lucifer, your presence is an offense."

Luc projected to the stage standing next to the general. He wrapped his arm around his shoulder and squeezed him as if they were an old friend. "One day, Palmer, the humans will realize that you're eviler than any of us." Luc hissed before he and the other demons disappeared at once.

"The monsters refuse to help. Will the Angels do the same? I know when Samael led, they would've done everything to keep us safe, but now God's army is led by a murderer." General Palmer's voice rang out over humans.

"I'm not here to debate with you sir. Samael sits at my right hand because he believes in my abilities to care for humans and lead angels. I am a healer, and no matter what you saw on the news, I don't go around murdering humans for the fun of it. I lead God's Angels who have one purpose, and that is to care for humanity, even in the darkest days." Wylie waved away the accusation in the man's pronouncement. "The world is ending. We didn't make that decision. It has an expiration date. We're here to make sure it goes smoothly. Unlike them— Wylie pointed toward Gabriel and his group —"it isn't a coincidence that the subhuman outbreak started in Louisiana."

"Why would we cause that? We're here to stop the world from ending." Gabriel turned from Wylie to the crowd. "Just because we have wings doesn't mean we can be lumped together."

"It doesn't seem to matter what your end goal is. The problem is that you all think you have the right to control us." General Palmer smoothed the podium with his hands.

"And where did you get this intelligence?" Gabriel asked.

"The Bible."

The humans erupted into both cheers and boos in response.

Wylie folded her arms; she'd heard enough. The humans were distancing themselves from the angels and she could care less. She had no agenda other than protecting humankind and even that was weak. She glared at Gabriel, her nails digging into her palms. She wasn't going to argue with this male in front of the world. The humans had caused enough drama on their own.

Wylie stood. "We will help Louisiana."

Gabriel followed suit. "Seeing as we are living in the middle of this disaster, we will use all of our resources to end this epidemic. Let us prove this to you, I myself, and my best warriors will join PPL as they work to eradicate the husks."

"God's Angels will do the same," Wylie said out of pure spite.

"Is this enough?" Garret's hands rested on his hips. He turned to the men that sat before him. "Are we in agreement?"

Wylie held back a scowl as they raised their voices at once. "Aye."

She walked out, feeling a terrible sense of disgust at herself for growing so far from humanity that she struggled to tolerate their fears and assumptions.

Wylie lifted her forearm to her fellow angels as she exited the balcony "*Pro summon bonum.*" She waited for their solute before exiting.

Before she planned for her little field trip to Louisianna, she needed to say goodbye to Samael. Her hand fell to her side, her fingers stretching.

Samael's hand slipped into hers and the fears swirling in her mind silenced, he new Scientia zinging under her skin with his contact. He pulled her passed the map room and out of the building, only stopping when they reached Luc's Ferrari.

Samael's hand slipped into Wylies. He pulled her passed the map room and out of the building, only stopping when they reached Luc's Ferrari. "Sit with me for a minute." He opened the door waiting for Wylie to slide in. "Luc will come back for me, but I think he had something he needed to take care of first." He joined her, his eyes lingering on her lips as he shut the door behind him, her breaths becoming pants when his hand landed on her thigh. "You're the most beautiful thing I've ever seen." He opened his mouth to say more, but she grabbed his cheeks and pressed her lips to his.

The spark that zinged from his lips to his belly sent a shudder through his body. Her lips were gentle, her tongue patient as it teased its way into his mouth. Had God created heaven with a kiss, he wouldn't be surprised.

As the kiss deepened, he lowered Wylie onto her back. Afraid to hurt her soft body as he leaned into her, he braced himself above her. They were hungry for each other and the push and pull of touching sent his hips rolling against hers. His hand shook when it landed on the bare skin of her thigh, the red silk had slid up to her waist and cascaded over the side of the seat.

Samael fingers squeezed on their own, loving the softness that gave her the curves he couldn't keep his eyes off of.

Her lips slid away, down his jaw and to his neck. Her tongue drew a circle before she sucked, pulling a moan from his throat. Samael's hands traced the curve of her hip with slow, decadent touches. "Wylie." He kissed her hair. She smelled like woman and desert skies before the rain.

Her hands wandered downward and he caught them before they found the fly of his pants. "Do you want this?" He pressed his length into her belly.

"I want it. I want you. I want all of you. I—" He cut off her words with more kissing.

He growled, licking and sucking at her lips, unable to form words as he freed her hands.

"If we are going to have sex—" her fingers fumbled "—there're things you'll need to understand first."

"They taught more on Ludus than how to dress like a human." He mirrored the movement of her hands with his own, pushing her thighs apart, his finger found her clitoris through her panties, eliciting a gasp. "I know this is your—"

"No, Samael." She ground against his palm; her voice breathy. "Don't say it."

"You want to teach me, but you won't say the words." He smiled against her lips. He pushed the fabric away. One of his fingers pushing inside her. "Does the words vagina and labia make you so embarrassed that you wish for me not to touch them?" His second finger slipped in, and he groaned. "How do you feel so good? How does this feel so good?" He meticulously explored. His chest rumbled in a low hum as Wylie moaned. "Why do humans waste time doing anything other than this?" He caught his breath as she gasped, enjoying the way the tight space in the car forced them close, cradling them. "Wylie, let me touch all of you. Touch all of you with my tongue. Dear God, with my lips and my hands. I want to rub my entire face against your genitalia."

Wylie burst out laughing, and Samael's hand dropped.

"This isn't funny. I've never wanted something so bad it hurt before."

"Is this the new you, Samael?" Her lashes dreamily fluttered, creating shadows on her cheeks under the setting sun.

"Yes, Wylie, this is me now. I want to say the things I think. And I'm thinking about tasting you. Tasting every part of you, but especially every place that would make you moan and writhe the most."

"Did you learn that the first time for a man can be short?"

Samael's brows lifted, a smile pulling at his lips. "What constitutes the 'first time'?"

"You know, sex. The man may ejaculate quickly."

"And that means we must be done?"

Wylie blew out a breath, the small worry lines on her face tempting Samael to kiss them. When she didn't respond Samael's fingers began to move again, this time in a rhythm. His free hand came to her breast. "Can I taste you here?"

Wylie nodded, so he pushed the silk of her dress aside and took her nipple in his mouth, rolling his tongue over the tender flesh. He pressed and then pulled and pressed again. His fingers left her core to take hold of her other breast, the crimson fabric turning maroon with her slick. "I want to taste all of you. I want to be inside you. Wylie I—" He pulled her tight against him. "But I can stop. Do you need me to stop?"

"No, Samael." Her hand found his length and began a long slow pump. "I want you too." Pre cum sent her hand gliding over him.

Samael's hands found her thighs, coaxing them to open. He kissed her chest, and her ribs, and then with both hands gripping her ass he scooted her further down the bench seat before resting his cheek on her belly. He stared down at the apex of her thighs, and as if his gaze could move her on its own, she lifted a leg, resting it against his shoulder. What she revealed had his mouth watering. "Can I?"

"Yes, yes to all of it. You're torturing me."

He spread her lips apart and licked a long slow line up her core, blowing a shuttering breath against it. Her thighs shook around him, encouraging him. He closed his eyes and kissed her with all the passion he'd shone her mouth, slipping his tongue inside and meeting her at every movement until she fell apart, crying out.

Samael paused. "Was that an orgasm?"

"Yes."

"Can you do it again?"

"C'mere." She pulled at him. "I want you inside me."

His eyes widened as he crawled up her body.

She tore at his slacks and gathered his cock in her hands. Soon she pressed it against her, her head falling back as he strained against her.

"Wylie," he moaned. "My heart. I'm going to die."

"You will, and then you'll want to do it again."

She was wet for him, but it still took a few rocks for him to enter her. "Fuck." She clung to him as he worked himself deeper with every thrust until their thighs slapped together each other.

Samael lost control the moment he was fully seated. He came up to his knees, his fingers digging into her ass as he pulled her against him with every thrust. His teeth bared, and his cheeks burned. He couldn't take his eyes off the way she matched his passion, holding on as moans fell from her lips like fever prayers.

The wave crashed. The earth split. The sky tore. The world stopped spinning as he dropped his mouth onto her neck and grunted the last of his passion into her skin. The weight of his body and the rock of his breaths were the only things keeping them from floating away.

"Thank you. Thank you. Thank you," he chanted, his lips pressing his words and his kisses just below her ear.

Chapter 19

Gabriel

Gabriel sent his team ahead of him, and projected. He took advantage of not having his "bodyguards" and stopped by the lab for an update on the subhuman numbers. *One million?* With a new weight on his shoulders, he headed to his office with a pile of paperwork.

A hand brushed over his shoulder as he reached the hall that lined his office and room. "Lexy?"

Fingers brushed his beard but no words came. He reached for her, but he couldn't catch her. "*Wylie can help you.*"

"*Râleuse?*"

Her familiar presence rushed away from him and he lifted his head to follow her flight. His eyes landed on his office. The door sat open a crack. He folded his papers and shoved them in his jacket pocket. "Who's there?"

Only Lex and himself could get through the wards he'd placed there. He stepped over the threshold, his watery wings present and ready to shield him at any moment. For the second time that day, he walked into an empty room.

A dripping greeted him, and he flipped on the light, his eyes landing on the wooden box on his bed. But it wasn't the familiar carving that got his attention, no, it was the crimson puddle that surrounded it, spilling off his desk and soaking the carpet.

Gabriel's hands became fists as he rounded his desk and sat in his chair. His head tilted, his eyes closed, and he rubbed his temple. The continued dripping setting his teeth on edge. The faces of the people he'd hate to find in the box flashed on his eyelids. But the truth was, Todd and his other bodyguards knew nothing about the box.

With a sigh, he reached forward and pulled off the lid. Binah stared at him with empty eyes. Her braids piled beneath her head like a beaded cushion.

A hand brushed his arm. "Who did this?"

She didn't answer. Her thought brushed against his consciousness. Her mouth was close to his ear. Her hands smoothed over his shoulders.

His breath came out in clouds, and the ghost of Lexs' hands solidified with crystals. His heart race, but he controlled his breaths. Last he heard from Binah she was going back to hell to negotiate. His eyes narrowed on a scrap of paper protruding from his friend's mouth. He pulled it out, unfolding it jerky movements.

You'll never be rid of your curse.

Gabriel crinkled the paper in his fist. He'd offered the world to Kami on a silver platter and here was the Queen of Hell's response. A double insult. She came into his home to leave the body of one of his angels. No, not the body, all she got was her head and an impossible amount of her blood. He thought more about the blood puddling at his feet. There was too much blood!

He lifted the box and studied the bottom. Nothing. The lid only held the carving of the trumpet. He reached inside, both hands gently lifting Binah's head. There, caked in clots, lay three Kanji symbols. It was a spell. It had to be.

He pulled out his cell phone and dialed Todd.

"Sir?"

"I'm sending you a picture. I need you to find out what they mean."

"Yes, boss."

Gabriel hung up and balancing Binah's head in one hand, took a picture and sent it. He didn't want Todd being involved, but he didn't trust anyone else. Gabriel gingerly returned Binah back into the box and replaced the lid. He pulled off his jacket, wrapping it around the wood to prevent it from dripping, and projected to the tool shed.

His angels forsook their Throne when they chose freedom. It was up to him to rejoin Binah with the earth. He grabbed a shovel, his teeth grinding with every scoop of soil. The demons would regret messing with one of his. Eventually, he placed Binah's head in the hole and began to cover her with dirt.

He'd pay Luc a visit. Kami would pay for this transgression with her son's blood. Raphael would be getting his distraction after all.

Chapter 20

Wylie

Wylie didn't know when she volunteered to help the PPL that she'd be expected to eradicate their little zombie problem. The barrier created around the state of Louisiana rose into the air, more than twice her height. Luckily, almost half of the state was lined by water, whether it was the gulf or the Mississippi River.

She'd expected to see her twin, they'd both volunteered for this job after all, but she didn't recognize anyone at the wall. She pushed past the strangers, ready to meet her cousin. Luc and his team joined Wylie at the southwest border of the state with plans to travel across the state to the epicenter and go from there. "How'd you get the devil to agree to help you?"

"How do you think? We made a deal." Wylie couldn't help but smirk. Luc's people were highly targeted by the subhumans, having lived with and as humans for most of their lives. Of course, he would want the subhumans stopped. Not to mention, his kind didn't all have muses, but when they did, they were highly treasured.

"I guess I should forget everything I learned in Sunday School?" The man in the army fatigues rolled his eyes.

Madoc stepped in front of the soldier, his wings appearing. "What does that mean?"

"Nothing, sir." He saluted with a shaking hand as if he had no clue what else to do. "Thank you for your service."

"Leave him." Ariel said when Madoc began rolling his sleeves up his tattooed arms.

Shafer tapped the toe of his boot, his eyes narrowed on the pair as Ariel pulled Madoc away.

Luc punched Shafer's arm. "Hell's halls, why are you being so creepy."

"Only teenage girls say 'creepy.'"

"Well, fuck you." He turned to Wylie. "Can we get going?"

"Don't look at me. You're the oldest, you get to be in charge."

"The hell he is," Madoc said under his breath.

Luc smirked. "You're lucky we aren't in hell, boy." He raised an arm. "Hey, Brute! Nyla! Time to go!"

The pair left their shady spot under a willow, Brute holding a low hanging branch out of Nyla's way. They stopped behind Shafer and Luc.

Luc straightened, his black leathery wings appearing. "Are you ready, soldiers?" The prince's neck strained with the volume of his shout.

"Yes, wing commander!" The three demons responded at once.

"Make 'em bleed." Luc took to the air.

"Make 'em bleed." Shafer, Brute, and Nyla rose behind him.

Wylie turned to Madoc with raised brows. She'd seen what angel military strength looked like, but these Archangels never taught her any of that.

"What? I ain't calling you commander." Madoc took a few steps forward. His wings spread and he followed the demons.

"Pro summum bonum."

"Huh?"

"Now's a good time to recite our motto." Ariel squeezed Wylie's shoulder and then took off parallel with the wall. She ran into flight. Circling back until she hovered with the rest on the other side of the wall.

Wylie held her apprehension in her chest, watching with amazement as the wing she'd created for Ariel worked just as well as the one she was made with. A familiar pride warmed her chest. She'd done that.

She smoothed her hands over her weapons, her wings burning

into life. She bent her knees and leapt skyward. The mob of subhumans rushed her, running straight into the flames, not stopping as they screamed their pain. Their fingers grazed her pant legs as she took to the air again. Her fellows waited for her in the air. They watched the fire spread, the bodies writhing and jumping as if somehow, they could pull the angels out of the sky.

"Well, that worked." Ariel returned her halo to her chest. "I'm not sure why you brought us."

The smell of cooking meat and burning hair made Wylie's eyes water. "We'd get done faster if I'm not the only one working."

"But it's just so much fun to watch you."

Wylie laughed. "Fuck you, Ariel. Get to work."

Wylie landed at the edge of the fire this time. A wall of flames came for her, and she took to the sky in seconds.

Madoc and Ariel landed and leapt, decapitating four or five every time they touched down. They looked like frogs or crickets when compared to Shafer and Luc, who carved a path through a mass of bodies with a steady pattern of spraying bullets and flying limbs, thanks to Luc carrying an ax rather than a shield. Heads rolled and bodies thudded on the ground.

Wylie found herself staying in the air longer than necessary. She couldn't keep her eyes off of Brute and Nyla. She hadn't known what to expect, but the two could've been an army on their own. Nyla's hand hovered at her waist, her face blank, her eyes unfocused and totally white. The movement of her fingers corresponded with ten to twenty subhumans falling to the ground lifeless. Brute then lifted his arms and the bodies rose in unison, turning on their fellow infected with the same rigor they'd fought for Scientia moments before.

They pushed forward in synchronized movements. Nyla a ball of power, and Brute her shield of muscle. Between Wylie's flame and the other's fighting prowess they carved their way to their first city. The sign read DeRidder, and Wylie remembered her times at the prison.

Luc joined Wylie where she hesitated midair. *What is it?* He pushed the question into her head as the wind screamed past her ears.

We have a friend here.

Let's go get them then.

An hour later, they arrived at a prison she'd once thought was haunted and landed on its roof. The subhumans surrounded the building totally unaffected by the bloody trail Wylie and the rest made to get there. Madoc lifted the hatch where the rope attached for a hanging. One at a time they dropped past the spiral staircase lined with prison cells, landing on the stone ground at the bottom.

"Kis?" Wylie called out as her boots crunched on the hard floors.

Wylie stopped when she heard a creak, and Ariel ran into her back. "I wonder what angels taste like."

Luc chuckled. "I haven't tasted one in a while."

Wylie rolled his eyes. "They probably taste like humans." Wylie continued to the entryway.

"I don't think so. I mean angels don't really exist here. I bet we taste like air," Ariel replied.

Another creak and something jumped out of the shadows. Arms wrapped around Wylie's middle. "You're here."

"Kis!"

"It took you guys long enough." Kis laughed, nervously patting his black braid. "I thought I was going to spend the rest of my days here."

"Have you been here the whole time?" Luc asked.

"Yep, it's been just me and the zombies." Kis' head tilted, his eyes widening with recognition before bowing. "You brought the prince?"

"Oh, stop with the formalities." Luc dusted his shoulder. "Brute, Nyla. Fall in." He turned to Wylie. "While this reunion is cute and everything, we should probably get back to work. I'll have these two escort Kis.

"We aren't calling them zombies," Ariel said stepping past Wylie and Luc. She pulled the Shadow's braid.

"Then what are you calling them? 'Humans that Eat People?'" He hooked arms with Ariel and led her to their former meeting room with the rest of the group following.

"Husks."

"Hmm, interesting choice. They're especially hungry for me." He held up his chin, the grin on his face faded. "There're a few people I know out there. They've gone wrong. They can't hear me, they can't speak. They just want in. Speaking of going wrong. How's Samael?"

Wylie ran her fingers along the table. "He's figuring things out. I don't think he'll ever be the same, but I think he's becoming a very good man."

"She'd know," Madoc said as he shut the door behind them.

"So, you two are . . ." Kis did a few hip thrusts, and then turned around to mimic himself kissing, his fingers running through his hair suggestively.

Wylie's cheeks burned, but then she remembered the way Samael's green eyes held hers. "You can't make me embarrassed of him."

"I don't want you to be embarrassed." Kis patted Wylie's back. "I'm glad he has someone to help him through this. There's no loss that can compare to what he's gone through."

Wylie took a seat and leaned back in her chair. She noticed a layer of who-knows-what baked onto her arms. She picked at it, realizing that the substance was definitely bits of the infected she'd roasted earlier. She rubbed her arms and watched the stuff flake off, mesmerized until an explosion rocked the building. "Kis?"

"That wasn't me."

Another explosion sounded from the other side of the outer wall. It caved in, and soon the moans of the subhumans filled the room as they forced their way through the rubble, even the ones injured by the blast. Wylie pulled out her halo and reached for her sword. She wouldn't be able to use fire in this small of a room. Taking a shaky breath she ran forward, hacking anything and everything that came at her. No amount of practice could have prepared her for this, and she realized how easy she'd had it earlier when she used her fire.

Her arms shook and her nerves short circuited every time the things got close enough to bite or scratch her. The virus didn't do anything to angels, at least not that she knew about. They fought their way out of the building. Each strike removing limbs or heads, her angel strength evident in how far the body parts flew before they landed. There was no end to the onslaught, and for a moment she worried that if they didn't make it out of the building where the monsters bottle necked, they wouldn't make it out at all.

The thought of retreating upward disappeared when another blast took down the door way to the spiral staircase. Her heart plummeted, but she pushed on, blood and sweat mixing together and replacing the layer that had crusted to her arms earlier. The hill of bodies they fought on top of soon closed off the only exit and the angels. This was their first chance for a break.

"Let's make a small hole so the subhumans can enter one or two at a time, we can take turns offing them." Madoc leaned against the pile of bodies, sweat making lines down his face. Wylie never saw the male out of breath before.

"I'll go first." Luc, Nyla, and Brute created the first hole in the wall of bodies, working like a well-oiled machine. Ariel played with her gun as the angels waited, pulling the piece apart and putting it back together.

A subhuman slipped past the demons and Ariel stepped forward. "My turn." She leveled the Glock and pulled the trigger.

"Shit!" Kis covered his ears as she unloaded the thing on the first two Scientia eaters that entered. He hid behind the upturned table. Shadows were known for being non-violent, and Kis could no more kill a living creature than he could leave this land. Wylie wondered how many angels were trapped in this state. And her stomach twisted as she realized many of them may not have been able to find safety.

A fourth explosion rocked the building, and the wince on Kis' face enraged Wylie. "Move!" she shouted over Ariel's gun shots. "I'm going to find out what the fuck is going on."

She knelt and just as Luc taught her, she placed her hands on the ground, pushing her Scientia through the earth in search of more power. She reached, her brow furrowing, her eyes closed. "There." She recognized the Scientia immediately. "Gabriel."

The earth rumbled, and a fine dust showered them as if in response.

"That bastard." Anger had her holding her breath. How could he attack them while she was cleaning up his mess? The mess that took

Lex from him. She wanted to make Gabriel suffer, but she was mad, not suicidal. She wasn't sure when it happened, but she'd started wanting to live more than she wanted revenge. She smiled to herself as she imagined Samael's hands on her body. No, she knew why she wanted to live.

"What the fuck? I thought we were working together on this." Madoc glared at Wylie like it was her fault Gabriel decided to turn on them, and it probably was.

Wylie turned to Kis. "There has to be another way out of here. My Scientia followed a path to Gabriel."

"We can try going underground. There used to be an underground tunnel connecting the prison to the capital, so that prisoners could be transported without being in full view of the public. But those tunnels haven't been used in decades. I don't know if they're still clear."

Everyone in the room froze as their head turned to Kis. The grunts of the subhumans outside filled the silence. "You mean there was another way out, and you were going to let us just kill our way out instead?" Madoc shook his head. "I thought you were a pacifist."

"I don't think we'll be able to get through that way."

"Let's check," Luc said nodding at Brute. "Follow the Shadow. We'll hold up the rear."

Nyla turned from the bodies. "Sire, this is not your battle."

"This is my family's battle and a Devil never fights alone. Let's make them bleed."

"Make 'em bleed."

"Make 'em bleed."

The ground bucked and bricks rained from the ceiling. The vibrations of the third collapse had Brute staring at the hallway that led to the underground tunnel. He leapt toward it, his tree trunk arms shooting out. Those muscles twitching as he prevented the hallway from crumbling in on itself with an invisible force. The building creaked and groaned with the intention of coming down on them and everyone. Madoc turned to Luc.

"Wylie, Ariel and Shafer, come with me. The rest of you take the tunnels and get the Shadow out of here."

Shafer scowled as Madoc squeezed Ariel's shoulder, whispering something near her ear.

"I'm fine. Just keep Kis safe." She shoved him toward the hallway and moved to Wylie's side. "Now what, Prince shit for brains."

He raised a brow before gesturing to Shafer. "Why don't you show your fated what you can do."

Gabriel

"Yes, *frangine,* I'm here." Gabriel tossed another ice ball at the building, and the stones crumbled beneath it. "Come out, come out. Bring Lucifer with you."

"She's no good incentive to come out. Look how the subhumans are swarming the building now that she's used her Scientia."

Gabriel side-eyed Dina. He was a poor replacement for Binah, but he was right. Gabriel checked his watch. He wouldn't give the angel the satisfaction of agreeing.

Subhumans crawled over each other like ants below. The swarm split in half between his building and Wylie's. "Why don't you go get them out for me?" Gabriel asked.

Dina snorted, his mouth opening for a retort, but shutting the moment he saw the seriousness on Gabriel's face. "They're buried under a mountain of bodies, sir."

"I've never seen a few bodies stop an angel before." Gabriel waved him away. "Take care of it."

Dina's wings blinked into existence. "Well, you heard Gabriel." He turned to the angels behind them. "Let's go get her."

Five Angels took to the sky, heading for the building. Gabriel hoped none of them would survive. Though many considered his rebel angels weak, they took chunks of the subhumans out effortlessly. Gabriel checked his watch, thirty minutes had passed, and it would get dark soon. He'd look a lot less dignified if he had to wait until dark. "If you want something done right . . ."

He jumped, landing on his feet hard enough to compress the soft soil beneath him. He reached out for the closest subhuman, flash froze him and every other husk in the front parking lot of the building. He shoved the solid being over and it shattered. He smirked and strolled toward the prison. He wasn't supposed to be killing these things Raphael had created, but there was something so satisfying about shoving his power into the subhumans so hard that some of them burst.

He crossed the street, and another pack froze as they rushed him. By the time he made it to the soft grass of the prison, the only living beings in the vicinity were his angels. He gestured to the pile of bodies clogging the hole he'd made in the building. "I shouldn't have to do all the work. C'mon, move them."

He took a seat on a park bench and steepled his fingers on his knee as Dina lead the team in removing the bodies. Upon creating the first small opening a cloud of blackness burst out. Knees buckled and his angels dropped to the ground as the blackness swept past them. He'd never seen anything like it. He stood. It was almost as if his team had released a black sandstorm, and now it had its eyes on him. He surrounded himself with his Scientia and waited for the demon wielding the stomp to show their face.

Chapter 21

Wylie had questioned her memory of what Shafer's tattoo could do several times since she'd first seen it fall off his skin like sand, but watching the grains of black sand fill the air her doubts evaporated. The bones tattooed to his hand glowed as he lifted it, and with a small gesture sent the floating storm through the opening the rebels had created in their attempt to get at Wylie. Her brother stood just beyond the line of falling angels, his Scientia whirling around him. Gabriel's ridiculous suit, sans jacket, fluttered in the wind. He wore a bullet proof vest and the smile the man always wore.

Wylie followed Shafer out of the building, Ariel glued to her back. These two were a power couple whether the Archangel wanted to admit to it or not. Wylie felt encapsulated by it. She was a freakin' fated mate sandwich.

Gabriel folded his arms over his chest as Shafer's sand returned to his tattoo. "Sandman? I've always wondered why they called your people that. It's all too literal, isn't it?"

"Hmm, somewhat like how we demons call you bastard?"

Gabriel coughed out a laugh.

"What do you want, Gabriel? I thought we were working together?" Wylie asked.

"*Fragine?*" Gabriel leaned sideways. "Oh sister, you're here? I'm not here for you. I'm here for the Prince of Hell."

Luc stepped out of the ruble with the last of Gabriel's words. "Who me?" The Devil pointed his thumb at his chest.

"You'll suffer for what your family did to Binah."

Luc projected and unholstered his gun. "I don't know what you're talking about." He pushed the barrel into the back of Gabriel's head.

"Aw, he knows what I'm talking about. Right, *fragine*?" Gabriel patted Wylie's cheek.

The sky darkened as the hammer of Luc's gun clicked back. "Step away from your sister."

Gabriel raised his hands, but instead of surrendering he spun to face Luc, his fist connecting with his chin. An icy breath escaped Luc's mouth and frost spread over his skin, his body freezing.

Wylie's heart froze with Luc, but her hands didn't. Her hands never did. She grabbed the back of Gabriel's bullet proof vest and jerked, but her twin didn't budge. Luc's skin turned blue, and Wylie slammed a fiery hand into Gabriel's head. Her eyes watered with the smell of it burning. Gabriel slapped at the back of his head as if batting away a fly and color returned to Luc's face.

Wylie didn't wait for Luc to reprimand her for putting herself in danger, instead she slapped his back and using Samael's Scientia sent the Devil away. She pulled her halo from her wrist and placed it atop her head, her blade appearing in her hands. "If you want the prince, you'll have to go through me." Her wings appeared and she rose into the air sending Shafer the location of where to find Luc.

Clouds gathered and rain dumped. The part of Gabriel's shirt that caught fire went out as he shot into the air after her. Steam rose from her wings, the heat of them keeping he back dry. Gabriel gave her one last grin before coming straight at her. The shield Raphael had given her blinked into life and smashed into her twin with a grunt, his wings propelled them toward a building.

They crashed like a shooting star, missing the building by a hair and skidding down a street before crashing through the wall of a house. The impact stole Wylie's breath. She gasped as she shoved Gabriel off her with the shield, and then brought it up smacking him in the chin. His head snapped back. He touched the blood on his chin, staring down at the red before grabbing her shield and using it to pull her to her feet he tossed her through the opposite wall.

Wylie flew through the brick. She caught herself with her wings and lunged forward sword first. Gabriel walked into the sword as ice formed around it, blunting the blade. Ice climbed the silver and up her arm.

Gritting her teeth Wylie willed it to melt, becoming so distracted that it took two ice shards cutting her cheek for her to remember Samael's precognition. She pulled his Scientia close, and her shield lifted as if Samael had stood behind her and lifted her arm himself. A volley of dagger-like projectiles rang against her shield. Samael's invisible arms wrapped around her waist and her chest burned for an instant before she burst into flame. Ice sizzled and melted joining the torrent of rain running downhill around her feet.

Gabriel jumped back, his hands up, his eyes squinting from the glare. "You can't stay like that forever," he shouted over the cacophony of rain and flame.

Wylie caught her breath as she burned brighter. Gabriel's outline backed away further and paced and stopped. He raised his arms and the rain ceased. Wylie smelled the burning before she saw it. Without the rain, the buildings around her caught fire.

Gabriel

The entire block was on fire in minutes. Panic widened his sister's eyes, and all the fight rushed out of Gabriel. He pulled down the rain once more, quenching the flame.

Wylie came to stand beside him, returning her halo to her wrist and looking at the destruction they'd caused. "I won't fight you."

"It's too late for that," he said halfheartedly.

"I don't want to die anymore."

Gabriel's eyes slid to Wylie; his teeth barred. "I know what you're thinking. You're thinking you're about to get a happy ending. No one gets a happy ending."

Wylie waved at the destroyed and vacant streets and the husk bodies littering the floor. "Does this look like a happy ending?"

"Goodbye, Gabriel."

He reached for her, but not fast enough. Her Scientia slipped between his fingers. He fell to his knees, his head hanging. Were they playing hide and seek? He shouted into the rain until his chest heaved and his voice grew hoarse. He needed to move on. If he couldn't have Luc, he'd take someone else. Kami had other sons.

Chapter 22

Lex

They were perfect. Everything about them. The way they looked at each other as Johnny held Persius. The way they talked as they made meals together. The way they used each other as touch stones throughout the day. They fit together like puzzle pieces. Their mannerisms reflecting what the others needed.

Not in Lex's greatest fantasies did she imagine her brother finding this. He just had to wait to die first because in no world where Frank, their war vet father, lived could be an out-of-the-closet Johnny. Even with heaven crashing down to the earth and Demons admitting to being real. Frank did have enough space in his heart for a stripper daughter and a gay son. Or maybe she wasn't being fair.

As far as heaven goes, she fucking hated the place. It was every suburban nightmare she'd ever experienced. She wondered if she'd been placed in Johnny's version of heaven, and once they deemed her healed, she'd be able to go off into nonexistence like she'd always dreamed about. Persius would stay here with her uncles. The only person who really grounded her was Justin, but the asshole spent more time away than with them.

"Are you ready to see Mom?" Johnny asked as he tilted the bottle so that Persius could get the last few drops. They sat on the couch next to a fire. The light flickering over their forms as they waited for Gary to finish prepping the sweet peace offering he always brought Dung.

"I don't want to see that bitch."

Johnny coughed, biting his lip to prevent a smile. "There's a park across the street if you need to escape."

"That's good to know. If I'm forced to spend too much time with her, I might punch her smug fuckface." The high ceilings barely contained Lex's tone, and she lowered her voice. "Don't pretend to be so shocked."

Johnny covered his smile with his hand. "I'm trying not to laugh."

"Why?"

"You think God would let you punch her."

Lex rolled her eyes. "Shit, Johnny, what am I doing here?"

He shrugged, repositioning her son on his shoulder and patting his back. The babe let out a belch and the siblings smiled at each other. "If I knew, Lexy, I'd tell you. I don't know what you got mixed up with after I left. I've heard things are looking pretty bad down there."

"Yeah, and why's that?" Lex stood, turning heavenward. "Because God fuckin' abandoned us."

Persius began crying with her raised voice.

She folded her arm around herself and glared at the babe. "I don't think I ever cried that much when I was little."

"Girl, you were just yelling at my ceiling like a mad woman." Johnny continued to pat Persius' back until he stopped crying.

"Johnny, do you want me to take the baby?" Gary came from the kitchen, untying a frilly apron from his waist. Without waiting for an answer, he reached for baby Persius.

"Thanks, sweetheart." Johnny kissed Gary's cheek. "Are you ready to go?"

Gary nodded and both men turned to their nephew, smiles on their faces. Persius' little eyes did the slow open and close of a milk-drunk baby.

"Grandma D will love you so much, little guy." Gary wiped the babe's drool from his chin and then combed his black curls with his fingers. "Johnny, go change your shirt."

Johnny smacked Gary's ass. "I think we need a baby. You look so cute right now."

Gary brushed his husband off, a smile on his face. “Go on.” Gary waited for Johnny to disappear into the hallway before turning to Lex. “Are you nervous, sis?”

“Me? Nervous? Never.” She really liked this man.

“Yeah, I mean I’m nervous. I’ve never thought that woman liked me.”

This confession had Lex ready to defend her brother-in-law. What kind of monster didn’t like Gary? And how was she allowed up here? “Are you allowed to not like people in heaven?”

“You’d be surprised by what you can do in heaven.”

Lex laughed, pulling on her septum ring. “I really don’t know what to expect. I’m surprised that woman came here. She totally fucked my life. Shouldn’t she be in hell?”

Gary twisted one of Persius’ curls. “Humans don’t go to hell.”

“Hmm, explains why I’m here.” Lex ducked her head pretending to retie her shoelace She didn’t want to see Gary’s reaction. She was starting to love him like an extension of her brother. The man was devoted to Johnny and everything about him was the sweetness her brother used as a pet name. “Sorry, I’m such a shit, Gary. I bet you never expected to end up dealing with an ass like me here.”

“You know, I suicided too.” Her head jerked up in time to catch Gary wipe a tear from his eye.

“I never would’ve guessed.”

“Life is hard. I . . .” The sound of Johnny’s steps interrupted his confession. “We should talk about it some time. If my journey has taught me anything, it’s that talking is key.”

“Yeah, sis,” Johnny interrupted. “Your voice is back; you need to talk and never stop talking.”

By the time Lex arrived at her mother's townhome she felt like the air in the car had disappeared. She flung the door open before the fucking engine was off and climbed out. She couldn't believe she was putting herself through this again.

Persius' car seat clicked into the stroller, and the men carried it to the door. "Johnny!" Dung hugged and kissed Johnny, waving everyone inside. Lex's breath caught when her mother turned to the car seat. "So, this is him. My grandson. He's handsome. No?" One wrinkled finger ran over Persius cheek. "Cưng." The endearment set her teeth on edge and filled her mind with images of Abbadon. And that's when her mother decided to acknowledge her. Lex remembered as the woman eyed her from head to foot why she was the bad guy in her story.

"Mom." Lex lifted her chin, not willing to let the woman cut her.

Dung straightened. "We have a lot to catch up on."

"I think, I'm going to take Persius to the park first." Lex couldn't meet her mother's eyes as she took the stroller and pushed it right back out of the townhouse her mother lived in.

Johnny followed her, helping her down the steps. "Putting it off is not going to make this any easier."

"I know," Lex spat out the words and Johnny flinched. "I'm sorry. It's just, fuck her, she can wait another hour." She squeezed his arm before heading to the crosswalk.

She did a loop around the park, appreciating the bluer than blue sky and birds chirping. She could've been walking through a painting. Every plant, every stone was perfect in detail. She hated it.

She slumped onto the first park bench she found. An older gentleman sat at the other end of the bench. His elbows on his knees as he leaned forward, his eyes on the swings where a man pushed a toddler. The toddler giggled, her curls flying in the wind as her onyx eyes stared at what must've been her father, with so much admiration that it made Lex want to wake Persius and stare into his eyes.

"Children are such a gift." The old man's accented voice jerked Lex into the present.

"Yeah." The asshole in her would have ignored the man, but there was something about the about the man's demeanor that made her want to make sure the smile he had on right now, didn't go away because of her.

"That's my son and granddaughter. She's two, she's my little princesa."

Lex nodded, the giggles, the glowing bronze skin, those pig tales. The kid was probably one of the cutest she'd ever seen. "What's her name?" She asked, knowing that this was the next expected question.

"Linda."

Lex smiled at the pronunciation. The name in Spanish sounded beautiful compared to its English counterpart.

"She's named after her great-grandmother." He gestured to her stroller. "How old is your little one?"

Persius stirred and snored in response. "I can't tell here. He's aging so much faster than he would on Earth." She pressed her sweating palms together. "He should be just a few weeks old, but you can see."

"Oh, so you're new here, welcome." The man smiled. The silver at his temples gleaming as he put out his hand. "My name is Roberto. Roberto Hernandez."

"I'm Lex."

"I know."

Lex caught her breath. "You know me?" Her words came out in a whisper.

"You know me too, don't you?" He raised a brow. "Or at least you know my wife."

"Who?"

"Wylie."

Lex gripped her seat. His black hair was more salt than pepper now, but he was definitely Wylie's deceased husband. "Fuck."

"Yeah, fuck." He nodded. "I know you guys didn't get along, but she never knew the whole story, and neither did you."

Lex eyed Persius, unsure if she should make a run for it. "How do you know me?"

"I was told that you'd come. To be ready to introduce you to Dean. Maybe fill in some of the parts of the story that you're missing."

"Then you must know why they let me in early."

"Because Earthside needs you, and they don't have time to wait while you spend a lifetime or two in purgatory."

"You think I would've been there that long?"

"I could've spent I lifetime there. But my son helped me heal, yours will too."

"Dean?"

"Yes."

"That man is Dean?" Lex remembered the pictures she'd once seen on Gabriel's desk.

"That was like three and a half years ago."

"I know you've notice how fast time goes here."

"Why?"

"I'm not the one to ask about that."

"Your wife is a fucking bitch."

Roberto laughed. "She's very protective. I can imagine she didn't like you."

"She didn't. She blames Gabriel, but she doesn't understand."

"No one down there does. They're all blinded by what's right in front of them."

Persius let out a wail, and Lex jumped to her feet. "It's okay." She unbuckled her little one and settled him against her chest. "Shhh." The babe grabbed Lex's shirt, his eyes wide and searching.

"You know, they're cousins. Our children are cousins." He smiled.

Just then Dean whooped and dragged his daughter from the swing and into the air, flying her from her swing to her grandfather.

"*Mijo*, this is Lex."

Lex's cheeks burnt as she shook another man's hand. Two handshakes in one day, must be a fucking record for her.

"Nice to meet you. I hope my dad hasn't been talking your ear off."

Lex nodded, unsure how to respond. She pulled Persius closer to her chest and kissed his sweet curls gathering her thoughts. "I've definitely learned a lot from him.

"Me too." Roberto stood. "I hope we see you here again some time. This is Linda's favorite park. We come here a few times a week."

Lex's head bobbed, once again speechless.

Roberto gave her a knowing smile as Linda found a spot on her grandfather's shoulders. The three of them headed for the path to exit, waving as they went.

Chapter 23

Samael

"She's in Louisiana now." Samael stared out the window switching the phone from one ear to the other. This would be his first day Earthside without her. He still floated on the high of their intimacy the night before. Since she left, he'd hit both the highest and lowest points in his life. It confused him. He caught himself checking his chest for the gaping holes.

"And you're telling me why?" David's voice was gravely as if he'd just woken up.

"Because I know you care about her." And the man probably understood the turmoil tearing Samael apart better than he did himself.

"Hmm." The sound from David irritated Samael. *"It doesn't really matter anymore, does it?"*

"You'll always be her muse." Samael grunted when David didn't respond. He had nothing to say about what tore David from Wylie, all he could feel was gratefulness that she was his now. "You told me to stay distracted." Samael blew out a breath. "It's harder than it sounds."

"That's why you're calling me? To distract you? Okay, well here's something: I think the world would be better if you'd died when you cut off your wings."

Samael cringed. Where had their relationship gone wrong? David had once been a sweet boy. He turned from the freedom of the outside. It was Jacob's death. All of this animosity started when his muse died. "I need to tell you what happened to your father."

"You can tell me whatever you want, but you and I will never be friends."

"I never wanted that from you, but it would be nice to visit Jane and not have you glaring at me."

David grumbled, something Samael couldn't understand. "Wylie misses you both."

"We miss her too. Jane misses you. She's worried." The phone crackled. *"So, tell me how you got my father killed."*

Samael rubbed his temples and then focused on Luc's grand piano. That Devil was always surrounded by pianos. "Your father became my muse as an adult, unlike your sister. I watched him grow up though, because his mother was my muse before that. I was treated like his uncle. He treated me like family. I *loved* him like family.

"The night he died I was away. He became curious about why muses and angels were connected and got tired of my explanation of 'that's how God made us.' He'd found a muse support group. I was against it, but Jacob asked very few things of me, and I wanted to give him that companionship he felt he was missing.

"What was meant to be a place for muses to talk about their shared history became a place of carnage. I projected there the moment I felt Jacob ripped away from the living. The police called it a robbery, but I recognized traces of Scientia. Something more was going on. I should've been there for your mother. I should've been there for you and Jane, but I felt it was my duty to find out what was happening. That year thousands of muses were murdered or kidnapped. I needed to stop whatever was happening, but the angel that was committing these crimes was always a step ahead of me. I wish I would've figured out it was Raphael back then. There were all these hints throughout the centuries, but I couldn't believe my brother was behind all these atrocities."

Samael groaned and walked up to the window, leaning his forehead against the glass. "Are you still there?"

David cleared his throat. *"I am."*

"I didn't tell you because in some ways, you're right. If Jacob hadn't been my muse. If he hadn't been born a muse. He would still be alive. I've lost hundreds of thousands of muses." Samael blew out a breath, his hand covered his face. "So much death. But I know, I know where they go is better than here." The wind picked up and the trees outside fought as if resisting the words he'd said.

"Why did you decide to tell me this now."

"Because now that my life has an expiration date, I need to know that I have a family. That I didn't waste all the years of my life building power and not love. I loved your father, David, but I also love you and Jane. I remember holding you as a baby. We played games. We passed a ball a few times. And suddenly those moments are more important than every war I won.

"I also wanted to tell you, I understand why you did what you did. I'm proud of you for trying to make a difference. I'm proud of you every day. For a long time, jealousy and apathy got in the way of that. And for that I'm sorry."

There was the sound of a door shutting and David's voice raised in volume. *"Jane misses you. You should come home to visit us before this is all over."*

Samael pushed a fist into his mouth to keep any involuntary sounds from coming out. He took two deep breaths, his eyes closing. "Thank you, David."

"Now, I have to go back to work."

"Goodbye."

The phone clicked off and Samael remembered why he called: Wylie. He missed her. Every small step he made toward becoming human, he did for her. He closed his eyes, missing the angelic senses that had let him feel her no matter how far away she was.

Samael got to his feet with the help of the couch. His legs hurt. He'd started training with Santana, Luc's little brother, and the Demon was merciless. Samael had trained with the Spartans, the Marines, and many other well-known military fighting forces. But he never fully understood what the humans had endured until now.

The pain, the aches, the sweat in the eyes, the burning lungs. He couldn't understand why humans would put themselves through it.

He was doing it to stay relevant. He looked down at the planes of his body. They carried the same edges, but those lines had softened. It had creeped up on him. And that's when he realized that he would need to work in order to maintain his prior physique. If he ate whatever he wanted as he explored his new tastes buds, he'd have to carve out the time to burn off the extra calories. Having cookies as his favorite food just increased the time Santana would make him spend in the gym.

"You're moving like an old man, brother."

"I am an old man." Samael smelled his armpit and flinched away. "A very smelly old man."

Santana laughed. "That's what happens when you spend over an hour praying on your knees. Ready for our jog?"

Samael had taken to praying every time he missed Wylie. He would take that ache in his heart and channel it to his fingers. With that energy he'd been able to do a few minor parlor tricks the best of which included scrying. This let him see her. It was one of the best things he'd learned from Mary.

Santana raised his brows. "Let me rephrase that. 'Let's go.'"

The insolence of this kid. "Fuck you." The words didn't sound right coming out of his mouth, and the youngest Devil son laughed.

"It's not my fault you got left behind, old man."

Samael grunted; he had no interest in arguing. He had the argument with himself enough times. He should have been allowed to go. He still knew how to swing a sword and hold a gun. He still had millennia of experience as God's general under his belt. If anything, he'd be in the least amount of danger since there was not one drop of Scientia left in his body.

Samael followed Santana out of the house and paused as the demon, walked up to his car. "We aren't running here?"

"No, dude, this is too easy for you." Santana pulled his car door open and climbed in. "C'mon."

Samael fisted his hands and marched the rest of the way to the car.

The engine roared to life as he climbed in. "Sometimes you remind me of an angel I used to know."

"There is no greater insult."

"We're not that bad."

"Sure, sure." Santana turned up the volume and shifted. The car growled as it picked up speed.

The bass buzzed in Samael's rib cage. He checked his seatbelt and he wondered if crazy driving was taught to the Devil boys when cars were first invented or if they all acquired the taste for speed separately. Samael's eyes wandered over the landscape and its patchwork canvas. He started counting cows when Santana slammed on the breaks.

"Shit!" The car swerved and Santana shifted down. "Who the fuck are they?"

"Gabriel."

"Damn. What do you think he wants?"

"I don't care. Meet me in front of the car. Be ready to get back in."

"I could just shift."

"Santana, trust me, we don't have a chance if we try to fight."

Santana's jaw worked. "Fuck it. Okay."

They climbed out. Gabriel stood in the middle of the street. Flanked by two angels Samael didn't recognize. Gabriel didn't need backup so the fact that he brought some, meant Gabriel wasn't there to talk. Samael walked with his hands raised, coming around the hood of the car, and meeting Santana. Samael didn't wait for Gabriel to speak and grabbed the gun tucked into the back of Santana's jeans.

Bam.

Bam.

Bam.

Each Angel collapsed as a bullet lodged into their brains. "Go!" Samael roared. Gabriel climbed to his feet as Santana reversed the car, spinning it around, his feet slamming on the pedals.

"Hell's halls, Samael. I didn't know you could shoot like that."

"Just drive faster."

Something landed on the roof of the car, and Samael raised the gun to the ceiling.

"Don't you dare!"

Bam.

"You bastard!"

The thud, thud, thud of a body rolling off the roof filled the cabin. The next angel landed on the hood of the car. Samael lowered the gun.

"If you do that, I'll never forgive you." Santana growled out before the bullet went through the glass and into the angel's forehead, next to the last entrance wound. The body slammed into the windshield. It shattered but stayed in one piece as it caved in. "Fuck you, Samael. This is my baby."

Samael ignored the whining. "Better your car than you." Samael unbuckled and kicked the glass out of the way before putting his belt back on.

"I'm sure they don't want me." The car engine roared as Santana found its limit. "Is that . . ." Santana narrowed his eyes. "Gabriel?" His face scrunched up, and his knuckles widened as he leaned into the steering wheel. "I'm going to run that bastard over."

"No, you fool! Go around!"

Gabriel's wings spread wide and his stance widened. He put his arms out like a linebacker.

"What is he doing?"

"Go arou—" They crashed into Gabriel, the car curling around him before flipping and rolling.

Samael's body flopped about. Pain like he'd never experienced sliced threw him until the dashboard blew open and the airbag smashed into his face turning the world black.

Chapter 24

Wylie

Wylie squinted toward the sun. They'd been in Louisiana for days now, and she was starting to grow numb. The screams of pain didn't touch her anymore, but she had a mother fucker of a headache. Smoke thickened as their newest city grew close. Buildings jutted out of the ground, empty and silent and Wylie knew to blame Brute for the fires. The necromance introduced her to his flaming flails on day two, and she couldn't help but add a little of her own fire to their flame.

"Luc said they'd meet us out here when they finished with the city." Wylie turned back to Madoc where he leaned against a tree, an apple in his hand. "It was nice of him to give us a break."

"Leave it to a demon to call genocide a break." Ariel gripped the nape of Wylie's neck. "Is there any human left in there?"

Wylie pushed Ariel away. "We all know these aren't humans anymore. In fact, the last few waves were stronger and faster than the last. Are they evolving?"

"Is Armageddon getting tired?" Madoc drawled as he chewed.

"Don't make me light you two on fire."

"I'd like to see you try." Madoc smirked until the hair on the back of his arms began smoking.

Luc projected beside Wylie before her and Madoc started brawling. "Did you miss me, cuz?" Luc had blood splattered over his chin and chest, but he pulled her into a side hug.

"I almost forgot the two of you are related." Madoc asked as he stood, dusting the ash from his arms. "Doesn't that make you a princess too?" He chuckled. "Now, everything makes a lot more sense, but what were you doing in that city that you didn't want God's army to see?"

"Nothing, I just couldn't stand one more second of Ariel and Shafer hate fucking each other with their eyes." He ruffled Wylie's hair. "I don't know why my man has to go crushing on an angel. I've never seen that work out." Luc released Wylie, his brows dipping as his mouth straightened. "Is it just me or are the husks changing?"

"I was just saying that." Wylie blinked a few times. She couldn't remember the last time her head actually hurt this bad.

Luc rubbed the flaking blood off his chin as he studied her. "You okay?"

"My head is killing me."

"Maybe we can stay somewhere nice tonight? Take showers? That would really boost morale."

Wylie turned to Ariel and Madoc who stared at Luc with the mistrust they shown since Samael cut off his wings, narrowing their eyes. "What do you guys think?"

"A shower would be nice, but I'd rather project to my muse." Madoc frowned.

"Same," Ariel added before Madoc finished speaking.

"Cool. Let's meet back up here tomorrow afternoon? I don't know about you, but I'd love to sleep in." Wylie held a straight face as Madoc sarcastically saluted her, and Ariel nodded.

"Later, bitches." Luc slapped Wylie's back and held up a middle finger to Madoc.

Madoc rolled his eyes before projecting away.

"That wasn't very nice," Wylie said in her mom voice.

"No, it's not, but look he listened and fucked right off."

Wylie almost slapped her forehead. "You two drive me nuts."

"But it's so fun to taunt that asshole."

"I've noticed." Wylie put her hands on her hips. "So where are we staying?"

"I'll show you." Luc gripped Wylie's shoulder and projected.

"Fuck!" They found themselves in front of the Westin's rooftop infinity pool. "You should warn people before you do that."

"You're here!" Shafer waved from the jacuzzi. "Come join us."

Nyla sat innocently across from Brute, wearing a t-shirt and gym shorts, her eyes on her hands. Brute sat shirtless. Scars and tattoos covering every inch of skin. A chain with a medallion hung down his chest and he leaned back with his eyes screwed shut.

Wylie didn't think she could get relaxed enough for a jacuzzi. "Maybe later. I'm going to call Samael." She went to the edge of the rooftop and dialed.

The phone rang until it went to voicemail, but he hadn't setup an inbox. Wylie called Samael every day. Which she always got shit for because the two of them had the hardest time getting off the phone, but this was the first time he didn't answer. She tried again, her stomach cramping with dread, and her head throbbing with a new intensity.

The last time she had a headache was before her Catharsis. She blinked back tears as her anxiety worsened the pain, and she dialed Samael a third time.

"Luc." She swung around the phone still pressed to her ear. "Can you call Santana? Samael isn't answering his phone."

Luc's smile fell from his face. "You look sick."

"I think there is something wrong with Samael." She held her head in her hands.

Luc pulled his phone from his pocket and dialed. The phone stayed at his ear for a few seconds before he pulled it away and glared at it. "His phone is off." He held the screen in front of his face, a hand dancing along it. "It looks like they left together this morning, but he knows better than to turn off his phone." He shoved his phone back in his pocket and closed his eyes.

Luc unsheathed a dagger, cut a symbol into his palm, and flung his blood into the wind. Scientia whooshed out of him in search of his brother. Wylie had heard of demon's communicating over large distances, but she never realized how.

"He's hurt and unconscious."

Shafer and Brute stood up at the same time. The water of the jacuzzi splashed as Nyla climbed out. "Where?"

"They're not Earthside." Luc's eye lids fluttered open and he braced the wall closest to him.

"Is Samael with him?"

"I couldn't tell." Luc shook his head. His fist hit the wall and he roared.

"Luc, I have the closest bond with him." Nyla stepped into the rage rolling off of Luc. She looked small next to everyone, but beside Luc she looked like a child. "I'll project there." She disappeared.

Wylie's head swiveled in Brute's direction.

"They're fated." Shaf answered Wylie's unasked question. "Like Ariel and I. Nyla should be able to find him anywhere. She can feel his pain and even hear his thoughts at times."

"Feel his pain?" Wylie gripped her head. Was the pain threatening to split her head in half Samael's pain?

Chapter 25

Samael

Samael touched the wetness that oozed from his forehead, his eyes blinking open to find his fingers covered in crimson. His throat burned and his body ached, but his head hurt more than any soreness tearing at his muscles.

"You're awake."

Samael's brain hesitated to translate the muffled words. He groaned and wiped at the blood leaking into his eye. "Where's Santana." Flashes of cows, a car, and then wings. "Gabriel?" He turned his head, diverting the bleeding from his face to his hair.

"How far you've fallen." Gabriel cupped Samael's cheek. "To think I grew up on stories of you and the epic battles you won."

Samael's eyes darted around the darkness, but no shapes hinted at where he was. "Where are we?"

"We're in the ninth circle. It was hard to find a host after little Lucifer chose sides."

"Where's Santana?"

Gabriel's face came into view, a spotlight outlining him. "Don't worry, I brought him too. His mother sent me a gift, and I need to return the favor."

Samael attempted to move his hands, but they were pinned in place. He couldn't believe this child had taken him hostage. Didn't he have bigger fish to fry? "For not wanting the world to end, you're about to cause a war like no other."

"You have no idea." Gabriel stepped aside and the light blinded Samael. "Don't you know the best civilizations rise out of the ashes of war and the highest profit comes from the largest body counts. Those who survive will be the ones who deserve to live."

Samael coughed, causing the throbbing in his head to multiply. "Raphael fed you these lines. I'm not impressed."

"Raphael will be the first giant to fall."

Shouts filled the room and Samael squinted, his head whipping sideways as he searched for the source. Santana hung from a rack naked with his face screwed in pain, a gag holding his mouth open. Gabriel ran a knife down the demon's torso and muffled obscenities spilled from his mouth.

Samael cringed. He didn't like seeing Luc's little brother harmed. "Santana is the youngest Devil son." Samael pulled on his bindings. "You're torturing a prince. They will kill you." Shame hallowed Samael's chest. The only silver lining he could find is that Santana hung from the rack and not Wylie. And that's when he realized all of this was for Wylie. Was Gabriel's plan to trap Wylie in hell permanently? There were too many possibilities.

"Your concern would be touching, if I knew it was for me."

Samael cringed. Would they kill Gabriel if they knew it meant killing Wylie? Yes, there's no way the Devils would allow someone to touch one of their sons and not end their life in the most painful way. He needed to escape. The room became clearer in increments revealing a torture chamber matching those medieval dungeons he'd once reigned over.

"I can see the wheels turning in your head. Don't worry we'll go on a fieldtrip soon."

"This is suicide."

"You might be right."

Santana's cries filled the space.

A warm piece of flesh slapped against Samael's chest. The hand sized patch carried the image of a spider. "Here, hold that for me, I want to bring Kami some proof that I have her son."

The pain in Samael's head worsened as the demon's muffled screams continued. He attempted to roll off the table, but all he succeeded in doing was cause the throbbing to travel into his neck and back. Gabriel ignored him, saying nothing about Samael's movements, and piled two more tattoos on his chest.

"Let's go." Gabriel loosened Samael's bindings and pulled him to his feet, placing the tattoos in a satchel and securing Samael's hands behind his back.

Chapter 26

Wylie

"Nyla, you have to take me." Wylie grabbed Nyla's sleeve and the slight woman glared down at her hand.

"Luc?" Nyla brushed off Wylie's hand.

"Wylie, they took him because they want you."

"Or they took Santana to get to you."

"Taking Santana will bring all of hell down on them. This plan of theirs won't work." Luc had projected them to a warehouse. Industrial shelves piled high with weapons created aisles of metal on metal. The prince pointed at Wylie. "You're staying here. They have my brother. I can't babysit you while I'm trying to save him."

"Excuse me?" Wylie stepped into Luc's space, but he caught her by the wrists.

He squeezed. "This is not an argument. You'll stay here on your own or I'll tie you down."

Wylie twisted away, her hands coming to her head as the pain intensified.

"You need your muse. Why don't you go see David, and by the time you get back we should be home with Samael."

Wylie opened her mouth to argue, but Luc set his hand on Nyla's shoulder and projected them away, leaving her alone in only God knew where. For a moment she considered pulling everything off the shelves, chucking them into a pile, and burning all the blades, guns, and ammo until the warehouse exploded.

Wylie let out a frustrated growl before projecting to David.

He sat on his bed, watching the news. "I was wondering when I'd see you again."

Dried blood and gore decorated Wylie's skin and clothes. This wouldn't be the first time she showed up in David's room like this, but his reaction showed how much their relationship had changed.

"You look like you need a shower?"

Wylie raised a brow. "And you look like you need a shave."

He smiled, and put the remote on the nightstand before leaning back. "I heard you've been busy."

"Just a little." Wylie's skinned crawled with tension. She couldn't read David. She felt his emotions, but they were all mixed up. The cocktail of love and hate made her heady.

"So, how's Samael?"

All the near misses of the last few days hit her at once. Her fight with Gabriel. Samael's capture. Her hands flew to her mouth as her chest heaved. She'd been holding things together so tight that she didn't realize that she'd already unraveled.

David's mask of indifference turned to concern when Wylie's tears created trails down her cheeks. "I'm sorry." He covered the space between them in seconds, his hand hovering over her back.

She shook her head, unable to speak, her throat closing.

David's hand met her back and she instantly curled into him. "It's okay, Wylie. I'm here."

Minutes ticked by, and Wylie calmed down in increments of relaxed muscles and renewed trust. Finally, she breathed in deep and let David's cinnamon peace wash over her. The rise and fall of her chest slowed and his hand came to her chin, lifting it. Those honey eyes captured hers and his head lowered. Wylie jerked away before his lips could brush her own. "Don't."

David straightened. His hand dropped to his side. "So, it's true?"

Wylie stepped back. "What's true?"

"You and Samael."

Wylie didn't respond. Couldn't respond.

David scrubbed his face, his eyes averted. "I did this to myself."

"No, David. We didn't work because it wasn't meant to be. We should've talked more. I've already forgotten why I was so mad at you. I hope you can forgive me for being a bad friend. I shouldn't have left you alone all this time. I was just so angry and afraid."

"That's not what I meant." He blew out a breath, his hand traveling over his scalp as his eyes flickered around the room. "I meant the distance between us. I knew I was right about Lex. That was never the concern. I should've done better convincing you. Maybe we could've —" David froze and turned up the TV. "Shit." He hurried back to the bedside table, and grabbing the remote turned up the volume.

"The quarantine lines have been broken in multiple places. Subhumans are escaping by the hundreds into Mississippi. Any attempts to close the lines have been thwarted by angels." The reporter ducked behind a car as an explosion went off.

David decreased the volume as he turned to Wylie. "What's happening."

"It has to be Gabriel." Her eyes narrowed on the screen, as if her twin would show up at any moment. "I came here because Samael was kidnapped. We thought it was a trap, but maybe this is what they were planning all along. It was a distraction." She pulled up her sleeves, suddenly too hot. "I need to get back to Louisiana."

David nodded. "Let me come with you. I want to help."

A "no" rolled around in Wylie's mouth as she contemplated what bringing him would mean. Life would be easier if her muse was with her. She needed to be at her most powerful if she was going into battle. "Okay. But I need to make sure that everything's clear. We're friends. You're my muse. These are two of the most important relationships in my life and they don't have to end just because we aren't . . ."

"Fucking?"

Wylie's brows scrunched together before she saw the smirk on David's face, and then remembered she was the first one to put it that way.

"I told you we were doing more than fucking." David put out his hand and helped Wylie up. "C'mon. You've got a lot of work to do."

Chapter 27

Gabriel

Gabriel jerked Samael through the tunnel. The huge male leaned against the wall every time Gabriel loosened his grip. For a moment, he worried that he'd permanently damaged Samael's human brain. And then he remembered that if his plan worked, the bastard would be dead within the hour anyway.

The light from hell's red moon had grown from a pin prick into an exit, and soon he dragged the stumbling Samael into an open field of dead grass. Hell was always so picturesque. Gabriel rolled his eyes, spotting the slight from of a woman sitting at a park bench.

"Gabriel."

He'd never heard his name said in that way. Had she just admonished him with one word? "Kami."

She rose to her feet, her eyes going straight to Samael's swollen face.

"Don't worry, not all of that blood is his."

"You have to know that I will kill you if my sons don't first."

"The Devils' are so good at making threats." Gabriel planted his heel in Samael's calf and pushed him forward. The man groaned as he fell to his knees. "You know what I want." Samael tossed his satchel at Kami's feet. "Break the hex, and I'll give your son back."

Kami bent down to retrieve the bag.

"No, Kami, he has Santana. You don't have to look inside the bag." Samael's head bowed as he spoke, his words slurred.

Kami's hand hesitated, her fingers skimming across the leather. "I know Samael. I can feel it." She flipped it open and pulled out her son's spider tattoo. "Santana received this tattoo after collecting trophy heads in a Nazca ceremony. They entangled their souls with the ash of the bodies and our royal tattooist inked their life force into Santana's skin. You just released twenty murderers and rapists." Though the woman seemed in control, her earthy Scientia rolled off of her in swirling tidal waves. "Why would you do this?"

"You murdered an angel under my protection. That can't go unpunished."

"I've done nothing to you or your angels."

"Luc claimed the same, but I found this with her head." Gabriel's lips flattened as he tossed the note of Kanji at her feet. She lifted a brow, and the paper floated into her hands. He studied the fine lines in her face as she read. The slant of her eyelids, the slope of her nose, all testaments to her origin. Most humans knew the woman by another name, and the stories of the atrocities she'd caused had been part of oral history since the beginning of time. What they didn't realize was Lilith had been the mother of sixty percent of the human population. While Eve. Who cared about Eve? Kami had been a God once. "Here's the deal, Kami. You will remove my hex, and I'll give you your son. Everything forgiven, I won't bring it up again."

Kami dropped the satchel on the ground and walked to Samael, lifting his chin. She studied his face. "I should call Raphael and tell him that his pet is out of line." She brushed Samael's hair back from his face. "But I have a feeling he's the reason you're here. Binah wasn't harmed by a demon. This I vow."

Gabriel ignored the words. He didn't care what Kami said. In fact, he didn't want to hear anymore. His revenge was more important. But Kami's familiarity with Samael did fill him with dread. Gabriel's ice wings came to life as his comprehension spiked. Wind whipped around them bringing up dust. He needed this to be an advantage, not the other way around. He forced Samael's blood to cool and smirked as the ex-Dominion turned blue. "I will kill him, or you will perform the ritual to release me from this hex."

"I will alter your hex, but I'll never forget this." Kami straightened to her full five feet and stepped up to Gabriel, her head tilting back.

"Oh, and when you get home, ask the last Dominion what happened to Binah." She dropped the note on the ground. "This says 'my son is a fool and so are you.'"

Gabriel opened his mouth, but a gasp came out instead of words. Kami's clawed hand stabbed into his side. Her fingers curled around his ribs and ancient words fell from her lips as blood poured down his side.

He took hold of her wrist, the bones crunching under his grip. He pushed his ice into her. The woman's free hand reached up, and she gripped his chin, her body stiffening until she became solid. Gabriel stumbled backward, Kami's hand coming free. He staggered to Samael, leaving Kami a statue.

"You shouldn't have done that," Samael said through chattering teeth.

"Shut up, or you're next. Now, let's go." He held his wound with one hand and yanked Samael back with the other. "Hurry, before she breaks through."

Chapter 28

Lex

Lex put little Persius into the toddler swing. Linda's giggles brought a smile to the muse's face. The little girl grew as quickly as her child. She'd graduated to the big girl swing a few visits ago.

"Auntie Lexy, push me." Linda giggled.

Dean smiled, wordlessly trading with Lex, taking over pushing little Persius.

"How high?" Lex asked as she stepped behind Linda.

"All the way to the moon." Linda giggled as Lex pushed. She'd fallen in love with the kid. The kid and his father. The grandfather wasn't that bad either. The asshole. She never thought she'd have family like she had here. She never knew what she was missing.

"Lexy." Roberto rested his hand on her shoulder. "How are things with Gabriel?"

Lex scoffed. "He hasn't been able to see me clearly since I came to heaven."

"Justin told me this might be the case."

"He's not very helpful, is he?" Lex shook her head. "Where's that bastard by the way?"

Roberto laughed. "Nowhere. Everywhere. 'That bastard' is more than he seems."

Lex frowned and stepped away from the swing. "Okay, Linda, show me how high you can go on your own." She turned to Roberto, her voice turning into a whisper. "If he's so special then why have things gotten harder since I got here? Gabriel's ignoring me, David has been left on the sidelines, and my father has done everything he can do." Lex wasn't sure what Roberto was involved in, but it didn't feel right. The intrigue he referred to would continue after death.

"Maybe it's time."

"For what?" Lex's hands came to her hips.

"For you to meet God."

Chapter 29

The airports were closed, stealing a car was easier than renting one and there wasn't time to drive to Louisiana. "If you want to go, you're just going to have to suck it up. We're in a hurry."

David had yet to agree on Wylie's proposition, but they were on their way up to the roof anyway. "I'm bigger than you, what if you drop me."

"You're not that much bigger than me, and I am stronger than I look. Remember, I'm an angel." Wylie threw the last part over her shoulder. The way he panted as he took the stairs should have been enough evidence to their differences.

They met the landing and David set his hand on her shoulder. She turned, their eyes meeting as she waited for him to catch his breath. "The truth is, I'm embarrassed."

"You've been my little spoon before. Let's think of it like that."

David shivered, his eyes closing. "I remember."

Wylie turned back to the door. "David, we are going to be okay." The wind wrapped around them in a frenzy. Angry clouds churned above.

He nodded; his face suddenly sad. He turned from her. "I'm ready."

Wylie took a step behind him, and leaning into him wrapped her arms around him. It took a minute for Wylie to figure out the best way to hold her muse. Since his pride wouldn't let her cradle him, she found herself standing behind him and crossing her arm over his front. She shook her head, the position didn't feel safe. She walked around him, ignoring the blush that bloomed over his face as she wrapped her arms around him and gripped his pants with her fingers through his belt loops to help distribute his weight.

"Now, hug me." She looked away from him as his hardness pushed into her belly. "Ready?" She wanted to say, *"really?"*

The shade of his blush deepened. He nodded and then flinched as her wings burst into life. His eyes squeezed shut, his arm shook with his grip, and he tucked his face into her neck as she slowly lifted them from the roof.

She fought the wind to keep them going forward and used her flame to keep David warm. She worked to rise above the clouds as she took them southeast. Madoc and Ariel were with Luc, leaving her no choice but to call Vice President Mendez or Mebahiah, now that he'd been stripped of his political standing.

He offered to meet her in Mississippi where he promised to bring a few more Archangel brigades with him. Since the casualties have continued to increase, their military couldn't keep up with the horde that swept north from the multiple mouths Raphael created in the quarantine wall.

Hours later, they landed on the capital building of Jackson, Mississippi. David's arms loosened, and his body leaned in as his snore rattled against her. "David," she said softly.

He jerked backward, his ankle twisting as his feet hit the ground. She kept him from falling, holding him until his eyes widened with awareness.

"We're here."

The crowded rooftop silenced upon their arrival and people backed away from Wylie's wings.

David's chest rose and fell twice before he gave her a nod and stepped back.

"Wylie!" Mebahiah, took her hand and shook it enthusiastically. "We are so glad you're here."

Wylie's name repeated in whispers around her, and she took in the scene. Stretchers lined the rooftop. She counted thirty from where she stood. The place smelled of death.

"Not all angels are gifted with healing. And that's what we need right now," The Power said.

"You're in luck. I brought one of my favorite doctors with me." She advanced through the crowd, curious about their resources. David stayed close to her back.

"We've secured ten rooftops throughout the city. Most buildings are packed with subhumans. Angels have been flying survivors to the rooftops. This unit is for soldiers. We have one for pediatric, another for burns, and so on and so forth. We've been saving the medical personnel and soldiers first, but I think we're past that point." The bustling returned. "Not all of the rooftops have electricity, but we were able to secure the top few floors of the local hospitals to work like ICC, umm, I mean IUCs, umm. . ."

"ICU."

"Yes, that."

"That's where David, my muse, should be."

Mebahiah waved to one of the men at the edge of the building looking down at the hoard below.

"Wait, Wylie, that's not my specialty." David put his hand up defensively as the angel approached.

"I know, but I can heal most things. Simple injuries will take less power, so if I can have the human medical providers focusing on the complicated cases. I can save some energy just in case I have to go on offense." She ran her finger through the hair of his beard before she could stop herself. His head tilted to the side. "I'll know if you need me. Stay safe."

He shoved his hands into his pockets. "Okay."

"Uthra, this is Armageddon's muse. You will protect him with your life. Take him to St Annes."

David spared Wylie a half smile before Uthra swept David in his arms without asking and took off.

Wylie's fingers tightened into fists as she watched Uthra carry

David away, suddenly feeling that every man who loved her was destined to a terrible end. She cleared her throat, swallowing back the fear before turning back to Mebahiah. "Let's take care of this first." She waved at the crowd. "Then the children, and then we need to start working on a plan."

"Take care of this?"

Wylie smiled, pulling on the confidence that Roberto and David and Samael nurtured in her. "Just watch." She closed her eyes and opened her palms. The rooftop fell silent as her Scientia thickened the air. She reached for the first soldier. She'd start one and a time. She'd never tested her ability to heal en masse, but if her brother could do it, so could she. The first patient had been crushed. Compartment syndrome had his legs swelling, purple, and blistered. They'd need to open things up or he would lose all circulation to his feet. He writhed in pain, his movements the slow, sloppy ones of someone whose pain medicine wasn't working well enough.

She soothed the swelling with her magic. Her invisible hands pushed fluid back into the vessels where it belonged. Wylie took the pain as she withdrew and found another body. In quick succession she closed wounds, stopped bleeding, and aligned bones. By the fourth or fifth healing, her Scientia had figured out how to enter more than one soldier at a time, and by the time her eyes opened, every human she'd healed stood watching her. The last rays of sun heated her back as one of the men turned away from her, fell to his knees, and prostrated himself.

Silence fell over the roof as all eyes fell on the praying man. A gratefulness settled over Wylie's shoulders. For the first time, she was thankful to whatever high power gave her the ability to heal. She'd always seen it as an extension of herself, but this tenor weighed upon the crowd heavier than her Scientia ever did. Her hands shook with the power of it.

The groaning of the subhumans brought Wylie back to herself. The reverence lay thick between her and the others on the rooftop. She turned to Mebahiah. "Let's go see the children." Without a word they jumped into the sky.

Lex

She shuffled through her meager wardrobe. She knew how to look sexy. She knew how to look inconspicuous, but how should she dress for a God? Lex figured he was a man, so she'd go with sexy.

She chose a long shirt that fit tightly around her breasts and pulled just below her ass. She looked in the mirror. Her tattoo remained, but her scars hadn't. She wished she had something to line her eyes with. Something to stain her lips with. Warpaint. Because no matter how supreme the being she was about to meet was, he'd still damned her to a life under Abbadon's thumb. A life of whoring and drugging and seeing herself as garbage. A life where she spent most of her adult life wishing it was over. Could she have respect for a God who allowed that?

She left sleeping Persius with his uncles and wandered into the kitchen and took a handful of cherries before going to wait on the front porch. She sat on a step and set her teeth against the red tender flesh of the fruit. "Mmm," she hummed as the sweetness burst against her tongue. She ran the juices over her bottom lip, remembering the magic of lipstick. Of how there was a time in her life when lining her lips with crimson gave her the strength to hold her head up as powerful men memorized her body with their eyes. Bite. Trace. Bite. Trace. Soon her fingers were stained red by the pits she rolled between them.

Roberto's headlights flashed over her as his car pulled up. She pulled open the door and climbed inside. "So, tell me, are we driving to God's house? Because I'm really curious what his diggs look like."

Roberto laughed. "I don't think he actually lives here." He put the car into drive. "So, did you decide to celebrate early with a food fight?" He gestured at her hands.

"How do you know it's not blood?"

Roberto shook his head and pulled out of the drive. They sat in silence. Lex's head was too full of apprehension to let her form words. Her mind spun like a top with every resentment she'd ever felt. Her eye drifted shut as they pulled onto a freeway, and next thing she knew Roberto was squeezing her shoulder to wake her.

"We're here." Darkness stretched around them, broken up by a dusting of stars above.

She opened the door and climbed out. The uneven cracks in the sand floor reminded her of running in Ethiopia and the angel she'd once worshiped. A bell chimed behind her and she swung around, the fear that Abaddon had somehow found her in the afterlife. Instead, she found a well-lit elevator had appeared behind the car. She rolled her eyes as Roberto pushed the up arrow. "Isn't this a little cliche?"

Roberto laughed. "Sometimes I think God is as bad at telling jokes as angels are." The elevator dinged, and the doors opened. Roberto gestured for Wylie to enter first.

Her palms sweat, and she suddenly regretted the cherry stains on her fingertips. The ride up took longer than the drive, and Lex's eyes drooped as she leaned into the corner. Roberto stood ramrod straight, a nervousness set his jaw, and through the haze of sleepiness, Lex realized that he was nervous.

The elevator came to a halt with a bounce, and Lex gripped the rail she leaned against as the doors opened, and a blinding light filled the space. The sound of high heels hit her before she could see who stood on the other side.

"Cherry Bomb?" Lex burst from the elevator and into the waiting arms of the stripper who'd shown her the ropes when she first took to dancing.

Cherry picked her up and swung her around. "Diamond Girl, you look so good," Cherry said in the falsetto voice that they often practiced together.

Flashes of the nights where Cherry cracked men's skulls together for getting too handsy and stuffing bras with anything they found in the changing room brought a smile to Lex's face. Now, here was a person who deserved to be in heaven. Speaking of bras. "Bitch, you got your top done! Congrats! Please tell me that happened before you died."

Cherry straightened to her full six feet. "Bitch, I never died." She took Lex's hand and pulled her further into the room. "It's me! God!"

Lex froze, and her hand slipped from Cherry's grip. Her heart squeezed in her chest and she turned back to Roberto. He smiled as their eyes met. "Are you seeing what I see?"

He shook his head. "I always see my *abuela*."

"Is this better?"

Lex recognized that voice. She turned back to God, her fingers locking behind her to keep her hands from trembling. "Justin?"

"I don't you think remember but I worked at Oregon State Hospital. I was the nurse that brought you extra—"

"Desserts for the first month I was there. All this time?" She shook her head. Had God really been with her this whole time? Playing with her septum ring, she decided it didn't matter. "Fuck you, Justin. Give me Cherry back."

She couldn't have chosen a better person to be God. She watched Justin become Cherry and realized how wrong she was about every assumption she'd ever made about God.

A grin broke over Cherry's face as she circled Lex and gripped her shoulders. "Stop being a bitch and let's go. I have some people I want you to meet."

Cherry pushed Lex further into the luxurious penthouse. The marble floors echoed their steps. The gold gilded crown molding sparkled with an otherworldly glow as it framed the rolling void of galaxies Lex had only seen in textbooks. Had God decorated their ceiling with the universe?

"This way." They took a left into a ballroom where hundreds of women stood, waiting.

Lex's feet dragged the last few steps. What the fuck was going on here?

"Everyone. This is Lex. She's the one who will put this all right." Cherry gestured at the women. "These are all the women who suffered under Raphael's experimentation."

A woman at the front of the group stepped forward, her raven hair had a dusting of white. Her obsidian eyes were surrounded by wrinkles. "I'm Ale," she said in a heavy Spanish accent. "We've waited a long time for you." She took Lex's hand. "Thank you for helping my children."

Cherry Bomb's masculine hand squeezed Lex's shoulder. "I have a few gifts to give you."

Lex's eyes closed as peace and warmth filled her and so did Ale's memories. Her kidnapping, the birth of her twins, her death, the lives of her children of which she watched from this place. The rush of memories came and went, but throughout Lex recognized the love transferring from the woman's grasp. A mother's love. She knew that feeling now.

Lex blew out a breath, her eyes fluttering open. "Don't worry. I've got them." Lex turned to Cherry. "What do they need to do?"

Between the moonlight and the glow of some of the Archangel wings, Wylie made out the captains of the two brigades that reported to her summons. Garrett, the PPL leader, had joined them and

Mebahiah stood at Wylie's side. The captains spread their wings, providing privacy, and Palmer's jaw worked as he pulled away from the feathers.

Wylie felt David from a distance. The intensity he wore while working brushed against her Scientia, and she shook her head to get her thoughts back on track.

"At this point the US is under martial law. We're trying to prevent more attacks by keeping our citizens inside. But it doesn't help that a few cities were hit before we were able to mobilize." Palmer's silver hair flashed in the moonlight as he took the time to make eye contact with every angel in the circle. Wylie heard his thoughts and knew the man was very well armed and often comforted himself with that thought. If only he knew she could pop a blood vessel in his head without lifting a finger.

Mebahiah nodded, unaffected by Palmer's glare. "Each Archangel brigade in North and Central America have been activated. We have mostly worked on saving those who haven't or cannot be turned. It is our belief that the subhumans only crave muses or angels but are willing to trample or chew through any human that gets in their way."

"And the infection? Can we stop it? Cure it?" Asked Garrett. The scars on his face created shadows that reminded Wylie of monsters.

The captain folded his tree-trunk arms, his shoulders bunching. "If we could cure it, we wouldn't be here."

"I'm sure that's true." Palmer lifted his chin. "What's happening to all the angels who've lost their muse?"

"Free will happens." Mebahiah scrubbed his face with both of his hands. "I've lost my muse."

"Then why are you here?" Garrett raised his brows.

"Just because I don't have a soul, doesn't mean I've stopped wanting to do my job."

"And what's that?"

"Protecting humanity."

"I see." Palmer turned back to Wylie. "Where are the demons and your brother?"

Wylie ignored him. Her eyes swept around the circle quickly as a slash of purple floated in her periphery. "What are our options now? The weather isn't going to allow for us to live on top of buildings like this for very long." Thunder clapped above them as if in agreement. Wylie closed her eyes to a burst of lightening and again caught a purple haze to her left. She shivered. She shouldn't be this tired yet. "Does America have a plan?" Wylie asked Garrett directly.

"We've mobilized our military, but there's much debate on the risks and benefits of sending more people into the maws of these subhumans."

"I think it's smart to let the angels deal with the subhumans." Mebahiah straightened. "The humans can work on evacuation. We aren't going to be able to stop the spread anymore."

"So, are you saying there's no hope?" Wylie reached for her shoulder where she felt a hand rest. She didn't look. She knew no one was there and didn't want to look foolish, but the invisible hand squeezed again and images flashed in her mind's eye.

"The hope is you, Wylie."

Wylie lifted her head to Mebahiah at the sound of her name.

"Armageddon is meant to be the midwife of the apocalypse. You will be their place of gathering."

A place? A flash of heaven's door flashed in her head, and the hand squeezed her shoulder once more. She nodded in agreement. "Everyone needs to get to the door."

"The door?" Garrett's hands came to his hips.

"The gate to heaven? Brazil?" The angel captains turned to each other. "It could work."

"What?" Garrett asked.

"I've opened it before." Wylie averted her eyes, remembering touching Roberto's finger's finger after prying it open by a sliver.

The angels gasped and at once straightened and lifted their forearms to cover their wide eyes. "We have faith in you." Mebahiah lowered his arm first. He turned to Garrett. "We need to get people to Brazil. To heaven's gates."

Garrett scoffed. "Are you all saying that the plan is to send everyone to heaven before their time?"

Wylie's palms grew slick with sweat, her heart racing to catch up with her thoughts. "This is why I was born. I am the place of gathering."

"I have no clue what that means."

"You don't have to. You just need to make it happen. I think we could move people south faster than this virus can spread. God's Angels can assist in transporting the willing, but we should use airplanes. It would be safer and we can move more people." Wylie turned to the Mebahiah. "Let's mobilize all the brigades in North America. We are going to have to split things up. I want some of our Archangels checking on the LACs who are unable to leave their land. Many of them may have lost their muse and may not know they can leave."

"So, this is it, the end." The Power frowned at Garrett. "What are we going to do once all you little shits are gone?"

That was a very good question. Not all the angels would perish once the muses were gone. Many of them have free will now. Wylie didn't want to think what was really going to happen. She wasn't willing to trade her muse for free will, no matter how many times he pissed her off. "Let's cross that bridge when we get there."

"And Gabriel?"

"Gabriel expects us to fight, and he also thinks we are weak since most of our fighting force are in hell."

"In hell? Why?"

"It doesn't matter. We're here and we aren't going to fight. Let's ditch the quarantine, just give him the whole mess. We'll see what he thinks of that."

Garrett nodded; his eyes distant. "Let's wait to withdraw until we have everything arranged."

"Can we help expedite anything?" Mebahiah laughed. "Humans are slow. Their governments are slower."

"How much time do you think we have?"

"With how fast the infection is spreading? Less than a week."

"Less than a week to evacuate Canada, the US, and Mexico. We don't work miracles like you guys do."

"I think we can carry the healthy. There are more of us than you know. An we'll reserve the planes for the weak and the children." Wylie scratched her head. "What do you think Mebahiah? How many could we fly out ourselves?"

"Maybe three hundred million if people are primed to cooperate."

Chapter 30

Samael

Santana's screams would live forever in Samael's mind. They never stopped. Sometimes they lowered to wails or hoarse shouts. Loud or quiet, they'd weaved themselves in Samael's being, and every time he closed his eyes, he saw Kami frozen in place, her hand reaching up almost tenderly.

"Everyone thought of Laoth as some kind of torture genius, but they always forget my father taught her." Gabriel leaned over Samael, their eyes connecting as he placed another of Santana's tattoos with the cooling collection on his chest. "This tattoo, must've been a special one. Can you feel the power in it, Samael?"

Samael closed his eyes.

"Of course, you can't. You're human." Gabriel smacked Samael's cheek with his bloody hand. "What do you think the Devils will do when they find their prettiest son torn to pieces?"

"Fuck you!" Santana shouted from across the room.

"You're going to make me regret taking out that gag, aren't you?"

"Hell's fury will find you, wherever you go. You will not survive this. My brothers will tear you limb from limb, and my mother will cook you until you're nothing left but nerves. She'll serve you for dinner. She'll display you on her silver platter, and I'll take the first bite. Your screams will go perfect with her gravy."

Gabriel shook his head, his eyes closing tight as he ran his fingers through his hair. "What did I tell you? She's dead! I killed her."

Gabriel stepped away from Samael, and Santana's words became incoherent shouts again. "Last one, little Devil and then we'll take our leave." This time he lay the warm flesh on Samael's forehead. It leaked down the side of his face and blood pooled in his ears. "Looks like it's time to say goodbye."

The lights in the room went out, and Samael shook uncontrollably as a chill took over his body. His teeth chattered as he discovered a new pain he'd never known. Cold. It cut him to the bone. It squeezed his lungs and threatened to skin him alive just as Gabriel had done to Santana. He concentrated on Santana's rough breaths, through the thousands of needles in his skin that competed for his attention.

"Are you okay?" Santana's voice came in a whisper.

"I'm sorry." Samael forced the words passed his tightly clenched jaw.

"Shut up, man. I'm not dying today. You, on the other hand, sound bad."

Samael's body jerked involuntarily and his eyes rolled into the back of his head. "It hurts."

"Yep, dude. It sucks to be human. So glad I don't have to put up with that shit, but fuck, am I going to scar. He freakin' left the water running. Fucking water. Fucking asshole. I'm supposed to be the pretty brother."

Samael's mind couldn't follow all of the chatter. Part of him thought he imagined it. Just as he dreamed of Wylie's hands warming him. The pads of her fingers smoothed his cheeks and then his forehead. She glowed, her curls floating around her. Her ebony eyes. Her ebony eyes.

Samael woke to Madoc lifting him from the table. "Wylie?"

Madoc, pushed Samael's arm down. "Rest. I'm taking you to her."

Samael vomited bile as Madoc's steps rocked him. Soon they were flying and Samael's couldn't be sure if he was really floating through the clouds or was in some strange form of human heaven. Blackness again.

"Wylie?"

A sea of olive drab surrounded them. Tents rose from the ground in every direction, and men marched about with determined looks on their faces.

"Wylie?" The rock of being carried.

Madoc pushed on. "She's close. I can feel her. Wylie!" Madoc shouted.

A tent flapped opened, and she stepped out with a confidence setting her jaw that Samael had never seen before. It all fell away when her eyes found him. The gasp that left her lips hit him in the chest like an arrow. His neck tensed, but he couldn't lift his head. Shame and fever burned him. He closed his eyes to the fear that creased her face.

"Where's the blood coming from?" Wylie held open the tent flap and Madoc hurried inside.

"I don't think it's his." Madoc settled Samael on the cot and sunk to her knees beside him. "How long were we gone?"

Wylie's hands cupped Samael's face before running down his body. "Two weeks, things got bad while you were gone."

"I've noticed."

"Samael, love, can you tell me what happened?"

Wylie lifted Samael's arms and checked between his legs, then the bottoms of his feet. She flattened her hands on his chest and warmth spread through him as her eyes darted up and down his body. "I can't heal him. I still can't heal him. Help me turn him, I need to check his back."

Samael moaned as Madoc tilted him. She palpated the bruises on his back and nodded to Madoc lowered him. "Can you have someone bring a medic kit. Maybe some food. Something easy to chew."

Madoc rushed away, his voice interrupting the mumbling from outside the tent. Wylie's fingers weaved into his hair and found the knot from the car accident. She traced it, and the pain their eased. "I felt this." She blew out a breath as she pulled her hands away. "I'm sorry, Samael. I'm so sorry."

Flames jumped to life in her hands, and she gently ran them up and down Samael's arms and legs. The stabbing pain in his limbs receded, and he licked his chapped lips before covering his face with his forearm. He wanted to tell her that her job was more important than him. That she shouldn't waste her time on a human, and this time when sleep took him, he knew that he'd wake up.

Chapter 31

Wylie

She felt more herself while placing an IV in Samael's arm than she had in months. The simple routine of it. She left Madoc sentinel at the front of the tent. And responded to the summons she'd received via text from David.

> DAVID:
>
> Meet me at the front gate. You're not going to believe this.

She rushed past the hive of people, her mind distracted by Samael's pain. Just as she considered turning back, something, no someone, slammed into her chest.

"Wylie!"

"Jane?"

Skinny arms wrapped around Wylie. David stood a few feet away, his arms folded, a hint of a smile lifting his lips.

Wylie squeezed the teen back. "How did you get here?"

"I drove."

"You what?"

"I drove. I found an abandoned car and packed mom inside. It was our first road trip."

Wylie looked and David pointedly and he shrugged. "I told her to stay where she was."

Wylie kissed the top of Jane's head. "I'm just glad you're safe."

"Now that's what you should have said," Jane quipped over her shoulder.

David frowned. “So, can she stay with you? Mom’s at the mess hall, but she’ll definitely need to stay with me.”

Jane stepped back. “What? I get to stay with Wylie, right?” Her puppy dog eyes widened as she clasped her hands together.

“Hold up.” Wylie brushed her fingers down Janes arm, her smile tight as she raced to think of a good reason not to bring Jane back to her tent. “A rescue mission just returned last night, and my tent is occupied.”

David lifted a brow. “A rescue mission?”

Even with his muse magic soothing her senses, Wylie’s eyes burned with unsplit tears. “Samael.”

David paled.

“Wait, Uncle Sam?” Jane ignored the way the adults around her stiffened and headed into the crowd of tents. “Is he okay?”

“How—”

“I told her. She knows everything,” David said, his voice barely above a whisper.

“Everything, but where your tent is.” Jane turned back to Wylie and David, who hadn’t yet moved to follow her. “Now, stop communicating with your eyes and show me where to go.”

Wylie’s head tilted as she studied David. Something was up, but before she could ask, Jane took her hand and pulled her forward. Wylie’s questions could wait. She released the teen’s hand and linked arms with her. “He isn’t doing well. The major stuff healed, but he’s pretty dehydrated and has a bit of hypothermia.” Wylie assumed the head injury was from a car accident by the abrasions on his face and the seatbelt bruise across his chest, but he hadn’t shared too much information with her and she didn’t want to push him. He’d returned the stoic silence he’d displayed in hell, and she hadn’t wanted to ostracize him further by asking.

Jane nodded her head slowly. “So, you’re saying he looks like shit?”

“Language,” David said from behind them.

“Yeah, he looks like shit. And he probably doesn’t want you to see him that way.”

"Tough nuggets." Jane grew quiet as they passed a group of angels who lifted their forearms when they saw Wylie coming.

Wylie let just enough of her Scientia go to touch against theirs. She was getting better at that. They lowered their arms, and Wylie walked past without saying a word.

"That's weird. I guess everything it says on the news about you is true." Jane giggled. "I knew you were a badass."

"Language."

The smile on Wylie's face fell when she saw Madoc. He stood at attention, his tattooed arms behind his back, his jaw sawing back and forth as he glared at her. "You can't bring them in here."

"It's my tent."

"He's my friend, and I know he'll be pissed."

This angel didn't have a leg to stand on. He'd treated Samael like shit since he became human. "Move, Madoc."

The angel held her gaze for a beat, and then with a growl marched away.

"See, badass."

"Jane," David groaned.

"Let me just check on him first." Wylie ducked into the tent and knelt as Samael's side. "I have someone here to see you." His moss-green eyes blinked open.

"No."

"This is part of being human, people visit you when your hurt or sick. Trust me, it will be good for you."

He took in a shuddering breath, his eyes closing. "Kiss me first.

Her hands cupped his cheeks, the stubble scratching her palms. Her lips brushed over his forehead, his chin, his mouth and both sighed, breathing each other's breath.

His hands covered hers, the tubing of his IV draping between them. He nodded.

Wylie held up the tent flap, stepping out of the way so Jane and David could enter.

"Uncle Sam!"

Wylie sat at the foot of the bed, her hand resting on Samael's shin as Jane pulled smiles and laughs out of him. The conversation became background music to the steady stream of anxiety racing through her veins. She was glad she brought Jane here, but something was wrong with David, and all she could think about was being alone with Samael.

Instead, she escorted Jane and David to the mess hall and found herself meeting with politicians and angels throughout the day and spent most of the night healing people. And every time the conversation lolled, she listened to the throng of subhumans that surrounded the camp. The slow move to Brazil taxed everyone. She'd attempted to heal a husk a few times. Twice, when a mourning angel brought their broken muse and begged that she'd try, once for a demon.

She decided if Samael had the chance, she wanted him to enter heaven when she burnt down the doors. He needed to take advantage of his humanity. With these thoughts weighing heavy on her mind she returned to her tent. She took a washcloth to his face. The crusted blood came off in layers, but Samael didn't move as she revealed he didn't wear his scowl lines in his sleep. She kissed his brow. "Are you awake?" She wiped his neck and chest. Guilt tightened her throat as she discovered the bruises she'd missed. She should've gone for him, but if she had, there would've been no home for him to come back to.

Gabriel's dwindling arms continued to fight and recruit, yet she hadn't seen her twin since before Samael went missing. Videos spread of the rebels herding subhumans to other continents, and she wondered where his former strategy had gone. The rebels were ruthless in a way she'd never seen before. Had the last of Gabriel's humanity died with Lex?

"Wylie."

"Hmmm?" Wylie returned her washrag to the now brown water.

Samael blinked at the light, his hands gripping the side of the cot.

"I'm here, Sam." Wylie patted his chest and then took his hand.

"Sam? You've said that a few times now." Samael's eyes finally settled on Wylie's face and something close to a smile showed at their edges.

Her cheeks warmed.

He shook his head. "I'm fine, you should get back to work."

Wylie ran her finger over his lip. "There is no point in me doing all the other things without you. That's the power that you have." She rubbed his ear between her thumb and finger, he closed his eyes. "You're my white horse. I need you."

Samael didn't answer, instead he tilted his head away from her.

Wylie pulled the sheet up to Samael's chin and started wiping down his lower half. She hummed as she went. He showed no sign of movement until she turned one of his legs out and wiped at his inner thigh. The sheet tented and she bit back a grin. She wouldn't say anything unless he did.

He grabbed her wrist as her rag went to his hip, a growl falling from his lips. "Stop."

She sat back on her heels, her hands raised. "Sorry."

With a grunt, Samael sat, throwing his legs over the side of the cot. The blood drained from his face but he held out his hand, stopping her from helping him. He took several deep breaths. "I'm not good at this, this . . ." he grumbled to himself as he searched the tent. "I'm not good at being weak, but that doesn't mean I don't appreciate your strength." He opened his hands. "C'mere."

She slid between his legs, resting her head on his chest. His hands went for her wild hair. "I worked so hard to help you become strong enough that you wouldn't need me, and now that you don't, I'm looking for my place."

She rested her cheek on his head, her eyes closing as she enjoyed his familiar scent. "Samael, there is nothing special about needing something. As humans you need to eat and drink. You need purpose and kindness. Your life is ruled by the things you need. It's the things you want that make life special. That gives us purpose. I'll never stop wanting you."

"Come here, sunshine." He pulled her into his lap. His arms shook around her as he held her close, lips rested against her ear. "Just let me hold you for a minute."

Her eyes blinked closed. Only he could make the fear and anxiety melt off her shoulders. She nuzzled the soft skin of his chest. "Can we sleep?"

He rolled back onto the cot, taking Wylie with him. She clung to him. "Does this hurt?"

He brushed her hair from her face. "I'm not hurt. Just grateful. So grateful you didn't come for me."

"Luc didn't let me." Wylie wasn't sure if Samael hadn't wanted her because he was worried about her safety, or he'd wanted her to stay on the throne he'd built her. She needed to set him straight. "Your kidnapping was a trap, but not for me. Raphael unleashed hell once Luc left. I hated not coming for you, but it was the right thing to do."

"It was. I'm proud of you." He ran his fingers down her back. "Now sleep, you can finish saving the world tomorrow."

"Hmmm." She held tight to his warmth, sighing when his baritone filled the air, reciting the prophecy.

From the water, she will rise
Born of death, raised in love
With black hair and blacker eyes
She is the peace of a dove
Angel, fallen, human, muse
For she is Armageddon
She must choose
She is the entrance to heaven

Chapter 32

Gabriel

Why are you letting this fucking happen?

"*Mon dieu*! I'm not, Lex. I'm *making* this happen." Gabriel made his hands into fists, resisting the urge to cover his ears. No one could hear him where he stood, but everyone could see.

"*Why are you doing this?*" Lex's insistent voice covered the sound of the horde below.

He'd been herding the subhumans across state lines since he returned from hell. Per Raphael's orders, of course. His conversation with Kami had left him questioning everything and everyone.

"I don't need to explain myself to a dead girl." He made the signal, and the wall between them and the horde exploded. Burning body parts flew with the rock like fleshy meteors. He looked away as the horde moved into the small city. He was a fool. His father had been right, and here was the ghost of the woman he'd loved making the same insinuation. Raphael had outmaneuvered him, and Lex hadn't only taken her life but made it impossible for him to see the birth of his child.

With the storm of the last few weeks at his back, he'd downed every barrier the humans erected between Raphael's monsters and their safety. 'The altered hex' hadn't stopped his father from taking chunks of Gabriel's life when he returned Earthside with the demons on his heels. Raphael punished him by showing Gabriel how truly powerless he'd become, and all Kami's little spell had done was make him conscious in his body after Raphael took control.

But his powerlessness wasn't the worst part. No, it was the fall of his empire. Soon he'd be fighting a war on both fronts, because even if God's Angels and the Fallen Angels didn't agree with each other, the fallen wouldn't forgive what Gabriel did. Wylie's plan to open the door to heaven wouldn't benefit the Demons, but they'd assist her if only to make his life miserable.

You and you, he pushed his command into the Dina and her sidekick's minds. *Stay here until the whole hord has entered.* Gabriel jumped from the building and flew away from the inhuman cries for help. He let the icy wind of the night cut into him, welcoming it even.

"See, you feel bad."

Gabriel's wings propelled him faster.

"You do. You feel fucking miserable."

"Lexy." Her name came out a moan. He'd failed at keeping her safe. He'd failed at avenging her. What was the point in ruling without his little savior at his side.

Her thin arms snaked around his back, her head buried in his chest, and her legs wrapped around his hips as he continued on his path. He let his face drop into her hair. She smelled like nothing, because she wasn't really there. She'd become the conscious he didn't need since she'd returned as a ghost. The one his father had beaten out of him before sending him to fancy boarding schools in France. All the education in politics he'd need to rule the world one day and here he was breaking down walls and herding subhumans.

"You were meant to do so much more."

His hands ran up and down her spine as if feeling those fine bones would somehow make all of her real again. "You don't get a say in what I do anymore."

"And neither do you." She bit his ear, and he flinched, his flight veering to the left.

"What do you want from me?"

"Your sister—"

"This is war—"

"I've heard this shit before." She bit his ear again, and he pulled her closer. *"Go to your sister, she needs your help."*

Gabriel spotted a clearing in the trees. He changed his direction, landing in the moonlight, his arms still tightly wound around his woman. He kissed the top of her head. "Let me see my son."

Their eyes met and she nodded, disappearing from view, his arms empty as if she'd never been there. Shaking off the feeling of loss, he paced, the wetness of the grass penetrating his leather shoes.

"Gabriel." Lex reappeared a little boy with black curls on her hip. Every parent thinks their child is growing up too fast, but Persius had gone from newborn to toddler in just a few weeks.

Gabriel stopped in his tracks. His hand raised to brush the babe's hair, but his fingers ran through empty air. Lex wasn't strong enough to make her and their son solid. Gabriel bent low, his eyes finding his sons. "I love you, *mon petit chou.*"

The boy smiled and reached, speaking his own secret language. Gabriel held tight to his smile but couldn't control the rain as it began to fall, soaking him to the bone and running through his little family as if they never existed.

Lex looked up at the sky and then at him. "You should get home." She pulled Persius close. "*We love you too.*" They faded away and Gabriel fell to his knees. He pressed his face into the mud and shouted his anger into the earth.

Chapter 33

Samael

Samael pulled Wylie into the first empty tent they passed.

"Sam, I'm trying to take you somewhere."

"But I needed a kiss." His nose ran along the side of her face and his teeth grazed her jaw. "I'll never have enough kisses from you." He whispered against her skin. "How can I with my bucket of life so full and my time with you only a drop?" He bit her kissed her collarbone.

"You can't distract me like this." Her head fell to the side giving him space. "We have places to be."

"Sunshine, let's escape for a few hours. Things have been moving quickly, this might be our last chance to be alone." He leaned away from her, unwilling to let her go yet. "How will I breathe without you as my air? Why did God wait so long to let me have you?"

Her hands came to his cheek, her eyes bounced between his. "Don't give up on us. I have to believe that we will build a new world and it will be perfect if not for anything but the fact that you're in it."

"You have so much faith. I used to be the one with the faith."

"I have faith in us. I have faith in this." She pressed her lips against his again and it felt like the first kiss. Every kiss from her felt like the first kiss. Like the world began when their tongues met. Like the magic of her taste gave birth to the universe and all he needed to do was continue his witness. She pulled away. "Tell me what happened in hell."

"I already told you."

"I've never seen you like that."

"I've never been so very human."

Wylie pressed her lips together. She had more to say. She had her tells. He couldn't read her mind anymore but the echo of her thoughts skimmed across his memory.

"It's okay, I learned a new magic while you were gone."

"You'll have to show me once we get where I'm taking you." Her fingers tightened around his, and she pulled him from the tent. "Keep your eyes closed, it's a surprise."

"Wylie, you really don't have time for this."

"If I don't make time for things like this, what's the point in all the rest."

Cool air caressed his face as Wylie pushed what sounded like a heavy door open in front of them. He instantly knew where he was by the smell. A mingling of incense and dust. His nares flared as he breathed it in.

"Watch your step." She slowed her pace and his feet slid from carpet to tile. "Madoc said that you used to love visiting places like this."

His hand brushed against the polished wood of a pew and he sighed. He'd missed the feeling of visiting God's house.

"You can open your eyes now."

Samael's lip lifted with the increased pitch in Wylie's voice. His eyes fluttered open and he found himself in a doorway before a grand naive next to a Mother Mary statue. Wylie took a step back. Excitement rolled off of her that Samael didn't need Scientia to feel. His fingers dipped into a dish of holy water and he whispered Latin words as he planted a wet cross on his forehead. He turned to Mary and brushed his lips with his still-wet fingers, they landed on Mary's paint warn toes.

He'd done this rituals as an angel, desperately trying to understand humanity. Now, even without knowing what it is to be a mother or to be a son, the love in Mary's eyes pierced him to the bone. The story of sacrifice reflected in the smile of every human he'd ever seen. He reached for Wylie's hand and led her down the naive. He wanted to show her what he'd learned while she was away. It wasn't much, but maybe in this place, he could do more.

He bowed at the end of a pew and slid down the row until he had the best view of the crucifixion before him. He pulled the kneeler down with a thunk and fell to his knees. "Join me." His hushed voice echoed around the chapel. "I want to show you something."

One knee at a time, she lowered herself, her eyes wandering as if worried she'd be caught.

"Now, close your eyes." He pulled her hand between both of his. She did as told and Samael did what he'd seen thousands of other couple do. He intwined his fingers with hers. Instand satisfaction tightened his throat. He brought their knuckles to his lips, was this the most beautiful thing he'd witnessed? Was there a better symbol for what he'd gained with his sacrifice? He hadn't just fueled the most powerful angel to roam the earth. He'd found this feeling. This feeling of completion. He'd chosen this and if given the choice now, he'd do it again.

It started as a buzz and soon became a rumble as he used his love for Wylie to pull energy from the earth.

"What are you doing," she whispered, her head swiveling, her eyes seeing something Samael's couldn't.

"I made you a shield." He closed his eyes, squeezing her hand as he shape the energy up and around them.

"It feels like you're burying the cathedral with earth." She closed her eyes again, breathing deeply.

"In a way, I am," he said his head tilting as he studied her face.

Wylie's cheeks rounded with a smile. "This is amazing Samael."

His lips itched to mirror hers. How is it possible that this goddess wanted him. He let his new found power fall away. He had more important things to do. Like touch all of her from her softly sloping nose to the scars on her knees. He froze as her lashes, gold under the chapel lighting, fluttered open. Green and black met and he cradled a gasp in his chest. *This isn't goodbye. This isn't goodbye.* The thought snuck into his mind, easing the sadness that had slowly consumed him as the world grew closer to its end.

She leaned toward him, her finger brushing the crease between his brows.

And that's when he knew. They were fated. That was the only way to justify how abruptly his millennia of searching stopped when he came into her life. Maybe he hadn't been looking for her for God alone. Samael had knelt in holy places all over the world. Worshipped with prayers from both living and dead religions. He'd called God many names in many tongues and had never felt the power of a creator like he did with Wylie beside him. He warmed from the sensation. The rightness that was at the core of all worship, and before he could show her the magic in what lay between them, he dropped her hand and turning pulled her face to his. Kissing her as if this would be their last, because that was what this moment was meant to be. One of their last chances at happiness before the world ended and all of angelkind dutifully faded into oblivion.

His tongue slipped past her lips with desperation, seeking to tangle with hers, seeking to devour her. His hands traveled down her body, guiding her hips with light touches until she stood before his kneeling form. He rested his cheek on her belly, breathing her in once before lifting her onto the pew before him.

Her legs hung at his sides, her ass swaying in mid air as he balanced her. She giggled, holding tight to his shoulders to keep from falling as he buried his face between her breasts. She held tight to his hair, forcing him to look at her. "We're in a church," she whispered.

"What better place to worship?" He stood, kicked the kneeler away, and lowered her onto pew. He slid to the ground.

Her chest heaving. His hand slid to the center of her chest, rocking with each of her gasps. He leaned forward until their noses touched and he sucked her hot breaths into his lungs. He wanted to live on them and them alone.

Her hand came to his cheek. "This isn't what I expected you to do here." She opened her mouth to add more only to have him capture it with his own. His body moved on his own, as did hers. Soon he balance on a knee between her legs as she rocked against his thigh. His kisses traveled to her neck and she covered her moan with her hands.

"Sam," she gasped as his tongue explored. She gripped the sides of his face.

"Hmmm?"

"We need to get out of here." Her hands slid behind his neck and locked together.

"Hang on."

She squealed and wrapped her legs around his waist when he cupped an asscheek in each hand and lifted her. He carried her out of the house of God and into His world. Samael's eyes darted from side to side, finding nowhere to go but the gated rows of headstones and tombs. For a split second he mourned the fact that they'd never make love in a bed, but quickly he realized anytime with Wylie beneath was a celebration of life itself, so he headed for the cemetery.

Wylie rested her head on his shoulder, her smile against his neck. "Never have I ever . . ."

"Hmmm?"

"Nothing."

He set her on her feet in front of raised slab with a concrete angel sitting on the other side. "I want to see you."

She nodded pulling off her shirt and bra. Her ochre skin stole his attention as she worked on her jeans. Soon she stood naked before him, her nipples pebbling in the cold. The perfection of her body had his knees locking and his mouth watering. He reached around her and let his hand lazily slide up the large curve of her ass and to the place where her wings belonged. "I want to see all of you."

Without a word she let her wings loose in a flury of flame. She pulled him close and wrapped her fire around him like a blazing vortex. "Remember the time you did this for me." The roar of the fire muffled her voice. She kissed his chest as she unbuttoned his shirt and Samael enjoyed the view as the warmth surrounding him had muscles relax, including ones he hadn't notice were tense.

Soon his patience got the better of him and Wylie laughed when he lifted her onto the slab.

"Lean back, sunshine." He pressed his forehead into hers and her cheeks shifted from gold to bronze as his fingers slipped between her legs.

Wylie moaned, pulling him closer as she moved against him. His fingers explored her wet heat. His body vibrated with the need to touch her there with his mouth and his cock, longing to do both at once. To cover her with the sensations driving him wild.

She reached for his fly.

He groaned in response, pushing her thighs apart. *One more time.* She could be all his, one more time.

She rested back on her elbows, the glow of her light flickering over her body as her wings draped on either side of the grave stone. His hands framed her breasts, watching them slide down her ochre skin until he cupped her ass. His fingers curled into her flesh, he'd never be able to touch enough of her at once.

Her wings became a light show as he sucked at her neck–her moans a chorus. "Samael, please." She whined his name, his arms too busy holding him up to do what her half lidded eyes begged for.

Sucking in a breath he freed himself from his pants and lined his cock with her entrance. His hand slid behind her and he gripped the base of her wings as he sheathed himself in her heat.

Wylie dug her heels into his ass, pulling him closer as he slowed. He wouldn't rush thing like her had their first time. Sliding from tip to hilt with each thrust, wishing to live forever between her thighs.

As something built inside him his infinite patients from moments before thinned, he lifted her hips off the stone and drilled into her, her screams of pleasure reassuring Samael that he could trust his body. That it knew what to do. That he couldn't break her, it only worked the other way around.

Flame danced around them, her body becoming an inferno as she shivered and then fell apart. He squeezed her ass, bouncing the last of her release out of her, his seed spilling as he took one more kiss.

This was their goodbye. Their last joining. And it hurt as much as it healed. Samael held Wylie's hand tighter now as they walked away from the cemetery. They had things to do. And none of it was together. There were so many balls in the air, he just hoped the end of the world wouldn't be the end of them. No outcome would be right. Not until he died of old age.

Chapter 34

Lex

The plan was solid. Now, she needed to wait in this happy place while Gabriel suffered. She'd taken to visiting him several times a day, wanting him to know that she was there. Lex couldn't be sure if she had more impact on his decision making now that she was dead or when they were sleeping in the same bed every night. A small part of her knew she was more likely to talk him into making the right decision as a ghost.

While Gabriel's exterior stayed sharper than ever, she knew he was being torn apart on the inside, and a lot of that was his doing. His body contained so much Scientia, like a shit ton, but he'd spread his muses out so far that he was reaching past stateliness to replenish what he needed. How could this broken person fulfill such a great destiny, and how can he be so fucking wrong about his role in it? All of them were so wrong, and somehow, they believed in their values enough to spill blood.

Twisting her septum piercing, she cradled the tablet in her hands. She didn't know what else she could tell the asshole. She'd never won their arguments in life; he'd always distracted her. Uncertain of how many more chances she'd still have, she gritted her teeth and turned on the tablet. She found Gabriel and reached through, but Gabriel wasn't alone, or himself.

Raphael sat behind Gabriel's desk, writing, his head bowed over his work. Gabriel kneeled on the floor next to him, his eyes emptily staring forward.

"We haven't had to do this in a while. That dead whore really did change you."

Gabriel's hands twitched where they sat on his lap.

"We used to do this every day when you were a child. Can you remember?" Raphael laughed as he leafed through his pages. "Of course not. But it was necessary. You were such a stubborn child. And that was a good trait, we just had to learn how to aim it in the right direction." Raphael leaned back into Gabriel's chair. "I didn't think we'd ever have to do this again after sending you to boarding school, but God only knows why you like to slip your dick in the trash."

Gabriel's fingers twitched again and Lex kneeled behind him. She pressed her chest into his back and wrapped her arms around him. "Gabriel."

He stiffened.

"Are you there?"

With an almost invisible movement Gabriel leaned into her.

"Dina!" *Raphael glared at the door until Gabriel's angel bodyguard came striding in, the grin falling from his face the moment he saw Gabriel on the ground.* "Sit."

Dina stepped behind the chair, his eyes still on Gabriel. "I'd rather not."

"I said, sit."

Dina smoothed his shirt and plopped into the chair.

"How did it go?"

"Exactly as Gabriel described. We were successful in spreading the virus, and—"

"I'm not asking about the virus." *Raphael waved a hand at Gabriel.* "Is he still acting weird?"

"You mean, is he still talking to himself?"

Raphael shrugged, picking up his pen.

"Not that I've noticed." *Dina laughed.* "He's a dickhead as usual."

"Hmmm." *Raphael checked a few boxes, the deep gouges of his tick marks the only proof of his temper.* "Where to next?"

"Brazil. Wylie hasn't kept her plans secret. She'll be there any day. We'll be ready to stop her."

"And my subhumans, have they changed?"

"They're getting faster. Some can even swim, which is creepy as fuck."

"'As fuck' is right. You have no idea what I went through to create this cure to the muse disease angels have been plagued with."

Dina's eyes shifted to Gabriel.

"Don't look at him." *Raphael's pen snapped in half.* "Look at me!" *He slammed his fists into the desk.* "I'm so tired of the way you all look at him. I'm the genius here. Your savior." *He dropped the pieces on the desk and flattened his hands on the surface.* "I started working toward free will before you were made." *Raphael rose from his seat.* "Do you know how many centuries Binah carried the key to this virus in her womb?"

Dinah shook his head, disgust leaving creases there.

"Fourteen!" *Raphael slapped his hands on Gabriel's desk.*

Lex had never seen Gabriel's father raise his voice before, but something about his frustration brought a smirk to her lips.

Dina's jaw clenched. "What an accomplishment."

"Was that sarcasm Dina?" *Raphael folded his arms, a stillness falling over his body as Dina shook his head.* "It sounded like sarcasm."

Dina opened his mouth to speak, but instead of words a horrible screech announced his detonation.

Lex's hands shook as chunks of the angel flew through her and landed on Gabriel's white shirt. She laced her fingers around Gabriel's stomach, jerking away when she realized she was sinking into him, seeing the room through his eyes.

He sucked in a breath when she pulled away. Raphael turned to his son, his eyes narrowing.

She squeezed Gabriel. *"I'm going to kill that motherfucker one day."*

Raphael's eyes connected with hers. "I see you there, whore."

Lex returned to heaven with a screech. She threw her tablet on the bed and tore off her shoe, throwing it at the mirror. The glass shattered, adding an instrument to the chorus of her screams.

Chapter 35

Samael

"Uncle Sam!" Jane ran up to him and jumped into a hug.

Samael grunted and squeezed her, lifting her from her feet. "You've gotten taller." He hadn't noticed when she'd visited him at his sick bed, but she'd become a woman. He held her at arms lengths.

Jane squinted her eyes, and a sly smile crept over her face. "And you've gotten older."

He pushed her orange hair back. "Are you ready for this?"

"To go to heaven?"

"I'll be escorting you and your family to the gate, but I won't be able to go in with you."

Jane hooked her arm with his and pulled him back into the encampment. "I have something I want to show you." She guided him to the other side of the tents where the army airfield bustled. "That's the craft we're taking. Look how big it is. It's called The Flying Eye. It's a flying hospital. It hasn't been used like one in a long time. They use it as a classroom of sorts now." Jane's words came out like a waterfall, uncontrolled and energetic. She pointed at the stretchers already boarding the craft. "Have you ever flown on an airplane?"

Samael shook his head. "I've always had my own wings."

"Not like this." She pulled his arm. "I'm glad you'll be with us. I feel safer knowing you will be there."

Samael thought of Wylie and the angel business that now took up all of her time. But before she left, she gave him one last assignment. She'd asked that he keep the Godwyns safe. That he'd see them through the gate. He'd agreed, though he had no intention of letting David go. He was one of the horsemen of the apocalypse. Wylie would need him. Jane and Emily would enter heaven without him.

Samael waited with Jane to board the aircraft. He counted the soldier to civilian ratio as he went and was sorely disappointed in the resources that were left for this mission. Gabriel's angels were weak, but not so much that a single armed human would have a chance. If he had to guess, it would take no less than three humans to take down one of the rebellion.

David stood between two beds giving rapid orders. Those working under him repeated his orders before carrying them out and he moved on to the next beds. The man looked older with all the hair.

"Isn't it cool to see him work?" Jane elbowed Samael in the ribs. "My dorky ass brother bossing people around like he owns the place."

Samael snorted. "I don't know what you're talking about, he always acts like that."

Jane giggled. "I don't think I've ever heard you tell a joke before."

"It's probably because this is the first time I told a joke that was actually funny."

"I like the new Sam."

He ruffled her hair. "Grown up Jane isn't that bad either."

"Speaking of grownups, I better go check on mom. She boarded earlier this morning. She doesn't like airplanes. I'll catch up with you later."

Samael grunted his agreement and watched him disappear behind a curtain further down the cabin. He'd caught David's eyes earlier, he knew the man would come when he was ready, so he monitored the steady stream of people entering the plane.

An hour later David approached Samael with his arms folded. "What do you think? Will Wylie's plan work?"

"As long as we are there for her."

"I'll always be there for her."

Samael clapped David's shoulder. "Thank you for that."

David scowled. "I'm not doing it for you."

"And that's why I'm grateful."

"Everyone, please take your seats and fashion your seatbelts. The plane will depart in twenty minutes."

A strange cramping filled Samael's belly as he followed David to the seats. "It will be strange to fly on someone else's wings."

"Better this than in the arms of an Angel. I will never live down that shame."

Samael forgot his nervousness, his lips flattening into an almost smile. "Whose arms?"

David shook his head. "I don't want to talk about it."

"Did Wylie carry you?"

David rubbed his temple. "I hate you."

"You sound like a man that—" The plane began to roll forward and Samael gripped the arm rests. "What was that?"

David shook his head. "You better buckle up."

Flight instructions echoed over the speakers, and Samael ground his teeth as the machine rumbled around him as if it were about to twist apart. He closed his eyes, remembering the feeling of wind in his feathers. God, he'd give almost anything to have his wings back.

Samael hated every second of the flight, but not so much that he couldn't appreciate the Human's ingenuity. A flying hospital? It was one of those creations with little to no Angel influence. Only a human would find such a contraption necessary and thank God they did. There were many onboard the craft that would have been unable to make the trip any other way. David and Jane had left him to manage for himself, and so he stared out the glass wishing she were on the other side of the window.

The landing jostled both Samael's bones and nerves. The throng of humans waiting at the gate covered the distance between where the plane landed and the entrance to heaven. Samael jumped off the plane with the rest of the soldiers. They were handed shields and batons. Robin Williams hovered above them, his face as stern as it could be. "We have transported some of the weakest of the humans still alive, we have made an agreement with the countries that are also evacuating to bring the sick and the weak closest to the gate, so they may be the first to enter heaven." A whisper interrupted William's speech, and he responded by beating his polycarbonate shield. The act didn't match his demeanor, and the soldier closest to Samael scoffed. "This will not be an easy task. Some of you who have experience with crowd control, please raise your hands."

Samael raised his hand along with six other soldiers.

"Right, you will take points. Remember, men, shield first, we aren't here to hurt people. They're all just as afraid as you are."

A man next to Samael whispered to his neighbor, and the captain narrowed his eyes. The creak of the cargo door opening made the hair on the back of Samael's neck stand. The man who'd scoffed earlier elbowed Samael. "Where did you get your experience? I did three tours in Iraq."

Samael paused, not sure if the man's comradery would continue if the ex-Dominion said with the Spartans or during the Crusades, so he stuck to his usual grunt and eyed the humans already pressing against the plane. It is as though they landed in the center of it all, though they had made a point to land a safe distance away. The crowd must have come to them. Samael couldn't see the trenches Ophanim had created out of all the lost angels through all the bodies.

"Take my son!" A father yelled in Spanish as he held the boy in the air, his leg in a cast.

"Help me!" Wailed a woman with a hunched back, her cane waving in the air.

The cries came as a chorus in a multitude of languages, Samael recognizing all of them, and though he couldn't get them to the gate any faster, a relief lightened the load on his shoulders to hear most continents represented.

"Hold." Came a voice over the megaphone. "Clear a path. We have gravely injured and sick among us who will be escorted directly to the gate. Bring your complaints and requests to the leaders of your country.

"What country?" An old man's voice rose above the rest.

Stretchers lined up behind Samael. A nurse stood at her patient's head giving breaths with an ambu bag, sweat dripping down her face.

The tension around them rose. People fell into the shields that made the point of their little caravan. "Let's go."

They cut through the humans like a butterknife in steak. A slow back and forth. The shield of his fellows shook as they continued to push through the throng. Dust rose with their movement, but they soon would be moving onto grass. Many of those pushed out of the way joined in and became their tail. Samael's arms ached with the weight of his shield, and he longed for his Scientia. His mind swirled around his inadequacies when the man who'd done his three tours in Iraq went down to a knee. Samael wasn't sure if the man had tripped or had been pushed. But the crowd was on him, yanking the shield from his hand and ripping him away from the group.

Samael moved to fill the space, but a second soldier screamed as hands grabbed at him. He swung his baton, his shield already taken from his grip.

"No!" Samael's instincts sent him reaching for his Scientia. But he was empty.

Now close your eyes and use what God gave you. Mary's words echoed in the foreground of his mind. He thought of Wylie, how her fiery wings felt in his hand and gathered that energy until he felt he would burst. He threw it out like a net, just as he would do if creating a human Reprieve with his Scientia. Those before him froze. "Help them," he bit out. His body vibrated with the strain of holding the humans still as his comrades untangled their fellows and pulled them back to their group.

"I have to let them go," Samael gritted out. He heard the wings before he saw the angel.

Robin Williams landed in front of him. "It's okay, you can let go. I've got you brother." Robin turned to the crowd, and Samael let go. "Bless you all." Robin's words came in countless languages. He used the Angel tongue, a universal language. He held out his hands to the crowd, and all the aggression drained from their faces. "No one here will be left behind. Now step aside." With that, a path was made, and Samael continued forward with shaking legs.

Chapter 36

Wylie

Wylie couldn't watch another monster with a human face burn to death. She unsheathed her sword and made like Madoc, decapitating the writhing subhumans as they ran away from the flames that engulfed them. Her heart grew heavier with each head that bounced to the ground. When the last body fell, she ran to clear the runway so the plane before her could take off.

Luc followed in his lion form, pushing his head into her hand. She scratched his mane as they continued to run. She ran faster as the engines revved and the propellers buzzed. She took to the air before the takeoff, avoiding the sound of takeoff as well as she could. She had another airway to clear, but she needed a breather first. She landed on the first bridge she saw. With no one in sight, she sat on the edge letting her legs dangle.

Picking at a patch of blood on her jeans, she watched the wind catch it as it flaked off. Every subhuman she killed became more painful than the last. She wished she could cure everyone. This evacuation was a joke. Yes, they'd easily moved six million people a day for the last week. But Brazil could not handle the influx of people. And humans were doing what humans do best. Fucking shit up. She needed to open the gate and open it soon.

"What are you thinking, dove?" Luc squatted beside her.

"Just a few more hours and everything will be well and truly fucked." The water below continued its turbulent babble, and for a moment Wylie wondered what it would be like to jump and just let it take her away. Probably a lot like how she felt right now. "What will your people do when this is all over?"

"Protect our muses. We don't all have ones, but the fallen that do are pretty loyal. Wipeout the rebellion. Those pricks have done enough harm. We'll just have to wait and see what's left of the world after all that."

"All that will be left are the stubborn humans who don't trust us and have somehow secured their city or town from the subhumans."

"Somehow?"

"Yeah, like how are these small pockets of society unaffected?"

"You know there are more of us than there are of you, right?"

Wylie turns to Luc and glared. "Really? You could be doing more?"

He smirked. "We're not on the same side, remember? I'm helping you out because I have two blood pledges I'm bound to." He shouldered her playfully. "You're not so bad either." Silence swept over them as the horizon cradled the sun, the last gaps of light making the water glisten and glow. "What are you going to do after?"

Wylie closed her eyes. "I haven't thought about that. I'm assuming that I'll be dead by then."

Luc grabbed a hold of her chin, pulling it until their eyes connected. "I'm not going to let that happen."

"That's sweet to say, but I don't think this will be over until my brother and I are gone from this world, and I don't mean heaven or hell."

"Hmmm." His non-response spoke volumes.

"Luc, do you know anything about heaven?" Wylie felt her eyes glassing over.

"I've heard stories, but you know the rules. My people don't go there."

"I just can't stop thinking about Roberto and Dean, you know. About how I can go whole days without thinking of them now. About how I will never see them again and I'm finally at a place where I've found a little peace with their absence only to know my life will be over soon."

Luc's hands came to her cheeks, his eyes searching her. "I will protect you."

"You'll protect me?" Something clicked in her head and she laughed out loud. "You're my black horse," she said in awe.

"You're just figuring this out?"

"But when will I save you?"

"You saved me when your brother attacked."

Wylie wrung her hands. "You didn't need saving."

"You never know, I could've." Luc chuckled. "Have you ever been blessed by a demon?"

"Huh?"

"I know you've been blessed by angels, but has a demon ever blessed you?"

She shook her head.

"Here." He pulled her forehead against his and a zinged buzzed through her that was stronger than peace and on the edge of giddiness. Her shoulder fell back, and her body felt the sudden urge to stand. Power coursed through her veins and layers of insecurities peeled back until and absolute confidence secured a smile on her face.

She stood, and Luc followed. "I feel like I just snorted Adderall."

He laughed "Well, dove, I've never heard it described that way before, but I'm glad you're feeling better."

"Better? Luc, I'm ready! Let's fucking do this!" She punched him in the shoulder. "And just in case I don't get a chance to tell you this later. I love you like a brother."

He snorted. "My mom would adopt you in a minute. When this is all done, we should go visit her. Zeke has been asking about you."

Zeke. The boy's name reminded her why she needed to find a way to survive this. She pulled in a deep breath of fresh air, the energy Luc gave her helping her find the strength to go on.

"Where to next?" Luc asked, rising behind her.

Wylie pulled out her phone and scanned through it. "West, we've got three more to go."

Luc's wings appeared. "Three more and then we make the biggest bonfire this world has ever seen." He winked at her.

Wylie smirked. “I don’t know how you always find a way to make these things sound fun.”

“It’s a gift. Lead the way.” He gestured to the sunset.

Wylie took a few steps back and with a giggle jumped off the side of the bridge.

Chapter 37

Gabriel

Gabriel had never seen so many people in his life. People spilled from Rio de Janeiro. Bodies lining from shore to rainforest. The door sat at the base of the green, blocking the view of the city when approaching from inland. The Corcovado was totally obstructed. He and his angels settled themselves amongst the humans. Observing God's Army as they escorted the humans to heaven.

He knew his sister expected an attack, and he wasn't shy about making his presence known. His father had ordered him to come here, but it was Lex, with her insistence that he needed to help his sister that made him come. Other than withholding the attack Raphael had demanded, he wasn't sure how he'd help Wylie turn the gate to ash. If the gate could be turned to ash. He had his doubts. He looked down at his watch. Wylie was late and Gabriel hated waiting. Almost as much as he hated this situation.

"This feels all wrong." He whispered to Lex as Wylie's wings appeared on the horizon.

"It's because the asshole is late. Don't worry. This is where you belong." An invisible hand with dainty fingers settled in the crook of his arm and for a moment he allowed himself to imagine they ran away when he'd wanted to. That they'd chosen this place to live their lives with baby Persius and little Zeke as they waited for his family to destroy the world. What a dream.

Gabriel looked at his watch again. This was reality. He was the evil, presiding over a crowd of victims trying to escape the world he'd help create. The hair on the back of his neck rose as a familiar presence cooled his back.

"Son."

"Raphael." Gabriel's hand grazed the piece at his back. "What are you doing here?"

"Just making sure you're doing your job." Raphael straightened a sleeve, sneering down at the throng. "Wow, they really tried to get everyone."

Gabriel saved his breath. He had a decision to make: revenge or give in and do what Lex wanted of him. And wouldn't that be its own kind of revenge. "I'm waiting for Wylie to attempt to open the door. We can cause the most confusion then."

"I see, I'd prefer not to wait, but I trust you son." Raphael's hand branded Gabriel's shoulder as his "father" left bruises with his fingertips.

Lex's body leaned into Gabriel's chest, her arms wrapping around him, and his decision was made. He lifted his chin, resisting the urge to leaned down and kiss the top of Lex's invisible head. "Yes, Father. You can trust me."

Chapter 38

Wylie

Wylie circled heaven's door three times. She didn't know where to land. She felt Samael somewhere in the crowd, but even with her angel sight she couldn't find him. If he was safe, he knew David would be safe. Her brother was there too. She didn't know what the angel was waiting for. Maybe he thought the door would kill her for him.

Wylie eyed the door; the thing had kicked her ass in the past and she wasn't sure if she was ready for another zap. With her wings moving languidly, she leaned into the door. It felt the same, heavy and impenetrable. She invoked the dream that brought them all here. Her memory of it was fuzzy, but its power still buzzed under her skin. In her dream she'd stood at the base of the door and had burned alive with the wood. She shook her head, even if this door opened, it would take days to get everyone through it.

Wylie backed from the door, her fiery wings gliding through the bright blue sky as she circled the city. People cheered as she sped around for the second time. If only they knew she was gathering the courage and momentum she would need to take this door down. On the third time around, she propelled toward the door with all the speed her wings could muster, slamming into it with her shoulder. It rewarded her with a shock that could have stopped a heartbeat.

She fell from the sky, momentarily losing consciousness. People swarmed her, helping her to her feet and dusting her off. She couldn't understand the words, but the encouragement was obvious. She shot back into the blue above, taking the slow approach this time. Wylie caressed the wood and then channeling her flame into her hands sent it traveling up and down with the grains. The door charred where her hands touched it. She pushed herself, her entire body lighting up, but all she did was make a larger black smudge.

This was the second worse possible outcome. The first being death. What was missing? She felt for Samael, suddenly needing his comfort, her fire brightened as she did so. That was it, she reached for David's Scientia and again she felt her body heating to the point of near pain. She needed her horsemen. As if in answer, someone slammed into the door next to her. She turned her head, her teeth gritted in concentration.

"I'm here." Luc called over the roar of fire. She took his hand, and he gripped it tight, the blaze around her growing. He groaned in pain but didn't let go. The door rattled under her hand. All she needed was her brother.

She closed her eyes and searched for him, her Scientia traveling through the door and underground until it reached Gabriel. His Scientia flinched away from her touch, but she wouldn't give up that easily. Some innate part of her knew his Scientia as well as her own. They belonged together, no matter how much she resisted it. Like a viper she dug into his magic, grabbing hold with all her spare strength. To her surprise, Gabriel didn't resist, in fact he did the opposite. Shoving his Scientia through their new sibling bond with such force that flame exploded out of her chest consuming the entire door.

She was back to her Catharsis, nothing but an inferno of pain as she took and took and took. She buried everything she had into that door and didn't stop until she heard shouting. The door was gone and people stampeded to get through first. Wylie blinked twice, and her wings disappeared.

Chapter 39

DAVID

She fell from the sky, and Samael couldn't catch her. Last time David watched her fall, Samael had been there to snatch her from the sky. Instead, the ex-angel stood with the first row of humans, his hands opened wide as he held her flames at bay with a static wall of . . . was that Scientia? David had shaken off whatever Wylie had done to him while she destroyed the door and dragged his sister and mother onto a boulder, while rows of people climbed to their knees and pushed forward again. He squinted from left to right. If Samael hadn't been there, humans would have lit up like kindling.

Samael's shield dropped and he stumbled with the crowd. "Wait here," David shouted at Jane over the sound of human struggle surrounding them. He jumped from his perch and pushed his way to the angel he'd called uncle all his life. "Samael!" David pulled Samael to his side. "I don't think they're going to let you in there."

"We did it," Samael slurred, turning to David. "We did it." The big man pulled David in an unwanted hug that felt a lot like childhood. "David, we need to get you and your family through."

David nodded, barely understanding what Samael said, but knowing from experience that the easiest way to get a patient to comply was to agree with them. All he knew was Samael was barely standing and would be trampled if he lost his footing. "Jane's over here, let's go get her."

David struggled to support Samael as they made their way to the boulder.

"Uncle Sam!" Jane clapped as they reached the rock. "You got him!" She and Emily reached for Samael, and David supported from below as his only enemy climbed to safety.

"You look almost as bad as you did the other day." Jane batted Samael's hands away as he reached for a hug. "No, you sit."

Tears blurred David's vision as Jane joined the big guy, their legs hanging off the boulder, his sister's head on Samael's shoulder. David recognized their angel-muse connection. The peace the relationship brought. He needed to find Wylie. He hadn't gone for her before because Luc had her, and Samael had no one. But no matter how strong Luc was, he could never be Wylie's muse.

Just as David decided to go looking for her, a tatted-up angel with the face of an asshole landed on the boulder.

"Madoc?" Samael attempted to climb to his feet but ended up staring at his hands when his body wouldn't cooperate.

"I'm here for David." And then the piece of shit gripped the muse's collar.

"Madoc!" Samael shot to his feet, his face going from pale to flushed in an instant. "Hands off." He grabbed the angel's wrist, pulling David free.

"No, I'll go with him. Wylie needs me. But dude if you're going to be an ass, I'm going to be one too." David folded his arms. "Take my sister and my mother to the gate, and I'll go with you."

"Really?" The angel looked from David to Samael who nodded with a proud lift of his chin. Madoc's hard gaze shifted from annoyance to frustration. "Fuck, fine. Who's first?"

Emily raised her hand. "Can't you take us both?"

Madoc's eyes narrowed.

"I mean, I've seen Samael juggle three people back in the day."

The Archangel snorted, his gold tip wings rising. "Fine." He opened his arms. "Let's do this."

David wanted to ask more questions but he saw the trust in Samael's eyes, and he knew that though the ex-Dominion was on his shit list, he'd never put Jane in harm's way. He pulled Jane to his chest. "Take care of mom. I'll join you as soon as I can."

"Love you, bro." Jane sniffled as she stepped away, only to pull her brother back in a hug. "I just wanted you to know you're the best brother anyone could ask for."

"Oh, I know." He rubbed his knuckle into her scalp. "Try not to get kicked out before I get there." He kissed her forehead and then reached for Emily, pulling them all together for one last time.

"Now, you're just wasting time, David. I want to go see your dad."

David's life changed as he watched his sister's ginger hair disappear as she passed into the gates of heaven. He hoped he wasn't making the worst decision of his life.

"They'll be fine. Jacob will be there," Samael said from David's side.

David turned his back to his uncle as he wiped a tear from his cheek. "I'm staying because I love her." Wylie had consumed him in a way his ambition had. Tearing him from the things that should matter most to him.

"She loves you too." Samael sat like an old man, his body stacking painfully.

David glared at the man's back. "Yeah, just not enough."

"Thank God for that." Samael's shoulders bounced with laughter.

"You're a bastard."

"Most angels are." Samael shrugged, his head lifting as his eye's followed his asshole friend's flight.

"Most angels are what?" Madoc spoke as he landed, as if he'd listened to the whole conversation.

"Bastards."

Madoc laughed. "Look at the two of you having philosophical debate, while the world is falling apart." He lifted his brows. "Time to go, David."

David's eyes ran over the angel's inked arms. "How are we going to do this?"

Madoc smiled wide. "Why don't you give me a hug."

"Fucking angels." David stepped into the angel's hold, his heart racing ahead to Wylie and how she'd fallen from the sky. Time for him to save his angel . . . again.

Chapter 40

Wylie

Wylie's world spun like a top. She hadn't felt this empty since she brought the Heavenly Planes to earth. No one could find David and Wylie refused to pull Scientia from the unsuspecting muses that waited for their turn to enter heaven. Luc loomed in the shadows, agitated and probably needing his muse as much as she needed hers. So she slid to her ass, leaned against a tree with her eyes closed, and gripped its roots as if they could still the earth. Twice she fell asleep and twice the world jerked her awake, Luc forgotten in the haze of her weakness.

"Wylie?" A hand rested on hers and the spinning stopped. "I'm here."

Wylie wanted to jump into David's arms, but she settled with pulling him into hers. He fell forward and she curled into him. "David, you were supposed to go."

"I couldn't leave you." He rested his chin on top of her head, his hand ran up and down her back. "What now?"

"I don't know, I'm waiting to see where Gabriel takes this."

"Gabriel is here?"

"Gabriel is one of my horsemen."

Luc stepped forward and Wylie jumped. "Speaking of your brother, I have a plan for him. I just need to get Shafer. I think he's helping the human's calm the fuck down." He squeezed her shoulder. "Stay here, I'll be back soon."

Once Luc had projected away, David sat back on his heels and lifted a brow, he took both of Wylie's hands. "So does this mean you and Gabriel are ready to work together?"

The question took her aback. She'd been so stuck in saving-the-world mode that she'd forgotten her hate for her brother. "I'm starting to question everything. David, I want to live."

David nodded, his eyes wandering back to the door and Wylie had to come to terms with the fact that she was the reason David was not with his family right now. Her Muse, who only wanted to save humanity. The physician who knew how to talk anyone from a ledge. If anyone deserved heaven, it was him.

"Maybe you should go," Wylie whispered.

David's head swung back to her, his eyes widening. She let his thoughts enter her for the first time in a long time and she knew he wanted that very thing. She heard his secret hope to be reunited with his parents and Jane. To be surrounded by unconditional love.

"I can already feel my Scientia replenishing. You should go."

"I can wait." He kissed Wylie's hand his words in contradiction with what he longed for.

"I know it's what you want."

He smiled his hands squeezing hers. "I want a lot of things I can't have. That seems to be my destiny."

Wylie's heart broke for him, but she couldn't be everything to everyone. There was no question in her mind, she belonged with Samael. There was an ancient love between them. Something that started before her birth. Something that lived at the core of her being. She loved him.

Wylie blinked, suddenly needing to stand. She loved Samael. The world was about to end and she never told Samael she loved him. She scrambled to her feet. Scanning her surroundings. They were two care lengths away from a cliff's edge. Lazy waves crashed below. Trees obstructed her view of the door. Or the place the door had been. The sounds of the crowd was barely a whisper.

"What's wrong?"

"I need to find Samael."

"What?" David rose, his face scrunching, his cheeks growing red. "Why?"

"I have something I need to tell him."

"Now?"

Wylie froze, thinking of the last time she kissed Samael. She should have told him then. She should have realized then. How was it that now she was surrounded by billions of people and waiting for her brother to strike she's realized something so integral to who she was. She loved him and he'd always loved her. Always.

"You must have seen him recently. You two flew here together. Do you know where he is?"

"We were." He turned toward the door. "I think Madoc was going back for him. He's probably going to be here any minute."

Wylie bounced on the balls of her feet, as if she could see over the mass of humans before her. "Are you sure."

"Yes, he said he'd be back." David rested his hands on her shoulders and his muse magic cinnamon scent infused her with peace. "He'll be here soon. You should rest until Gabriel shows himself."

Wylie turned to the sky, scanning for Madoc.

"Hello, *fragine*?" A voice came from the tree behind them.

Wylie swung around, pulling David behind her.

Gabriel laughed, but his eyes were too wide for humor. "Hey David, how've you been?"

Chapter 41

DAVID

David had felt how similar Gabriel and Wylie's Scientias were. He'd known they were twins from the first time he laid eyes on Gabriel, but seeing them together. A chill ran up his spine. They were the same person. If it wasn't for that surge of power surrounding Wylie since Samael made his sacrifice, he wouldn't be able to tell her power from his.

"So, you brought daddy dearest?" Wylie asked, her black curls bouncing as she tilted her head and as if on que a slim, well-dressed stepped out from the rubber trees. "Hello, Raphael."

This angel David had yet to meet, but he knew from the stories the sharp male was responsible for his fathers death. A spike of anger cooled his chest as he remembered just how human he was. The impotence that came from discovering the angel world framed his view. His eyes lowered and he took a step back from Wylie. He really should run. He was useless here. Maybe he could help in the aftermath, but now?

Raphael's perfect white teeth showed as he shrugged his jacket off. "I forgot how hot it gets here." Raphael leaned against a tree, his ankle crossing as he draped his jacket over his forearm. "Ignore me, I'm just here to enjoy the show."

Wylie shifted, her body going from blocking David from Gabriel to facing Rapheal. "Were you hoping to watch your son die? It doesn't matter who wins here."

Raphael smiled. "You're right, it really doesnt matter." The Dominion tilted his head to his son. "Go on son."

Gabriel closed his eyes. "We either fight like this or–"

"Ah, ah, ah, don't give the surprise away." Raphael straightened his jacket, his hand smoothing the velvet.

Gabriel's jaw ticked and his ice sword formed between his hands.

David fell several paces back as Wylie removed her halo from her wrist. There was sure to be fire next and though he was certain he wouldn't survive this, death by fire was not something he was willing to try.

"Fine." Kushima appeared, Wylie's knuckles whitened as she choked the hilt. She lowered into a ready stance. "Let's do this?"

Gabriel nodded, his reluctance reflected on his face as his eye met David's. *Run*! The word popped into the muse's head and without a second thought he turned on his heels and sprinted, stumbling as he heard the first clash of metal. His palm scraped painfully across a tree trunk as he caught himself. He needed to talk to Lex. His friend never warned him this could happen. What should he be doing now?

He glanced over his shoulder. David needed to do something and soon. He knew nothing about swords but Wylie barely blocked Gabriel's blows. Each one came faster than the last. David froze as the male's blade ran across Wylie's cheek, remembering to run as the wound healed before her blood dripped to her chin.

David caught a glimpse of the gold tipped Archangel wings in his periphery and veered in that direction. The tattooed asshole angel was back and he was carrying Samael in the same awkward way he'd carried David. Maybe if he got to them, they could tell him what to do. Every stride he took away from Wylie wedged a bigger pain in his heart. He'd been told to run, but had he ever ran from an emergency before? No. He was trained to run towards them.

David joined the pair, eyeing the cliff's edge only steps away. "What should we do?" He asked.

"Just stay behind me." Samael didn't meet David's eyes, just stepped in front of him.

"Watch yourself, girl." Beside them the Archangel threw his hands in the air as if he were on the sidelines of a football game. Wylie righted herself, landing a blow with the hilt of her sword to her brother's cheek. "That's fucking right! Keep moving!" The angel shouted. "Yeah! Like that!"

"Madoc," Samael growled with all the command he'd held as an angel. "Stop shouting and help me–"

"Wylie! Duck!"

Wylie dropped to a crouch at Madoc's command just as a shot

rang out. Everyone turned at once as Raphael's bullet hit the space where Wylie had once stood.

Madoc and Samael opened fire and David dropped to the ground too. David army-crawled away from the barrage of bullets and stopped when he ran into an invisible wall. He lifted his eyes following the shimmering barrier to the cliff and back to Samael. David reached out, touching the barrier as a bullet grazed off it. The wall felt like Uncle Sam. Almost as if it were made of memories. Memories of riding on the big guy's shoulders and chasing him with a water balloon.

A thud sounded behind David and he turned to find Madoc downed, laying on the ground in an awkward angle, blood running down his forehead.

Samael emptied his clip and patted his belt coming up empty. He turned to David. "I'm sorry."

Raphael appeared on the other side of the barrier. "Oh, brother, did you think this would keep you safe from me." Raphael rested a finger against the invisible wall. He smiled and then poked a hole in it. Using both hands, he stretched the opening until he could reach inside.

David shook as he climbed to his feet but he couldn't just watch. He was trained to run toward the emergencies after all.

Raphael rested the muzzle of his Glock on Samael's forehead. "Goodbye, 'brother.'"

David leapt forward pushing Samael out of the way. The gun went off.

He was falling. Pain lead to blackness and then peace.

"Jane?"

Chapter 42

Wylie

Wylie found a hole in Gabriel's defenses and bolted, her legs pumping, her wings coming to life and soon her arms wrapped around David as he followed Samael over the edge.

She held David's limp body close to her chest. Her mind diving into his wound and failing at correct it. Nothing happened. Half of his face was gone. Her muse was gone. *David was gone.* She held her breath as she landed on the bottom of the rock quarry. Her front was soaked in David's blood.

Samael brought her back to the present. He'd fallen. He was human. Maybe she could save him. With an aching heart she searched her surroundings and then stumbled to the broken man she never said "I love you" to. She lowered David next to Samael and fell to her knees. His eyes stared blankly skyward and blood bubbled from his mouth, her mind screamed *I can't heal him,* but she had to try. She remembered to be a nurse and felt for a pulse. Nothing. The heel of her palm found his sternum, her finger's interlocked, and she started compressions.

Wylie'd listened to thousands of heartbeats in her life. She knew what was normal and could guess the rate after just a few beats. But this heart she'd memorized. She'd slept with his chest as a pillow. She wasn't ready for that song to be gone.

God, please, bring him back.

She knew a fall like that would leave a man brain dead or dead dead and that her hands couldn't do what a defibrillator could. Or a surgeon.

She heard Gabriel before she saw him. Her brother hit her from the side and they tumbled away from the bodies. Wylie couldn't see anything through the tears, but she felt that this was not the twin she'd fought with before Raphael pulled out his gun. Empty of emotion and soul he wordlessly hauled her to her feet by her hair then dragged her to the wall of stone and proceded to smash her face into it. She screamed as the flesh peeled loose. Self preservation replacing the numb sorrow he'd pulled her away from. Wylie pushed her Scientia between her and the rock but still her nose crunched and grated.

When he pulled her head back and slammed it forward again she realized he meant to kill her like this, no weapons, no powers, and maybe she should let him. She'd opened the gate to heaven, she'd found love, and made love, she'd had a child. She'd done more than any angel before her.

She thought of David and Samael and knew she couldn't let it end like this. Gabriel killed everything she'd ever loved. Gabriel's death would be her final act. What was left of the world would be better without them both.

Wylie went up in flames and Gabriel fell back. He lifted his hands and rain fell, but the water didn't touch her, instead a cloud of mist surrounded her as her fire expanded, eating up all the oxygen between the drops.

"Today you die." Wylie shouted through the crackle and hiss their elements made as they met. She lowered her head an charged, Kushima reappearing in her hands.

Gabriel met her blade with ice and Wylie found herself using her sword like an ax. A prickle at her side from Samael's Scientia warned her that something flew her way. She turned in time to melt the volley of ice shards in mid air and leaned into Samael's Scientia like she never had before. Throwing three fireballs without aiming she guided them with the Dominion's magic. The first two missed but the third caught Gabriel in the chest sending him back. Wylie's throat erupted in pain as the skin over her breasts bubbled up with blisters. *Fuck,* this was going to hurt. She continued her onslaught as she marched toward him. Her sword was ready but she projected the moment she reached him.

Strong arms wrapped around her from behind and she did what came naturally, she brought her wings to life. Gabriel and Wylie cried out in pain at the same time her flaming wings pushed him off. She fell to a knee with a moan, but didn't allow herself any time to recover. She took to the sky, ignoring the hail stones pelting her as she went.

With her vision impaired by the storm, her hearing gone for the same reason, she didn't stop until lightning whizzed past her, singing her flesh. The flash was all it took to find him. She projected to where he stood, her sword already in his side. She pulled it free and ducked sideways his icy steel whizzing past her ear. She fell back a step, bringing up Kushima to block. Two blows and then a thrust. She twisted sideways to block him from where he'd projected, Samael's Scientia telling her where he'd be and forcing him to the ground like dozens of long arms extending from the ball of power she'd become.

He fell to his back and Wylie stomped his shoulder, her blade against the flesh protecting Gabriel's heart. "Die."

"Mom!"

Wylie froze as a man's voice so like her husband's cut through the buzzing in her ears.

"Mom! Stop!"

She didn't have time to decide, her blade just strayed from its path, digging into the rocks between Gabriel's ear and shoulder before clattering to the ground.

"Dean?" Wylie lifted her head, her eyes immediately eating up every inch of the man before her. Chocolate eyes, chiseled cheeks, how his eyes slanted down. "Dean." She clutched at the ache in her chest as she stumbled away from her enemy. "Son."

He opened his arms. "Hi, mom." And soon they were wrapping around her, his wiry body curling so he could hold her.

"How?" The word came out a whisper.

Dean kissed the top of Wylie's head. "Your destiny. You fulfilled your destiny."

Years of sorrow came out of her then, her knuckles whitening as she clung to his shirt. “My son, my son.” The two words matching the only thoughts her brain could summon. Her son was here. Her baby.

Dean ran his hands up and down his mothers shoulders as she wept. “Mom, there’s one last thing you need to do,” he said when Wylie quited. He retrieved Kushima. “What will you do with my uncle?”

Guilt wracked her body, had she almost killed her brother in front of her son. Wylie took her sword and followed Dean’s gaze to Gabriel.

Chapter 43

Gabriel

"*Gabriel!*" Lex's voice brought Gabriel back to the surface, if not giving him full control. He was losing a fight, in truth, any result of the battle would be a loss, and Raphael knew it. He felt his father's will like a binding around his soul.

Wylie planted her foot on Gabriel's shoulder, and he squeezed his eyes shut as her blade came down for the last time.

"Mom!" A man's voice shouted the endearment. "Stop!"

Wylie's blade crunched onto the gravel next to Gabriel's ear, and he opened his eyes as his sister's foot slid from his chest.

A glowing man reached for his sister. Something inside Gabriel broke. He saw Persius in this man. He saw a future without the threat of Armageddon, and a world where God and angels and demons left families alone long enough to flourish. A place where Dean could hold Persius, and he could hold Lex, and they'd watch the cousins grow up together.

Blood from a cut on Gabriel's forehead dripped into his eye as he sat up, transfixed by the scene unfolding before him.

Wylie let go of her son to wipe the tears from her eyes, and the man turned to Gabriel. Putting out a hand, he helped Gabriel to his feet. "Uncle?"

A weight lifted from Gabriel as he nodded. He'd kept pictures of the boy in his desk for all these years. "Are you alive?"

"No. I just came to remind my mother who she is." The man pulled Gabriel into a hug. "I'm glad I got here in time."

Gabriel refused to feel shame for his actions but looking at this man he knew the boys death was his worse sin. "Dean, I did the best I could."

Dean squeezed him tighter. "Lex told me all about you, and I couldn't be prouder to call you family." Dean released Gabriel from his hold and turned back to his mother.

Gabriel leaned forward bracing his knees. "Lex?" He formed his mouth around her name, but it refused to leave his lips. "Lex?" He tried again. In a small part of his mind he still believed he imagined her interventions.

"Yes, Lex and your son Persius," Dean said over his shoulder as Wylie pulled him into another hug.

"Gabriel, end this or I will." Rapheal's voice came from behind him and Gabriel remembered the reason he had to choose between his family's blood and saving the world.

"Father."

"Now, son." Raphael gripped Gabriel's nape and the pain at his side told him that he would soon lose control. "It's time you finished this."

"I'm here. Let me in."

Do it. Gabriel opened his arms wide and welcomed his woman to take control. Suddenly everything made since. The bone fragment, Binah's death, Kami's alteration of the hex. The pain in his ribs subsided as Lex and the magic carved into his bones became one.

"Raphael!" Lex shouted with his voice, spinning and once again pulled the gun from the small of his back.

Raphael's eyes widened in surprise. "Son?" A gunshot interrupted Raphael's last word, sending him crumpling to the ground.

"He's not your son, mother fucker!" Lex sent ice after the bullet to seal the wound, making it permanent. Gabriel's boot connected with the downed Dominon's side. "That was for Ale, asshole."

Chapter 44

Wylie

Dean walked Wylie over the rocky trail the twins had made in their battle and stopped at David and Samael's feet. Though Wylie never wanted to let go of her son again, her legs wouldn't hold her up, and for the second time in her life she crawled through blood to get to her family. "Not again." She reached for each man's sleeve, her vision too blurry to make out Samael's chiseled features. "Not again. Not again. God, please, not again."

Someone smoothed her hair, and she assumed it was Dean until they spoke. "You've lost so much, *cielo*."

Wylie closed her eyes, afraid to look and not see her husband. "Roberto?"

"David is with his sister and his parents where he belongs. And Samael—"

"Samael . . ." She breathed the name, but her mouth remained open in a silent scream.

"And Samael will never leave you." He stroked her curls.

"He's gone, David's gone, you and Dean are gone. Everyone leaves me." Her words came in staccatoed moans, between gasps and tears.

"Wylie, look at me."

She lifted her head and Roberto, *her* Roberto, stared back. Was this a dream? Something her grief stricken mind made up to keep her from imploding?

"You're not alone." He brushed his thumb over her cheek, catching a tear. "Come." He pulled her up, taking his time getting her to her feet. His hands lingered on her side, her hip, her shoulder, and when she swayed before him, he pulled her to his chest.

"I was a little late because I caught something on my way down." He rubbed circles on her back, letting his words sink in, but Wylie didn't understand. Nothing made sense, not Roberto's gentle touch or the absence of it as he pulled away, helping her lean onto Dean. Her husband knelt next to Samael and rested his hand on the Fallen Angel's chest. "Your turn to come home, *hermono*." Samael's body jerked, his eyes opening wide.

Wylie gasped and clung to her son as Samael's wandering eyes found her. Surprise. Hope. Fear. So many emotions swirled around the depths of his eyes, but the warmth of his love gave her the strength to stand on her own.

"Now, let's get you up." Roberto helped Samael to sit, and Dean joined him at Samael's other side.

Wylie's head fell back as she looked up at the three men.

"We have to go," Roberto said, and before Wylie could protest continued, "but we want to leave something with you to remember us." Roberto nodded to Dean and with the big cheesy grins that ran in the Hernandez bloodline, they began to fade. The shadow of their beings morphed and glistened under the sun, until they evened out, forming into feathers and spreading into wings.

Chapter 45

Gabriel

Gabriel fell to his knees his vision clearing enough to see Lex's slim legs. She looked so solid. His hands wrapped around her ankles, and his cheek rested on her feet. "Are you real?" He kissed her feet and then her shins, her knees, her thighs. His arms wrapped around her hips and found a toddler in her arms. Gabriel pressed a kiss into Persius' back. "Is he real?"

"Papa," said the toddler in response. "Papa."

Gabriel's ribs crowded his lungs. He couldn't breathe. This couldn't be real. He listened for Lex's thoughts and heard nothing. "This can't be real."

"Take him. You'll see." Lex's voice was the smooth alto he'd heard from her mind when she was alive. He shivered at the sound of it. Lex held out the boy, and Gabriel took him, sitting back on his heels as he turned the boy around.

"Persius? Son?"

The little boy smiled, his puggy arms rising to cup his father's cheeks. "Papa."

Their black eyes met, and Gabriel saw his future in his son's eyes. He pulled the boy close. "I love you, *cheri*. I've missed you."

Persius played with his father's hair and babbled in a language no one but he could understand. That's when Gabriel lost all self control. Lex wrapped her arms around the two of them making a sandwich out of their child. She held them as Gabriel's shoulders silently bounced.

"I'm so sorry you've had to do this alone. I promise, I'll never leave you again."

Leaving one arm around his son, Gabriel reached for his woman. His hand found her hair, and he pulled her mouth to his. His lips as demanding as his grip. "Never again."

Epilogue

Lex

They held each other like their lives depended on it while the world burned around them. "Gabriel, I fucking love you."

Lucifer the third walked by, his second at his side. "Shit, I almost forgot about them. I've got to meet with Palmer and let the fucker know the world is his now. What's left of it, at least. Satan save us all. " He narrowed his eyes, and Gabriel's wings appeared opening wide. "Shafer, take him away." And Luc strolled away with a scowl on his face.

The sandman stepped forward, but Lex stepped in front of Gabriel and her son.

"Lex, move," Gabriel growled.

"Fuck that," she spit over her shoulder. "If you're taking him anywhere, we're going with him."

Shafer's shoulders sloped, and he pulled his cowboy hat off, pressing it against his chest. "Are you sure ma'am? The place I'm taking him to isn't very nice."

"You can't have them." Gabriel held Persius out for Lex, but she didn't need a hero. She needed him.

Lex lifted her chin. "Hey asshole, don't hand that baby to me. It's time for you to be a dad." She gave Gabriel a hard stare. "You said 'never again.'"

Gabrie's eyes fell from Lex's to Persius, lingering for a moment before pulling the child to his chest.

"That's right." She turned back to Shafer. "First, who the fuck are you calling ma'am? Do I look like a ma'am to you? Second, I'm not very nice, so you're taking me or you can fuck right off." Lex put her hands on her hips.

Lex felt Gabriel's shoulders shake next to her.

"What?" She ruffled Persius hair as her father threw his head back and laughed.

"*Ma petite râleuse,* only you would stare down a demon." He kissed Persius' cheeks. "Only your mother."

Shafer blew out a breath. "Fine."

Black tendrils of smoke danced around the family's feet as Shafer lifted his hands.

Gabriel pulled Lex close, wrapping his wings around his family before a weightlessness signaled they traveled between planes.

Two hundred years later . . .

Samael

Samael tangled his fingers in Wylie's raven curls and pulled. She moaned, her body arching into him. God, he needed this. His knee landed between those thick thighs as he kissed his wife's neck. It didn't matter how many centuries went by, he still preferred to be between her legs than anywhere else on the planet.

"Sam." His name came on a gasp as her nails dug into his back. "I need you."

He tasted her. "Mmm." He trailed kisses between her breast and to the apex of her thighs.

"Sam, please."

"Yes, 'Sam, please.'" Came a mocking voice from the other side of the door. "Don't you guys know it's noon outside? The rest of us actually have to work for a living."

Wylie swept the sheet next to them up to her chin, covering Samael as she did so. "Luc! Didn't I fucking tell you to call ahead!" Samael attempted to sit up, but Wylie locked her legs around him. "Don't you dare move," she whispered.

"I heard that, and I'm not leaving until I talk to one of you. I don't really care which."

"Oh, go fuck you yourself." Wylie stuck her head under the sheet. "Look at me Samael. We can't let him keep doing this. Don't you dare."

"The world might be a shithole, but there're still plenty of ladies out there willing to help me with that."

Both of them were speaking at the same time, and Samael couldn't keep up with them. He never could. They argued like siblings. Samael sat up on his heels, making a tent of the sheet. "Let me get rid of him, Sunshine." He smiled, a talent he'd perfected in the mirror only recently.

"Samael, don't . . ." her eyes softened even though her tone carried that note of warning.

His smile grew, showing teeth and waited for her to smile back before crawling off the bed.

"Be quick."

He nodded and headed for the door.

"Samael." Wylies snapped her fingers. "You're still naked."

Samael grinned, "I know." He stepped out of the room, and Luc crossed his arms at the other end of their humble dining room.

"Really?" He lifted his chin. "You think you can intimidate me with that? I'm a Prince of Hell."

Samael strolled passed Luc and out into the sunshine. He stretched, his eyes scanning the horizon. The Corcovado glowed white just as the entry to heaven did. Samael and Wylie had guarded the entrance for so long that Samael had forgotten any other horizon, and he was okay with that.

"I know you and Wylie have your hands full here, but I can really use some help with the PPL. They sent another spy to Pearl, and I can't help but think there's something special about her." Luc took a step next to Samael. "What do you say, can Sunny come help her old uncle out? I can't deal with the husks *and* the PPL on my own forever."

Samael lifted his brows. His daughter was everything he wasn't. Sunny was sweet, well spoken, and funny with a heart of gold to match her mothers. "Uncle" or not, he didn't trust his daughter in Luc's care.

"She's not a child anymore."

"Hmph."

"What's the worst that could happen?"

Samael raised a brow. "My answer is 'no' Luc."

"If you don't give her the chance to experience the world, she's going to end up in trouble one day."

"Let me raise my daughter the way I wish, and one day I'll do you the same favor."

Luc scoffed. "You know as well as I do, I'll never take a bride."

Samael sat in the grass and stretched out, his fingers digging into the soil. "No matter how long I live here, I can't forget my siblings who make up this land." When Luc didn't reply Samael squinted up, shading his eyes. "What?"

"Doesn't that make your ass itch?" The demon's disgust bled into his words.

"I'm talking about thousands of fallen brothers and sisters, and all you can think about is how the grass is treating my balls?"

"You said it." Luc pulled off his cowboy hat and fanned himself.

"Samael." Wylie's voice came from the house. "Come in, it's time for lunch."

"I'll take a hint, cuz." Luc rolled his eyes. "I'm not sure how the two of you get anything done."

"I'm not sure either."

They shared a smile before the prince projected away.

Samael climbed to his feet, glancing at the entrance to heaven and it hit him, if the entrance was before him and behind him, he must be in heaven now. He turned to his wife. "Coming, sunshine." Samael strolled back to their cottage, ready to eat his fill.

ABOUT THE AUTHOR

C L Cabrera is a Labor and Delivery nurse and a mother of three girls from Washington state. Her love of writing started in second grade and never stopped. Now, she spends every free moment putting the worlds she made up in her mind on paper.

The Heir's Querida
THE PRIDE OF THE FALLEN
C. L. CABRERA

ALSO BY C L CABRERA

THE HEIR'S QUERIDA

1 Peter 5:8 - Be sober, be vigilant; because your adversary the devil, as a roaring lion, walketh about, seeking whom he may devour

Tommy unbuttoned his jeans with shaking hands. I pulled up his undershirt, revealing his beer belly. It spilled over his belt, milky, pale, and soft.

I ran my thumb over his cheek. "Is this your first time?"

"Yes, ma'am."

I pushed him onto the bed. "Don't worry," the bed dipped as I straddled him. "I'll take care of you."

My fingers found the crevice of his neck where his pulse drummed against his skin.

He shivered, his body going rigid. I rolled my hips against him and rested my hand on his bare chest. Our eyes connected, and I drew a sip of his life force through our skin-to-skin contact. I waited for him to relax before sliding my consciousness into his skull. Slow. Inches at a time. His awareness stretched as I filled his brain with my own thoughts.

My body convulsed with pleasure, and I slipped all the way in. Waiting for my heart to steady, I studied the man's face. My invasion had emptied his eyes. "I hope that was as good for you as it was for me." I lightly smacked his cheek and climbed off, heading to my recliner in the room's corner. "Tommy?"

"Hmmm?"

"Tell me how long you've worked at the cement plant." I crossed my legs.

"Five years."

"And what do you know about the owner?" I felt bad for the bastard. He might be dirty and a little pudgy, but he loved his mama, loved his church, and volunteered at the animal shelter. It's too bad I'd be sending him off still a virgin.

"His name is Luc Devon. He's thirty-six years old, and drives a Ferrari."

"Does he have a girlfriend? Any close friends? Family?"

"Not that he brings around the plant."

The questioning went on for another thirty minutes. *Time to send him off with good memories.* I couldn't have him getting suspicious. I reached for the side table. *The Virgin Princess* fell open to page one-hundred-and-twenty-two, where I'd broken the spine. I cleared my throat and read aloud. "Their bodies moved together as he spread her legs wide . . ."

After reading Tommy his happy ending, I sent him on his way, his mind once again his own. I left my apartment moments later, my hands shoved deep in the pockets of my leather coat.

Vacation time! Satan, get me out of this shithole.

I landed in Diamond Falls three months ago, and ever since, the slow pace squeezed the life out of me. My skin crawled with claustrophobia. The small-town vibes suffocated me whenever a woman leaned over to whisper into her neighbor's ear as I walked by.

A splotch on the bible belt's buckle; this place expected its citizens to hold themselves a notch tighter than the rest of the nation. People here didn't like me. Maybe the red lipstick scandalized them. If not, my wardrobe did the job.

If only they knew.

Diamond Falls had a demon problem, and I'm not just talking about me.

Technically, I'm a succubus. Or at least that's how I registered when I joined the PPL, *or The People* as we like to call ourselves, sent me undercover in this bullshit town. The Paranormal Protection League plucked me out of the foster care system after I sucked the life out of my first girlfriend with our first kiss.

But Querida, you ask, *how can you stick out like a sore thumb and work undercover?*

Easy, they think I'm a prostitute.

If only my customers knew they were my personal food delivery service. I'd drink my fill, take their cash, read them a scene or two from my latest romance novel, and they'd leave thinking I showed them the time of their lives. Easy-peasy. Their human brains soaked up every word as I shared images of tongues and hands and thighs, of panting and sweating and fucking. They'd walk away silly with blood loss, fatigued from sharing their life force.

Diamond had more demons per capita than New York or LA, which explained why the place clutched their pearls as tight as they held onto religion. The humans adapted by grabbing for the only defense they had: God.

I resisted holding up my middle finger as I passed a church, making it to the Greyhound station just in time. *Payment, ticket, fuck you Diamond.*

While I called these monthly meetings a vacation, checking in with my handler wouldn't be cambion's play either. He likely wouldn't be impressed with my findings. We'd suspected the cement plant for a couple of weeks now, but I took the damn tour and couldn't smell anything nefarious under the sharp sting of chemicals in my sinuses. And the only thing suspicious about Luke Devon was that he's a dude with two first names.

I stepped onto the bus. My three-inch heels announced my presence. Several heads lifted. My eyes scanned the faces of the passengers. I picked the prettiest girl and slid in next to her, shoving my bag and jacket under the seat. She wore rose-colored cowboy boots and matching lipstick. *You don't belong here either, do you, sweetheart?*

"Hi. I'm Tonya, I'm heading to Tennessee. I'm going to be a country singer." She pushed her blond braid over her shoulder.

I smiled, guessing I picked a talker. "I'm sure you already are." I flashed my pearly whites and grazed her elbow with my hand. She caught her breath and leaned close. "I go by Querida."

"Nice to meet you." Her freckled nose scrunched. "You're beautiful."

Humans always reacted to my kind this way. Mesmerized. Filterless.

I ran a finger down her outer thigh. "That's nice, girlie. You're pretty." I might have kissed her neck then. *Why*? Because my kind were always hungry.

"Oh." She slumped back as I took just enough of her life force to top me off.

"Yes, oh." I smiled against her skin. *This was going to be a fun trip*. I slipped off my heels and suck in my teeth.

I woke to the sound of the bus screeching to a halt. Moonlight glowed through the windows, outlining everyone with silver. *We shouldn't be stopping yet? We aren't supposed to get to DC until the morning.*

My arms stretched up as I breathed in the emotions surrounding me. The salty smell of sleep emanated from the passengers. A hint of tangy fear wafted from the driver. The breeze from the air conditioner sending it splashing into my face. He leaned over the driver's wheel, his head swiveling on his neck as if someone rounded the front of the bus. He jerked up with a cry before slumping forward. The horn pierced the silence as he slid off the steering wheel and his seatbelt stretched tight.

None of the passengers stirred. *A sandman?* I turned to Tonya, whose head rested on my shoulder. I pinched her thigh hard. She nuzzled my neck, her eyes still closed. Now that I knew what to look for, I sucked her scent in. She smelled of magic. *Shit! Devil's spawn! Satan's staff!*

A soft snore escaped her as I pressed her against the window and ducked down laying on her lap. I wrapped my fingers around her wrist and pulled it to my teeth, just a few more gulps for strength. The accordion door screeched as someone forced it open. I licked my lips.

"She's in there. Tommy said he saw her board." A man's voice. He smelled like the sleep of the passengers. *Maybe the sandman?*

"This better not be a waste of time." The voice that answered reverberated in my chest and then my lower belly and thighs. He smelled like leather and bourbon and pine and incubus but stronger. My mouth watered. *A lot stronger.*

Banshee fucker! I ignored my body's natural response to the demon's power and closed my eyes.

"Wait out here. Her powers won't work on me." Again that smooth bass. Well, it didn't matter if my powers worked or not, I could defend myself in other ways. I slipped a dagger from the holster under my shirt and closed my eyes at the sound of boots climbing the steps. *I'm supposed to be on vacation.*

I held in my sigh of relief as I heard the man walk past me. The metal crunched with each step, the sound becoming louder again as he turned from the back of the bus.

"There you are."

Big hands pulled me out of my seat, his fingers curling around my rib cage. My back hit his chest as I planted my dagger in his thigh. Blood gushed.

"Shit!" He released me and I lept forward. The collar of my shirt cut into my throat, choking me. He dragged me against him, holding tight to the fabric with one hand and grabbing a handful of my hair with the other. "Now stay still, brat."

"Go to hell."

He snorted, a puff of his breath combing the back of my ear. I threw my head back, and his nose crunched under the blow. With one swift move, I removed my dagger from his thigh and cut off my hair. My shirt went next and freedom.

I shot out of the bus in nothing but a bra and a miniskirt. Demon blood crusted my dagger hand, and an icy wind bit at my naked skin. I melted into the darkness, jumping off the road and into the tree line. I dodged shrubs and fallen branches, using my nose to choose which direction to run. A light flashed behind me, and I made the mistake of looking back.

"Shit!" I glimpsed at his bloodied face for a split second before I ran into the wall of his chest.

His arms wrapped around me. "Hey, brat, I thought I told you to stay still." He lifted me off my feet. "Now, Shafer."

The sandman's magic hit me in the back at full force, knocking the breath out of me. I sank into the male who held me, my vision blinking out, and the cotton sensation of his magic clogging my brain. I was too strong for the bastard to put to sleep. If only my body could realize that. My legs hung limp.

The male holding me adjusted me in his arms. My cheek fell against his peck, bouncing with every step.

Lucifer's balls! I don't have time for this.

"Luc, man, slow the fuck down. I'm running on empty."

Wait, is this Luc Devon? Maybe I do have time for this. Did I just fall into my target's lap?

"Do you need me to carry you too?" The rumble in Luke's chest as he spoke vibrated against my cheek. If I had control of my body, I would be crossing my legs. *Hey, bad guy, do you mind repeating that while I'm sitting on your face?*

"I'm just saying, we've got her. There's no race."

Fingers pushed my hair from my face. "She doesn't look anything like Tommy described."

Of course, I don't, dumbass. When you look at a succubi . . .

"When you look at a Succubi, you see what you want to see."

"How do you know?" Asphalt crunched under us, my ride growing smoother.

"My cousin married one. Let's just say when I found out the homely chick in the wedding photo was the bride I danced with, I was floored. He thought he was marrying a young Megan Fox but ended up with Sarah Jessica Parker after a beating with an ugly stick."

If he's related to you, sandman, she probably married up.

I absorbed Luc's chuckle. "Are they still married?"

"Twenty plus years. To each their own." A car security system chirped. "Here, let me get the trunk."

The trunk? My heart raced at the prospect. *Please don't put me in there.* Memories of dark nights locked in small spaces itched at my skin.

"Nah, you drive. I'll ride in the back with her."

"Are you sure?"

"Shut up and open the door."

Yeah, Shaf, shut the fuck up.

Luke climbed in, buckled his seatbelt, and keeping me cradled against him, rolled down the window.

What no seatbelt for me, buddy?

The engine hiccupped to life, and Shafer revved it like an idoit.

"It's cold. What's up with the window."

"She's hot. I'm sweating back here."

You're right, I am hot.

"Another reason she should be in the trunk."

Go suck satan's staff, Shaf.

"I'm tired of your shit tonight, Shafer."

Yeah Luc, way to stand up for me.

"I'm just saying, when we're done finding out why the PPL's following us, we're going to have to put her down. It's best not to get attached."

Put me down? Like I'm a puppy or something? What's he talking about, Luc?

"Have I ever had a problem with that?"

My fingers curled around his sleeve, and I forced my eyes open.

"She's not asleep."

I couldn't manage much else, so I glared as hard as I could. I couldn't see any outward sign of what demon type he belonged to. Neatly parted black hair, heavy brows, thick lips, strong jaw, damn this man was the whole package, too bad he planned to kill me.

"Hey, brat, are you awake?" A smile pulled at his cheeks as I studied his moss and oak colored eyes.

"Stop playing with your food, Luc."

Luke pulled me tighter to his chest, his chin lifting. "I'm getting really tired of you telling me what to do."

"You're acting weird tonight."

"Well, I did get stabbed."

True, true. He did get stabbed.

"Don't be an imp."

Yeah, Luc, stop your whining, I didn't stab you that hard.

"Fuck you."

"Maybe after I'm done with your mama."

"Your mama jokes dont work on me. Plus, when my father spawned me, he was fucking your mama. So, we're basically brothers."

If only I could roll my eyes.

"You've met my mother."

"I've also known her."

"Stop, please." The car swerved at the sound of my voice.

"Shit, she is awake."

"I told you."

"I'm surrounded by idiots." My body still wouldn't move. "I'm not going to talk. You might as well just throw me out of the window so I can finish freezing to death."

"Trust me, brat, you'll talk."

"Trust me, ass, I wont."

Luc leaned forward, his nose at my hairline. "She doesn't smell like succubus. Are you sure that's what she is?"

"Well, now I'm not sure either. That blast should've knocked her out for days."

"You mean that tickle."

"Can you do it again, so she'll shut up?"

"I'm driving, why don't you do your thing?"

"His thing?" I sucked in a breath. "Not his thing. Oh, no."

"I bet you're wishing you put her in the trunk now."

"You could always pull over."

"No. No. No. I'm good. I'll be good."

"Like you know how."

"Shut up, Sandman."

"That's it, I'm pulling over."

The car swerved again and the tire squealed as he hit the brakes.

I pulled Luc's sleeve, my eye boring into his. "Please, please don't put me in the trunk. I'll be good."

"Come on, Shaf, did you hear that? She said she'd be good." Luc pushed open the door as he spoke.

"Luc, please. I can't move. Please."

"You heard the driver. Brats get the trunk."

My hip hit first, then my head, and the truck lid slammed shut. I screamed, memories instantly flooded my brain.

Someone's foot landed in my belly. Holy oil splashed over my face, stinging my eyes. The closet door crunched my fingers again and again. And then the words came.

"Saint Michael, the Archangel, defend us in battle; be our protection against the wickedness and snares of the devil."

My fingers and my ribs throbbed, but I beat on the door with my fists, screaming every curse word I knew. My child-mind knew I was going to die.

"May God rebuke him, we humbly pray. And do thou, O Prince of the Heavenly Host, by the Power of God, thrust into hell Satan and all the evil spirits who wander through the world seeking the ruin of souls. Amen."

And that's when they threw the lit match inside.

"Fuck. Is she dying?" The trunk opened, and Luke lifted me.

"What's wrong with her?" The sandman's hand rested on my forehead for a split second before he yanked it back. I felt my memories trail behind his touch as if he pulled them out. "Shit, humans. Hell, I'm sorry."

"What?" Luke looked from me to Shafer. "What?"

"Here, let me get her to sleep. She'll let me this time. Right, angel?"

I nodded, unable to make a smartass remark if I wanted to. His hand covered my eyes, and warmth and oblivion spread through me.

Made in the USA
Columbia, SC
12 July 2024

38291327R00180